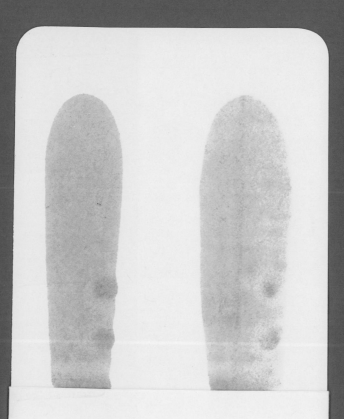

W9-CBM-716

The Columbia Book of Later Chinese Poetry

TRANSLATIONS FROM THE ORIENTAL CLASSICS

The COLUMBIA BOOK of LATER CHINESE POETRY

Yüan, Ming, and Ch'ing Dynasties (1279-1911)

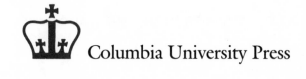

Columbia University Press

Translated and Edited by

JONATHAN CHAVES

New York 1986

Library of Congress Cataloging-in-Publication Data
The Columbia book of later Chinese poetry.

(Translations from the Oriental Classics)
Bibliography: p.
Includes index
1. Chinese poetry—Yüan dynasty, 1279–1368—Transla-
tions into English.   2. Chinese poetry—Ming dynasty,
1368–1644—Translations into English.   3. Chinese
poetry—Ch'ing dynasty, 1644–1911—Translations into
English.   4. English poetry—Translations from Chinese.
I. Chaves, Jonathan.   II. Series
PL2658.E3C663   1886   895.1'14'08   86-2302
ISBN 0-231-06148-X
ISBN 0-231-06149-8 (pbk.)

Book design by Laiying Chong

Columbia University Press
New York   Guildford, Surrey
Copyright © 1986 Columbia University Press

Printed in the United States of America

Translations From the
Oriental Classics

To John M. Crawford, Jr.

"This painting will never be rolled up
                        and put back in its case:

leave it on the wall,
                        watch it give birth to mist and fog."

(Yün Shou-p'ing)

Contents

List of Plates

1 **Wu Chen** (1280–1354). *Fishermen.* Handscroll: ink on paper. H. 9 3/4", W. 17". The Metropolitan Museum of Art, Promised Gift of John M. Crawford, Jr., 1981. (L. 1981.126.58)

2 **Yang Wei-chen** (1296–1370). Calligraphic colophon to painting by Tsou Fu-lei, *A Breath of Spring* (dated 1360), detail. Handscroll: ink on paper. H. 13 7/16", W. 88" (complete work). Courtesy of the Freer Gallery of Art, Smithsonian Institution, Washington, D.C.

3 **Ni Tsan** (1301–74). *Wind Among the Trees on the Stream Bank* (dated 1363). Hanging scroll: ink on paper. H. 23 1/2", W. 12 1/2". The Metropolitan Museum of Art, Promised Gift of John M. Crawford, Jr., 1981. (L. 1981.126.27)

4 **Chang Yü** (1333–85). *Spring Clouds at the Pine Studio* (dated 1366). Hanging scroll: ink on paper. The Metropolitan Museum of Art, Gift of Douglas Dillon, 1980. (1980.426.3)

5 **Hsü Pen** (1335–80). *Streams and Mountains* (dated 1372). Hanging scroll: ink on paper. H. 26 7/10", W. 10 1/5". Mr. and Mrs. A. Dean Perry Collection.

6 **Shen Chou** (1427–1509). *Poet on a Mountain Top.* Leaf from an album: ink on paper. H. 15 1/5", W. 23 7/10". The Nelson-Atkins Museum of Art, Kansas City, Missouri. (Nelson Fund)

7 **T'ang Yin** (1470–1523). *Ink Bamboo,* detail. Handscroll: ink on paper. H. 11 1/4", W. 59" (complete work). The Metropolitan Museum of Art, Promised Gift of John M. Crawford, Jr., 1981. (L.1981.126.33)

8 **Wu Wei-yeh** (1609–72). *Landscape with Man in Boat.* Fan: ink on gold-flecked paper. H. 6 2/5", W. 19 4/5". Asian Art Museum of San Francisco, The Avery Brundage Collection.

9 **Yün Shou-p'ing** (1633–90), after. *The Hundred Flowers,* detail of chrysanthemums. Handscroll: ink and colors on silk. H. 16 1/2", W. 255 1/2" (complete work). The Metropolitan Museum of Art, Promised Gift of John M. Crawford, Jr., 1981. (L.1981.126.42)

Acknowledgments

FOR SUPPORT which made possible the preparation of a substantial portion of this book, I am grateful to the Translations Program of the National Endowment for the Humanities (an independent Federal agency), and especially to the director of the Program, Susan Mango, whose vision and understanding have facilitated the appearance of a number of major contributions to our field.

The Columbia Book of Later Chinese Poetry

Introduction

THE IDEA that the history of Chinese literature falls naturally into a generic periodization is a powerful one. Traditional Chinese scholars of the T'ang (618–906) or Sung (960–1279) and later dynasties saw classical prose as having reached a high point in the Han dynasty (206 B.C.–A.D. 220), particularly in the writings of China's brilliant historian, Ssu-ma Ch'ien (145–?86 B.C.). The classical *shih* type of poetry was seen as having reached its zenith with Tu Fu (712–70), Li Po (701–62), and other poets of the "High T'ang" period. Although such views developed over the course of centuries, they reached the status of mainstream orthodoxy in the pronouncements of the so-called Former Seven and Latter Seven Masters of Ming-dynasty (1368–1644) literature.

In the twentieth century, the range of literary genres which modern scholars such as Hu Shih (1891–1962), Lu Hsün (1881–1936), and others were willing to accept as serious forms of literary art expanded under the pressure of western influence to include fiction (short stories in both classical and vernacular language, and novels), drama, and poetic forms other than *shih*—primarily the *tz'u* or "lyric," and the *ch'ü* or "aria" (so-called because they constituted the sung portions of plays, although *san-ch'ü* or "separate arias" not embedded in any play text were also written). But the ancient appeal of a system of periodization in which each period—indeed, each major dynasty—was dominated or characterized by one or two particular literary genres continued unabated from the past, only this time a greater variety of genres was granted entry into the realm of serious literature. Thus, the T'ang was the great age of *shih* poetry, the Sung of *tz'u* poetry and early vernacular fiction associated with the art of the professional storyteller, the Yüan of drama, the Ming and Ch'ing of novels.

But this scheme, while certainly corresponding in a rough manner to what might be interpreted as a sequence of Golden Ages in the history of Chinese literature, if too stringently applied has the deleterious effect of obscuring the accomplishments of writers working in the various genres in periods other than the dynasties primarily associated with those genres. As is now well known, significant fiction was already being written in the T'ang dynasty, and what might be loosely termed protofiction in the Six Dynasties period prior to that. *Tz'u* poetry was being introduced already in the mid-T'ang and some of the greatest *tz'u* poets lived *before* the Sung, just as others lived *later* than the Sung. Ming drama is at least the equal of Yüan drama, and some of the greatest plays of all were written in the Ch'ing.

But of all the Golden Ages, the one most firmly ensconced in people's hearts is that of the High T'ang period for *shih* poetry. Now, already in the late Ming dynasty, certain bold critics such as Yüan Hung-tao (1568–1610) and his brothers Tsung-tao (1560–1600) and Chung-tao (1570–1624) were challenging the absolute primacy of High T'ang—not rejecting it, but calling rather for recognition of the accomplishments of Sung poets such as Su Shih (1037–1101) in the realm of *shih* poetry. Their views came to represent one side of an ongoing debate in later Chinese literary criticism: did Sung *shih* poetry reveal a hopeless falling-off of quality, or did it in fact contribute a legitimate transformation of poetic style? By and large, those who argued in favor of Sung were the individualists or iconoclasts, while the orthodox arbiters of literary taste such as the Former and Latter Seven Masters tended to maintain the immutable preeminence of the High T'ang. And even among the iconoclasts, those who made serious efforts to champion post-Sung *shih* poetry—*shih* poetry of the Yüan, Ming, and Ch'ing dynasties, here termed the "later period"—were few indeed.

In modern times, the increased attention to *tz'u* and *ch'ü* poetry has replaced traditional orthodoxy as the primary obstacle to paying serious attention to later *shih* poetry. But the great Japanese authority on Chinese literature, Yoshikawa Kōjirō, in his important book, *Sōshi gaisetsu* (An Introduction to Sung *Shih* Poetry), published in 1962, made the strongest statement on record in favor of restoring a proper balance. As translated by Burton Watson, Yoshikawa wrote:

> As in the past, the mainstream of poetic literature [in the Sung dynasty] continued to employ the *shih* form, and the most important expressions of feeling were entrusted to this form rather than to the *tz'u*. This was the way the Sung poets themselves viewed the relative importance of the two forms, and the way in which, if we examine the facts objectively, we must view it today. (Kōjirō Yoshikawa, *An Introduction to Sung Poetry*, trans. Burton Watson [Cambridge: Harvard University Press, 1967], p. 9)

Ironically enough, although Yoshikawa is undoubtedly correct in his description of the traditional Chinese attitude, given the main thrust of modern scholarship in this area, his remarks actually constitute a challenge. Even bolder, however, were his comments in his subsequent volume, *Genmin shi gaisetsu* (An Introduction to Yüan and Ming *Shih* Poetry), published in the next year (1963):

> That which in this period (Yüan and Ming) as well [as in earlier periods] was conceived of as being at the center of literature, and that which consequently constituted the most serious arena for the expression of emotion continued to be *shih* poetry and nonfictional prose—especially *shih* poetry. (p. 12; my translation)

Because I believe Yoshikawa to be correct—and I would add, as I am sure he would, the Ch'ing dynasty to the Yüan and Ming— I have chosen in this book to stress poetry in the *shih* form, while giving examples of *ch'ü* by possibly the greatest master of the genre, Ma Chih-yüan (?1260–?1334) and both *ch'ü* and *tz'u* by Yang Shen (1488–1559), one of the freshest *tz'u* poets of the entire later period. *Tz'u* by other poets are included as well and are always labeled as such. But the vast majority of poems translated here are *shih*.

1. YÜAN (1279–1368)

The Mongol accession to power elicited a complex range of responses from the Chinese scholar-officials. Some withdrew from public life and went into various modes of retirement. Of the poets represented here, Tai Piao-yüan (1244–1310) was an example. He had held office under the Sung, and felt loyal to the Sung. His subtle protest against Mongol rule was expressed through his refusal to hold office in their administration coupled with his overt self-employment: taking students for a fee and actually selling his writings for a profit. This kind of mercantile activity, which seems so out of harmony with traditional Confucian imprecations against profit *(li)*, had started to develop in late Sung and by Yüan times became a recognized kind of withdrawal (from government service) and protest. If scholar-officials in power, the argument might have gone, are abusing their positions by giving in to selfish corruption, I will paradoxically demonstrate *my* purity by openly and unabashedly selling my writings—which in better times ought to be used to aid the Emperor in wisely governing the realm—to make a living. In addition, a tradition of actually praising riverine merchants for their untrammeled freedom was developing and would continue to provide a vehicle for taking a gentle swipe at the world of social obligation. The early Ming poet, Chang Yü (1333–85) would write:

> In this floating home of his,
> there's nothing to tie him down,
> and his name has never been entered
> in the tax-collector's books!
> (see below, p. 82)

Hence Tai Piao-yüan's selling of his own writings in historical context had a tinge of moral protest to it.

Ma Chih-yüan (?1260–?1334) and others, by contrast, withdrew from the official sphere into the realm of popular entertainment in the form of *tsa-chü*, or five-act plays with both spoken and sung portions. Combining romance with historical elements and episodes derived from contemporary life, these plays afforded a means of protest in their actual content but also by dint of the very act of writing them, rather than devoting one's energies to more traditional matters. Ma was also a master of *san-ch'ü*, poems written in the same form as the arias in the plays, but written separately as self-contained poems. Some of Ma's poems in this genre are landscape vignettes which owe much to earlier developments in *shih* poetry.

Still others might turn to a subtlely expressive type of painting known as *wen-jen hua*, "literati painting." Wu Chen (1280–1354) and Ni Tsan (1301–74) were two of the greatest painters in all of Chinese art history. Wu, both in his paintings and in certain poems, emphasized the image of the fisherman as an exemplar of freedom and harmony with nature, while Ni Tsan went further than any predecessor in deemphasizing any human presence whatsoever in his highly austere paintings with their sparse brushwork. Yet the poems inscribed by him on his paintings, as in the case of the quatrain on *Wind Among the Trees on the Stream Bank* (see p. 70 and plate 3), interject the element of emotion, and we realize that these seemingly pure landscapes are in fact expressive of loneliness and lamentation for something lost or absent.

But then there were those who opted to serve in government. Not that they too did not yearn to withdraw. Chao Meng-fu (1254–1322), a descendant of the Sung imperial family and therefore under a degree of moral obligation to withhold his services from any subsequent dynasty—let alone a non-Chinese dynasty—nevertheless did take office under the Mongols, and yet while contemplating a painting of the imaginary paradise, Peach Blossom Spring, he wrote:

> Where in the world is there a place
> just like this painted scene?
> I'll move my family there right now
> to live up in the mountains.
> (see p. 23)

Is it possible that one of Chao's feelings was guilt? Be that as it may, history's later judgment of Chao was mitigated somewhat by the recognition that his painting and especially his calligraphy set standards which were to prevail in the centuries to come.

Historians were, however, far kinder to those whose *entire* loyalty was legitimately to the Yüan dynasty. Yü Chi (1272–1348) was such a man. He rose to an eminent position in the Yüan admin-

istration and is known as one of the major poets of the period. Yang
Wei-chen (1296–1370) as well, although never more than a minor
official, chose to lend his abilities to the government.

The *shih* poetry written by these poets (with the exception of
Ma Chih-yüan) ranges in style from the quiet landscape imagery of
Tai Piao-yüan or Yü Chi (echoed in some of Ma Chih-yüan's *ch'ü*)
to the expansive, freely expressive *yüeh-fu* ("music bureau") poems
of Yang Wei-chen. They all turn back to the T'ang poets for inspi-
ration, but find it in different places. Tai, for example, evolves from
the late Sung burgeoning of interest in late T'ang landscape poetry,
introducing a somewhat darker tonality and broadened vision, while
Yang Wei-chen demonstrates affinities with Li Po and the later T'ang
master of macabre grotesquerie, Li Ho (791–817). At the same
time, he has a moral concern largely lacking in Li Ho but reminiscent
of the New *Yüeh-fu* poems of Po Chü-i (772–846). In general,
then, all these men are establishing a pattern of turning back to
T'ang poetry but then using the inspirations thus garnered to forge
new styles umistakably their own.

2. MING (1368–1644)

The Ming is the central dynasty of the later period, both in
terms of chronological position and of importance in poetic history.
The sheer quantity of Ming poetry, the quality of so much of it, and
its stylistic richness and diversity all cry out for serious attention.
And yet once again modern literary scholarship's tendency to stress
fiction and drama (and to some extent *tz'u* and *ch'ü*) in the later
period have ironically left the field of Ming *shih* poetry by default to
scholars in the field of art, who are familiar with the poetry of some
of the most important figures because of one of the salient charac-
teristics of Ming culture (foreshadowed in the Yüan): an unprece-
dentedly high percentage of the Ming poets were painters as well.
The so-called *wen-jen* ("literatus") ideal of the poet-painter-callig-
rapher had been fully developed by Su Shih and his circle in the
northern Sung, and evolved further in the Yüan with such men as

Chao Meng-fu, Wu Chen, and Ni Tsan, but in the Ming the painter-poet comes almost to occupy center stage.

But actual center stage in the Ming—at least in terms of offical literary history—was in fact occupied by the Former Seven and Latter Seven Masters. Of the poets represented in this book, Li Tung-yang (1447–1516) was a forerunner of theirs, while Wang Chiu-ssu (1468–1551), Li Meng-yang (1473–1529), Wang T'ing-hsiang (1474–1544), K'ang Hai (1475–1541), Pien Kung (1476–1532), and Ho Ching-ming (1483–1521) belonged to the Former Seven, and Hsü Chung-hsing (1517–78) and Tsung Ch'en (1525–60) to the Latter Seven.

The insistence of these men that *shih* poetry had reached an unsurpassable zenith of excellence in the High T'ang, and that all a later poet could hope to accomplish was to emulate the High T'ang masters, was matched by the actual stylistic consistency of their poetic output with Tu Fu, Li Po, or Wang Wei (701–61). Just as many Ming Che School academic paintings in modern collections were for years wrongly labeled "Sung," the poems of these poets often appear to be stylistically indistinguishable from High T'ang poetry. But art historians have recently made it possible to differentiate stylistically between true Sung paintings and Che School works, and the same should become feasible for poetry as well, once scholars of literature have turned their attention to this matter. In general it may be said that such poets as Ho Ching-ming and Li Meng-yang—probably the two best of the orthodox masters—introduce a kind of expansive looseness at least into their *ku-shih* ("ancient-style poetry") which is perhaps the literary equivalent of the bolder, broader axe-cut strokes in the brushwork of some Che School painters. Interestingly enough, the painters whose work inspired some of Ho's and Li's best poems-about-paintings in the Tu Fu manner were precisely the Che School masters.

But running parallel to the orthodox, T'ang-derived tradition in Ming is what might be considered a more individualistic, even eccentric or iconoclastic stream whose representative poets derived inspiration not only from High T'ang poetry but from later T'ang poetry and Sung poetry as well (both of which were anathema to the orthodox writers). This tradition, harder to pin down, may be seen as debuting with a group of four poets of the very early Ming whose names are linked together: Chang Yü (1333–85), Yang Chi (c. 1334–c. 1383), Hsü Pen (1335–80), and Kao Ch'i (1336–74). All of them—except for Kao—were themselves painters, as opposed to the orthodox poets who liked to write about painting but did not actually paint themselves. Most characteristic of their work are serene, lucid landscape vignettes drawn from the life of gentle withdrawal in the tradition of such later T'ang poets as Chia Tao (779–849) and Yao Ho (fl. c. 831), and in particular of their Sung followers—Lin Pu (967–1028), P'an Lang (d. 1009), and the so-called Four Lings of late Sung. But Kao Ch'i was also capable of such a large-scale masterpiece as *The Song of the Man of Green Hill* (see pp. 123–25), in a manner ultimately derived from Li Po, who was also a favorite of the orthodox poets.

Lest it be assumed that such poetry was exclusively practiced by recluses or men who never rose high in the official bureaucracy, stylistically comparable poetry was written by two of the powerful Grand Secretaries of the following generation, Yang Shih-ch'i (1365–1444)—one of the canniest players on the early Ming political stage—and Hsieh Chin (1369–1415). They are in fact among the most aesthetically successful poets among officals of such prestige in the history of Chinese literature.

With Shen Chou (1427–1509), T'ang Yin (1470–1523), and Wen Cheng-ming (1470–1559), the painter-poet tradition reaches its greatest height. These men were three of the greatest painters in Chinese art history, while their associate, Chu Yün-ming (1461–1527), is recognized as the single most important calligrapher of the Ming dynasty. As poets, although they differ among themselves (Shen being characterized by serenity, T'ang by expansiveness, Wen by a brooding sadness, and Chu by quirky eccentricity), their poetry can be said to echo the various voices of Sung poetry rather than T'ang. And a certain ambiguity among later critics as to their status in literature—some declaring it unfortunate that their fame as artists obscured their reputation as poets, others denigrating their poetry—seems from a larger perspective to form a part of the ongoing debate as to the value of Sung poetry itself as opposed to that of T'ang.

Loosely related are a number of poets who do not really fit neatly into any grouping but might be considered to constitute a stream of individualist eccentrics. Yang Shen (1488–1559) was a master of *shih, tz'u,* and *ch'ü,* but in his *tz'u* and *ch'ü* especially seems one of the Ming dynasty's most emotionally expressive writers. Li K'ai-hsien (1502–68) and Hsü Wei (1521–93) carry bizarre eccentricity to new lengths. Li reminds us—as does T'ang Hsien-tsu (1550–1616), better known as a playwright—that in Chinese literature eccentricity can be linked unexpectedly with an almost ludicrous degree of pedantic bookishness.

The individualist strain in Ming poetry culminated in the late-Ming Kung-an School, which centered around Yüan Hung-tao (1568–1610) and was partly responsible for making the late Ming to early Ch'ing probably the most exciting period in the entire later three dynasties. Yüan openly called for self-expression in poetry, and explicitly ridiculed the orthodox masters' insistence on emulation of earlier styles. He did not reject the poets of the past, but only excessive reliance on them to the detriment of one's own creativity. Like his predecessors in the individualist tradition, he was a particular admirer of Sung poetry.

3. CH'ING (1644–1911)

The fundamental dichotomy in Ming poetry—orthodox poets who followed T'ang and individualists who followed Sung—can be said to have continued into the Ch'ing dynasty. Wang Shih-chen (1634–1711) probably best represents the orthodox stream, although Wang manages to achieve greater real authority as a poet in his own right than any of the Former and Latter Masters of the Ming. Wang was a virtuoso of poetic style, capable of a complex exercise in historical allusion such as the *Song of the Ch'ing-Dynasty Mirror* (see pp. 410–12), or quiet landscape quatrains reminiscent of Wang Wei.

The painter-poet, Sung-related tradition also extends into the Ch'ing. Yün Shou-p'ing (1633–90), one of the finest masters of the *chüeh-chü* (quatrain) in Ch'ing poetry, is an example, although as a painter his name is somewhat confusingly linked with those of a group of "orthodox" early Ch'ing painters. Tao-chi (1642–1707) is the most highly respected of the "individualist" masters of early Ch'ing painting; his poetry at times has an almost purposefully clumsy and oblique quality characteristic of one mode of Chinese eccentricity. This characteristic is further developed by two of the Eight Eccentrics of Yangchou, Chin Nung (1687–1764) and Cheng Hsieh (1693–1765), like Tao-chi far better known as painters than as poets.

Standing outside any identifiable school or grouping are a number of early Ch'ing poets whose very refusal to fit into a category helps continue the fascinating richness of late Ming cultural life into early Ch'ing. Ch'ien Ch'ien-i (1582–1664) and Wu Wei-yeh (1609–72) are often mentioned together, although stylistically Ch'ien's immensely difficult diction often renders him nearly impenetrable, while Wu, although he too employs dense language, leavens it more consistently with delicate and even romantic lyricism. Indeed the combination renders Wu quite possibly the single most original—and indeed, simply the best—poet of the entire later period. His shorter poems employ bold imagistic fragmentation to conjure up an atmosphere of melancholy and loss suitable to Wu's purpose of capturing the mood of the late Ming–early Ch'ing transition. His long narratives, such as the *Ballad of Yüan-yüan* (see pp. 362–67), form one of the most impressive bodies of poetic work in Chinese literary history. Although they may be seen as deriving from Po Chü-i's lyrical narratives, especially the *Song of Everlasting Sorrow (Ch'ang-hen ko)*, Wu goes even further than Po in conveying narrative through fractured lyrical imagery and oblique allusion, without however losing the emotional thread.

Another side of Po Chü-i may be seen as having provided the inspiration for Wu Chia-chi (1618–84) in his stunningly effective narrative poems. Almost in diametric opposition to the style of Wu Wei-yeh, he presents the core narrative line in unrelenting progression, step by step, until the episode reaches its sometimes tragic conclusion. Po Chü-i's New *Yüeh-fu* would underlie Wu Chia-chi's poems in this mode, although Wu is fresh and original in tightening the drumbeat of inexorable narrative progression to such a degree.

Still a third aspect of Po Chü-i bore fruit in Ch'ing poetry in the form of Yüan Mei's (1716–98) delightful poems of understated everyday experience. The gentle, self-deprecating humor and simple, straightforward diction are familiar from Po's poems in this mode. Yüan Mei can thus be seen as representing the culmination of a certain stream of low-key poetry derived from the poet's undramatized personal experience which began with Po and continued to play a central role in Sung poetry.

Ch'ing poetry ends with distinction in the recently rediscovered and published poetry of Liu E (1857–1909), who was previously known almost exclusively for his great novel, *The Travels of Lao Ts'an*. Liu has some of the Po Chü-i/Yüan Mei type of humor which can be so delightful, but in such poems as the five which make up the sequence, *Waiting for the Ferry at Inchŏn* (see pp. 473–75), he demonstrates an extraordinary ability to fuse the centuries-old sensitivity to nature's most ephemeral moments as revelations of something eternal with an expansiveness and complexity of vision that looks ahead to later twentieth-century developments.

A truly comprehensive anthology of Chinese poetry from the later period would be almost impossible to fit between two covers. A good deal of picking and choosing is necessary, and no two anthologists would select precisely the same poets or the same works by a particular poet. I have omitted a number of major figures either because I could not find an appropriate way to translate them effectively or because they were simply not to my taste. On the other hand, I have included some fairly obscure poets who I think deserve to be better known. Many scholars would undoubtedly have preferred to place greater emphasis on *tz'u* and *ch'ü* than on *shih*. On the whole, however, I believe that the major trends are all in evidence here and that the general picture that emerges is an accurate one.

The perennial problem of stylistic flattening needs to be addressed as well. When one translator undertakes to translate many different poets, there will be an inevitable tendency for them to sound more similar in translation than they do in the original. I have taken some pains to capture nuances in the diction of Wu Wei-yeh and certain other poets here, but I must admit to the ultimate intractability of the problem.

Chinese poets often provided annotations to their own poems, as did T. S. Eliot in *The Wasteland.* These might be printed as headnotes, or in smaller characters right between the lines of verse, or at the end of the poem. In the translations, such annotations are presented as much as possible in accordance with their positions in the original texts. Sometimes they appear between the lines enclosed within parentheses; sometimes they are identified as "poet's notes."

Most of the translations in this book appear here for the first time. The Yüan Hung-tao poems were published in my book, *Pilgrim of the Clouds: Poems and Essays from Ming China by Yüan Hung-tao and His Brothers* (New York and Tokyo: Weatherhill, 1978). Other poems have previously appeared in the following magazines: The Antioch Review, Asia, Choice, First Issue, The Greenfield Review, The Hudson Review, Ironwood, The Malahat Review, Parabola, The Seneca Review.

For more detailed biographical information on most of the Ming and Ch'ing poets included in this book, consult: (1) L. Carrington Goodrich and Chaoying Fang, eds., *Dictionary of Ming Biography,* 2 vols. (New York and London: Columbia University Press, 1976); and (2) Arthur W. Hummel, *Eminent Chinese of the Ch'ing Period* (Taipei: Ch'eng Wen Publishing Co., 1975; reprint of 1943 publication). For other books useful for the study of later Chinese poetry, see the entries on the individual poets.

I

YÜAN DYNASTY
(1279–1368)

TAI PIAO-YÜAN (1244–1310)

T AI earned his *chin-shih* degree and briefly held office under the Sung dynasty (960–1279), but with the accession to power of the Mongol Yüan dynasty, he went into retirement, supporting himself by accepting students and selling his own writings—a practice rare in earlier periods but increasingly common in late Sung and Yüan. He was recommended for various offices under the Yüan government, but avoided service on the grounds of illness and old age. A close friend of the great poet, painter, and calligrapher, Chao Meng-fu (q.v.), Tai is associated with what is considered to be a revival of interest in late T'ang poetry among Yüan writers.

Returning to Yin-ch'eng Early in
the Year *Ting-ch'ou* (1277)

Three years ago I left these city walls;
my windblown hair now is touched with frost.
In poverty, much has turned out wrong;
unskilled I stand, my back turned to the times.
Bird prints left on sand—news from the battlefield
where oceans of dust smell of dragon blood.
But my solitary poet's heart lives on:
brush and inkstone are always by my side.

(p. 233)*

The Supervisor, Han Chün-mei,
Has Shown Me Five Poems He Has Written
Called, *The Trees Flourish in Early Summer*.
I Have Therefore Written Down
My Own Ignoble Feelings and
Sent Them Via Inspector Juan.
At This Time, Chün-mei Is
Lecturing to the Various Scholars
on the *I-ching*.

As I see it, T'ao Yüan-ming
was something like the hermit, Tuan Kan-mu.

---

* For works indicated by these page numbers, see "List of Poets with Editions Used,"
pp. 477–81.

While books of poems and letters filled his house
his wife and children never got much food.
He would gaze up where breezes swayed the branches
and look below at valleys filled with clouds.
Who could bear, just for the sake of foodstuffs,
to suffer being fettered and tied down?
Because you, Sir, have sent your noble verses,
my vision, inspired, goes back a thousand years.

(p. 210)

——T'ao Yüan-ming: The great nature poet, T'ao Ch'ien (365–427). He returned to his country home after a brief period of government service.

——Tuan Kan-mu: A man of the Warring States period (480–222 B.C.) who climbed over the back wall and ran away to avoid an offer to serve in the government of Marquis Wen of Wei.

As My Way Passed Through T'ung-ch'uan, I Wished to Visit the Policy Critic of the Right, Mei, But Did Not Know Where To Find Him.

T'ung-ch'uan is a beautiful place:
on all sides, emerald hibiscus!
A tall pagoda guards the pass, alone;
a clear stream embraces city walls.
The marketplace resounds with accents of Wu visitors;
some shrines bear dedications from Han days.
I want to visit the Immortal Hermit, Mei,
but which mountain is he hiding on?

(p. 230)

Cheng-tao Temple

Twisting, circling, the green path slants:
this is home for the rustic monks.
Swelling the gullies, waterfalls splash from cliffs;
piercing sky, stone teeth stand in rows.
The brazier is cold; some pine cones remain.
The trellis is silent; vine blossoms fall.
The monks remember when people fled the troops;
then, noble carriages flocked to these gates.

(p. 231)

In the Year *Chi-hai* (1299), While Returning by Way of Purple Fungus Mountain at Springmouth, I Lamented for Lecture Master Chin

The way is still clear, as if in dream;
I enter, but the man's already gone.
The mountain, dark blue—ancient Buddha's hair;
the clouds, ink-black—the patriarch's robes.
We gambled at chess, equally bad players!
Now, looking at his portrait, it seems a bit too gaunt.
But who can avoid this in a hundred years?
All one can do is stop scheming and be calm.

(p. 235)

A Painting of One Hundred Wild Geese

Close up they're seen in fine detail,
            far back they disappear;
sky and water, vast and open, riverside or lake.
How fortunate they were not noticed
            by the hunter's eye;
instead they're captured in their leisure
            by this painted scene.

                                        (p. 246)

The Painting, *"Mist and Rain on the Spring River,"* by Hsiao Chao

Wavelets like rippling trees,
            trees that look like mist;
truly an atmosphere of spring clouds drizzling rain.
Where did he catch those fish? Where did he drink wine?
—Beneath cabin-roof of bamboo sheaths he sleeps,
            raincoat tossed aside.

                                        (p. 249)

——Hsiao Chao: A painter who served in the southern Sung painting academy in the
mid-twelfth century.

Following His Rhymes and Answering the Poems of My Friend Next Door on Recent Events

(Poem no. six from a group of six)

South of the house, north of the house
            young men plant the fields,
singing field songs as they work,
            tunes that ring out loud.
How different from the young "knights-errant"
            of the neighboring town:
daubing rouge upon their faces,
            falcons perched on arms!

(p. 250)

CHAO MENG-FU (1254–1322)

A MASTER poet, painter, and calligrapher, Chao set new standards in all these fields. His calligraphy in particular was the basis of a Yüan-dynasty typeface and of an entire calligraphic tradition. As a painter, Chao is seen as a key figure in the evolution of the literati style. Chao was a descendant of the Sung imperial family; his willingness to serve the Yüan government and his rise to eminence in it led to his equivocal reputation in later Chinese historiography. For more on Chao Meng-fu consult Chu-tsing Li, *Autumn Colors on the Chiao and Hua Mountains* (Ascona: Artibus Asiae supplementum, 1965).

In the Ancient Manner

The long night drags on and on—
will the cold cock never crow?
I am traveling in the wilds,
my hat-strings frosted with dew.
Tigers and wildcats howl beside the road;
bears and grizzlies lumber back and forth.
In front of me, ghosts whistle loudly;
behind me, skunks and weasels cry.
I look all around—deserted, no one there;
the Northern Dipper hangs high and bright.
The Way of Heaven, truly deep and far:
my heart trembles in useless fear.

(ch. 3, p. 28)

Fisherman's Lyric

Floating, floating on misty waves
        in a little boat;
trees shed leaves in western wind,
        autumn on Five Lakes.
Friends with gulls and egrets,
        contemptuous of kings,
who cares if all the fish below
        never bite my hook?

(ch 3, p. 34)

Inscribed on the Painting, *Spring Dawn at Peach Blossom Spring,* by Scholar Shang Te-fu

Overnight clouds begin to scatter,
        green mountains stand moist;
falling red petals flutter down,
        stream waters flow fast.
In Peach Blossom Spring, most of the year is spring;
at the cave-mouth, springtime mists
        sway the hanging vines.
Hanging vines sway in mist, dangling from sheer cliffs;
flying water tumbles down, plunges three thousand feet.
Jewel-like plants everywhere cover gully slopes;
towering pine trees, stark and noble, penetrate the sky.
Roosters crowing, dogs barking,
        villages naturally form,
the folks in one village their entire lives
        not knowing the folks in the next.
This immortal of the isles of paradise
        knows the road to take:
his dots and washes of red and green
        he brushes on delicate silk.
Where in the world is there a place
        just like this painted scene?
I'll move my family there right now
        to live up in the mountains.

                  (ch. 3, p. 35)

——Peach Blossom Spring: The Shangri-La-like paradise stumbled upon by a fisherman in a famous account by the poet, T'ao Ch'ien (365–427).

——Shang Te-fu: Shang Ch'i, who served as court painter under Emperor Ch'eng-tsung (r. 1295–1307).

Song of an Autumn Night

The trellis, shorn of grapes,
        has let fall its red jade;
cold dew in the distant night raises gooseflesh.
Dark cicadas nestled in the grass
        chirp dissatisfaction,
vainly laboring to weave a tapestry without threads.
Soul in dream, alas! so short,
        the road, so long;
deep among ten thousand mountains—
        this is not my home.
The lampwick flutters in the jar,
        fireflies enter the room,
the parting wild goose, the coming letter,
        surely are foretold;
my waking eyes are glittering—ten thousand
        pints of grief.

(ch. 3, p. 35)

Poem of Prefectural Judge
Yang T'ien-jui Righting a Wrong

In the *chih-yüan* period, the year being *hsin-mao* (1291),
there was a Commandant in Chien-ning
        and his name was Ma Mou.
Because a band of robbers had risen in Chien-yang,
he wished to lead an army out to rape and pillage now!

He heard among the people that a family named Chang
had a daughter called Moon Maiden, beautiful and pure.
He set his mind on this young girl,
                he wished to ravish her,
and so he wrongly claimed the Changs
                were on the robbers' side.
Moon Maiden wanted to escape,
                there was no way she could,
and so, together with girls next door,
                she was defiled then.
Having had his will of her,
                Ma wished to end her house:
father, mother, relatives were taken prisoner.
Of that one family, nine men and women
                were all sent to their deaths!
The pain sank deep, unto the bone,
                no way to cry to Heaven.
Five other people in the family
                also came close to death:
they were beaten viciously,
                their flesh all torn and split.
By misfortune, this family had produced a lovely girl:
and the family was destroyed through no fault of her own.
His Excellency Yang T'ien-jui
                was Prefectural Judge;
he was suspicious that this affair
                was not what it appeared.
His whiskers bristling with righteousness
                he leapt into the fray
and insisted that Ma Mou
                be implicated in the case.
Moon Maiden's name was exonerated,
                her reputation cleared,
and he got the other innocents
                out of the local jail.

These people's wrong—outrageous injustice—
               in a single day was righted;
the documents were all sent up
               to the Secretariat.
His Imperial Majesty, Son of Heaven,
               was truly perspicacious:
he proclaimed that his royal decision
               be announced at Heaven Gate.
"Ma Mou is to be executed for his heinous crime";
when people in the streets heard this,
               they sighed in admiration.
The local people built a shrine
               to His Excellency while he lived:
meat and wine aplenty there they offered reverently.
His Excellency's righting of a wrong
               is something rarely seen:
surely, he would be promoted
               and a monument be built.
Political position should be based on moral rectitude:
seniority alone can't show the man's true character.
Today, already twenty years have passed
               since these events;
and still he's not turned in red sash
               for a shirt of blue.
Only with wise rulers like Kao and K'uei
               will sages come forth to serve:
please chant this poem of mine for them:
               The Piece on Righted Wrongs.

                                   (ch. 3, p. 36)

——*Red sash,* etc.: I.e., he's not yet been promoted.

The Pavilion-Where-the-Crane-Came

—In the K'ai-yüan Shrine in Hangchou. I once visited the shrine,
and a crane happened to come while I was there, so I
calligraphed the two words, "Crane Came" as a name for the
pavilion.

When I visited this shrine of Truth
a crane came to the paradise garden.
Brush in hand, I wrote out two large words
happily expecting they'd last a thousand years.
It cried out as moonlight shone through pines,
danced and danced as wind swept the bamboo.
The road to heaven, how vast and far it is!
You and I will go there together.

(ch. 4, p. 40)

A Eulogy of the Sagely Virtue of His Imperial Majesty Emperor Shih-tsu (Kublai Khan, r. 1260–95)

East the ocean, west the Himalaya,
        dwelling for great monarchs!
Southern barges, northern horses
        throng the royal capital.
The great man of this period
        descended from heaven above;

over ten thousand miles—standard axles and script:
          no precedent in the past.
Ch'in and Han were powerful,
          but tyrannical and cruel;
Chin and T'ang were beautiful,
          but lacked a noble scheme.
Weaving heaven and earth together,
          far-reaching in its rules;
generations of godlike grandsons
          will venerate your Sagely Plan.

                    (ch. 4, p. 45)

Living in Retirement at Te-ch'ing

Already, no more dreams of going to the capital;
only noble feelings of learning the hermit's life.
Quite poor, still I'll pawn my clothes
          when I want to buy a painting;
invalid, I want to throw away my inkstone,
          tired of requests for writing.
The stableboy burns piles of firewood
          to scare off tigers at night;
a young girl knocks at the gate each morning,
          come to sell us fish.
Tired, I rest my head on my books,
          hungry, I just eat;
I laugh at myself for having such a simple plan for life.

                    (ch. 4, p. 46)

To a Pyrotechnist

This wondrous art in the human realm
        rivals nature's skill:
concocting formulas, igniting lanterns,
        turning night to day!
Willow catkins flutter downwards,
        carpeting earth in white;
peach blossom petals drop and scatter,
        covering courtyards with red.
Bursting, spreading, scintillating—
        just like stars that fall;
bubbling, boiling, roaring, blasting—
        like warfare by fire!
Some other night, again you will unfurl brocade of flowers:
no need to grieve that they have scattered in the eastern wind.

(ch. 5, p. 48)

Lamenting the Taoist Wei Kung-yüan

Your residence on earth, a floating, nothing but a dream;
you wake, and your empty lodging
        has returned unto the Void.
The stove for herbs, the alchemical furnace
        are covered now with dust;
the feathered wand, the patterned carriage,
        lost in darkest mist.
White walls glimmer still with moonlight
        in this autumn home;
green pines continue breathing wind
        through the nighttime windows.
The Taoist saints are transcendent in their view of life:
no need to grieve and sadly mourn
        the uprooted tumbleweed.

(ch. 5, p. 49)

Inscribed on a Landscape by Mi Yüan-hui

Limpid river
    rippling in dawn light;
green peaks
    hugged by strands of cloud.
Who is that
    in that boat, alone?
He must have left
    the world of men behind.

(ch. 5, p. 50)

——Mi Yüan-hui: Mi Yu-jen (1074–1153), son of the great Sung-dynasty painter, callig-
rapher, and critic, Mi Fu (1051–1107), and himself a major landscape painter.

Inscribed on Sun An-chih's *Painting of Pines and Catalpas*

The family tombs
    are ten thousand miles away;
on official business
    I've traveled five years now.
What man is there
    who has no mom and dad?
I cover the painting
    and weep tears for a while.

(ch. 5, p. 50)

——Pines and catalpas were often planted around graves.

(Five Selections from) Twenty-Eight Poems Inscribed on T'ien-kuan Mountain

1. Dragon Mouth Cliff

Sheer rock, four walls stand;
cold waterfall sends two dragons flying.
In the human realm they're suffering from heat;
in these immortal mountains, autumn winds are here.

2. Spirit Pool

—Above the pool is a pavilion called "T'ing yü" ("Listening to
   Rain")

The Spirit Pool is never polluted;
its depth, impossible to tell.
Rest a while: the pines and bamboos whisper—
sighing, sighing, mountain rains now fall.

3. Thunder God Cliff

The Thunder God rouses sleeping dragons;
for the nation, lets fall heavy rain.
Flying lightning flashes golden serpents:
"Who is there who'd dare insult me now?"

4. Stone Man Peak

This mighty god is tall as heaven:
when did he turn into stone?
Here alone he's stood a million years
unrecognized for all antiquity.

5. Cutstone Pond

A magic dragon may hibernate in here;
a cave of stone leads to his watery home.
Do not let the children pester him:
he might fly up and bring thunder and rain.

(ch. 5, pp. 50–51)

Inscribed on a Wall [Painting] of Assembled Immortals

The immortals come and assemble
              in the Palace of Flowers and Pearls;
blossoms fill the jeweled mountains,
              kingfishers fill the air!
Jade pendants, coral ornaments
              amidst five-colored clouds;
and halfway to heaven, cranes and phoenix
              dance in springtime winds.

(ch. 5, p. 56)

An Admonition to Myself

Your teeth are loose, your head is bald,
              you're sixty-three years old;
every aspect of your life
              should make you feel ashamed.
All that's left that interests you
              are the products of your brush:
leave them behind to give the world
              something to talk about.

(ch. 5, p. 57)

MA CHIH-YÜAN (?1260–?1334)

IN THE Yüan dynasty, plays with alternating spoken and sung sections became immensely popular. Ma was one of the major playwrights, creating such masterpieces as *Autumn in the Han Palace,* the romanticized story of the Han-dynasty beauty, Wang Chao-chün, and her tragic, forced marriage to a nomad chief. The sung portions of these "operas" were called *ch'ü,* or "arias." Some poets also wrote separate *ch'ü* or *san-ch'ü,* unattached to any play text, and these became a major component of Yüan poetry. Ma is considered perhaps the greatest master of *san-ch'ü,* and all his poems translated here are in this genre. *San-ch'ü,* like *tz'u* ("lyrics"), are written in set tune-patterns of uneven line lengths, but go even further than *tz'u* in introducing colloquialisms into their diction.

Two Poems to the Tune, *Po pu tuan*

1. Staying in a Mountain Pavilion on a Summer Night
Tall stand the peaks;
I take off cap and pin.
Rays of evening sunlight cast wild shadows
                            in the pines.
Palace Pool, limpid, calm, holds
                    the moon's reflection.
A breeze blows, vast, across the water,
                    tearing tinted clouds.
After wine, boy servant!
                don't disturb my sleep.

                                        (p. 41)

2.
Among men of plain clothes
ask about heroes.
What's the use of plans to be king or hegemon?
Grain crops sway on palace sites of six dynasties;
catalpa and paulownia grow from tombs
                        of thousands of officials.
The whole show, one bad dream.

                                        (p. 43)

——These poems and all the others by Ma Chih-yüan are *ch'ü*, "arias."

To the Tune, *T'ien ching sha*

Autumn Thoughts
Withered vines, old tree
                and crows at dusk;
little bridge, flowing stream
                and bank of sand.

Ancient highway, gaunt horse
         in western wind.
Evening sun descending to the west;
desolate, a man at edge of sky.

(p. 43)

Three Poems to the Tune, *Lo-mei Feng*

1. *Returning Sails at a Distant Shore*

(One poem from a series of eight on the Eight Views of the Hsiao and Hsiang Rivers)

Evening sun sinks;
wineshop banner hangs.
Two, three boats
         have not yet reached the shore.
Water fragrant with falling petals,
         night comes to thatched roofs;
from the old bridge, fish peddlers leave for home.

2. *Evening Bell from Misty Temple*

(One poem from a series of eight on the Eight Views of the Hsiao and Hsiang Rivers)

Cold mist, sparse;
old temple, pure.
Close to dusk, the man so tranquil
         worships Buddha.
With west wind, three, four strokes
         of the temple bell:
how can the old monk ever meditate?

3.

Dew on roses,
rain on lotus,
chrysanthemums, chilly in frost,
       perfuming courtyards.
Flowering plum: the moon slanting above
       casting someone's shadow.
Alas, the man of little feeling
       betrays each of these seasons.

                    (pp. 44–45)

——The flowers named are characteristic of the four seasons in sequence.

To the Tune, *Shui hsien-tzu*

—Echoing Lu Shu-chai's poem, *West Lake*

Spring wind, proud rider!
       a youth from Wu-ling;
warm sun, West Lake, third month of the year.
Winds and strings play on water,
       this market of orioles and flowers!
Those who don't know music never visit here,
perfect for songs, perfect for wine,
       perfect for poetry.
Mountains washed by rain:
       dark eyebrows, knit.
Willows trailing mist:
       piled silken hair.
How truly beautiful, this Hsi Shih,
       fresh from her long sleep.

                    (pp. 45–46)

——Lu Shu-chai: Lu Chih (?1246–?1309), another major *ch'ü* poet.

——Hsi Shih: A legendary beauty of ancient times. The Sung poet Su Shih (1037–1101) had written that West Lake was like her in its beauty.

Two Poems to the Tune, *Chin-tzu ching*
(The Sutra in Gold Characters)

I.

Catkins flying: floating white snow;
fragrance of fish, wind through lotus leaves.
For now, to the river to be a fisherman,
in poverty.
A man who's "Not Yet Crossed,"
dream of wind and waves,
arena of illusion.

(p. 46)

——Not Yet Crossed" *(wei chi):* The name of the sixty-fourth and final hexagram of the *I ching.* It indicates a transitional stage where an important affair has not yet been successfully completed.

2.

At night, in west wind
nine heavens high the eagle flies.
Exhausted, a common man in the central plain,
in grief.
Are his friends aware?
He wants to ascend a tower,
but has no ladder to climb to the sky.

(p. 47)

Three Poems to the Tune, *Ssu-k'uai yü*

1. Enjoying Retirement (i)
The wine just purchased,
fish bought fresh,
cloudy mountains like a painting
                    far as the eye can see.
To the cool breeze and bright moon I return
                    my debt of poems.
Basically a lazy person,
with no financial sense,
it's time to retire, now.

2. Enjoying Retirement (ii)
Beside green water,
below blue hills,
two acres of good land and a little house.
At peace, I have leapt beyond the red dust.
Purple crabs, plump;
gold chrysanthemums in bloom,
it's time to retire, now.

3. Lamenting Life
Walking with the moon,
traveling by the stars.
Cold Food Festival in lonely inns,
                    then autumn back home.
Wife and children put on weight,
                    I just wither away,
sad on my pillow,
grieving on my horse,
only death a rest.

(pp. 49–52, and Kyc, p. 185)

Four Poems to the Tune, *Ch'ing-chiang yin*

1. Feelings in Nature (i)
Forest and brook—who has gone
             into retirement here?
A man has arrived, a pure breeze.
He may become "prime minister in the mountains,"
caring nothing for worldy affairs.
Why should he struggle for that piece of paper,
             fortune and fame?

2. Feelings in Nature (ii)
In the western village the day grows long,
             little going on;
an early cicada hums,
soon will come the blooming of sunflowers.
Also early, a swarm of bees buzz by.
Aloof, on my pillow, in dream
             I chase a butterfly.

3. Feelings in Nature (iii)
The woodcutter wakes as mountain moon hangs low;
the fisherman comes in search of him.
"You throw away your ax,
I'll cast off my boat.
We'll find a place to sit and be at peace."

4. Feelings in Nature (iv)
Bamboo fishing coat, purple official gown—
             which do you prefer?
Neither of them is any good at all!
Even if you are a fisherman,
you still must work the windswept waves.
Neither's as good as finding a place to sit
             and be at peace.

(pp. 52–54)

YÜ CHI (1272–1348)

YÜ was a major official and scholar of the Yüan dynasty, declared by P'an Te-yü (1785–1839) to be the dynasty's greatest poet. Many important paintings by Yüan masters bear *t'i-hua shih* ("poems inscribed on paintings") by Yü, as this was a genre in which he particularly excelled.

Sent To Be Inscribed on the Temple of P'u-jun (Universal Fructification) at Lou-fu Mountain

—This temple is located eighty *li* south of the city of Fu-chou. It is the shrine of Ch'an Master P'u-jun of the T'ang dynasty. The Master's [lay] surname was Weng. On the eighth day of the second month of the first year of the Yüan-ho period (March 1, 806), he died in meditation at T'an-chou. Miraculous omens appeared. The people of that place ornamented and [lacquer-] sculpted his actual corpse. Later, he appeared in dream to the Prefect of Fu-chou, who ceremonially returned [his body to Fu-chou] and enshrined it there. To this day, his body is as firm and whole as ever, and he still responds miraculously [to prayer].

This spiritual man left the world behind
but never forgot his feelings for home.
His divine bones returned ten thousand miles;
his deep gratitude remains through the years.
The grain crops here are bountiful each harvest;
the people never suffer infection.
The ancient temple holds meditation's joy;
a high mound brings mother's love up near.

——To the right of the temple is the tomb of the Master's mother; it is known as Weng Family Grove, and corresponds to the location of the Master's original home in lay life.

An imposing structure has risen from the ruins,
a new hall that breathes in flower-rich air.

——Built by the current abbot, His Excellency Ti Yün-fu.

The eastern neighbor is a certain scholar;
with high-peaked cap, he chants the *Odes* and *Books*.

——This refers to Yüan Cheng-chün, Ch'eng-fu.

In clear autumn I pledge with cane and sandals
to pull my way up the thousand steps,
                pine branch by pine branch.

——Behind the temple is a mountain called Thousand Steps.

(ch.28, p. 253)

——The notes appended to several lines in this poem are the poet's own.

——Fu-chou: In Chiang-hsi Province; not to be confused with the famous seaport in Fukien, which is written with a different character.

——For the process of lacquer-mummification in China, see the reference in my book, *Pilgrim of the Clouds* (New York and Tokyo: Weatherhill, 1978), p. 66.

Traveling Early Through a Snowy Valley

Piled snow hugs the bramble gates;
travelers emerge from the village.
At stream crossings some encounter tigers;
no monkeys are heard from the tree tops.
Mountain pavilions touch cantilever roads;
tree roots prop up a wood-plank bridge.
Driving their carriages, they climb the layered slopes;
looking back, they see the rising sun.

(ch.2, p. 31)

Getting on Horseback

My eyes are dim, my hands are clumsy:
getting on horseback, I fear the windblown sand.
Best for me to lean on a cane
as I creep along the hedges to view the falling leaves.

(ch.3, p. 45)

Following the Rhymes of Bamboo Branch Songs in Response to Yüan Po-chang

Sand birds fly east, they flee the spread net;
my boat bobs in pursuit of them, no matter how far!
The Yüeh mountains are green, green,
                    the Yüeh girls so white:
from now on, both of them will trouble my dreaming soul.

(ch.4, p. 48)

——Yüan Po-chang: Yüan Chüeh (1266–1327), another major poet of the Yüan dynasty. Yü Chi has used the same rhyme words as Yüan in a "Bamboo Branch Song," a quatrain derived from a certain type of folksong.

What Family?

What family has built a house beside the rapids here?
In the fifth month, the rapids' gurgle
                    sounds so cool inside.
They've planted trees—already large enough
                    to tie a horse—
and opened windows—from them you can drop
                    a fishing line.

(ch. 4, p. 48)

Going to the Ministry with Chao Tzu-ch'i

The sun comes up, wind starts to ripple
        the waters of T'ai-i Pond.
Below carved bridges, a thousand feet long,
        a painted barge floats by.
Beside the bridges, the willow trees
        are deeper in their green:
perhaps they have been favored
        with an extra wash of dew.

(ch. 4, p. 50)

Sitting Alone in the Courtyard

In what place in years to come
        will I lodge my life?
In the mountains? By a river?
        Both would suit me fine!
For no reason, the tall pine trees
        growing round the house
catch the sound of wind and turn it
        into sounds of rain.

(ch. 4, p. 50)

Inscribed on a Painting

The pines are capped with snow
        from the mountains of paradise;
the bamboos hum with winds
        from the shores of distant seas.
At midnight the moon rises—
        who is there to watch?
Only the old man from East-of-the-River
        practicing with his sword.

(ch. 4, p. 51)

Following the Rhymes of *Autumn Night Song* by Meng Tzu-chou, Signatory Official of the Board of Rites

Heaven expands, autumn arcs high, the night still long.
Floating particles of dust, utterly vanished;
        fog fills the air.
Pure, pure, solitary moon
        turns above the high wall;
the golden well sounds: it is the dropping of the dew.
The jade stairs show no color, then—
        they look like frost;
no human voice is heard, only
        the cicadas' chant.

(ch. 4, p. 54)

A Little Landscape by Chao Ch'ien-li

This prince of a former dynasty
   had no love for arms;
he held a brush by his quiet window
   and painted river banks.
Cloud fragments over distant waters,
   here three hundred years,
and still the pines and bamboo groves
   are moist with springtime rain.

(ch. 21, p. 194)

——Chao Ch'ien-li: Chao Po-chü, a descendant of the first emperor of the Sung dynasty
and a major landscape painter early in the twelfth century.

A Little Landscape by Yen Wen-kuei

He's walked each path beneath the pines,
now floats downstream in a boat.
If the emperor presented Mirror Lake to him,
he'd spend all day among its waves.

(ch. 21, p. 194)

——Yen Wen-kuei: One of the great landscape painters of the eleventh century.

When I Was Young, I Stopped by a Wine Shop in Chi-men and Wrote This Poem, Inscribed It and Signed It, "Written by Lien the Eighteenth." The People of That District Have Since Taken It To Be a Poem of [the God] Lü Tung-pin! I Have Recorded It Here as an Amusement.

Sight and hearing finely tuned,
          there is a real man
who flies to all eight corners of the sky,
          constricted by the world.
His sword spits forth white snow,
          exterminating demons;
his sleeves waft spring breezes,
          bringing the withered back to life.
As full of energy as two national heroes
          intoxicated with wine;
as full of feeling as ten thousand heavenly beauties
          surrounded by flowers.
But now he has left—no one knows where he has gone;
all that remains is his shadow in moonlight
          high up in the sky.

(ch. 29, p. 261)

Inscribed on the Painting, *Solitary Crane*, in the Collection of Jao Shih-ying

When ocean breezes blow the moon,
          he remembers the precarious nest;
in pure night air, he preens his feathers,
          snow filling up the pond.
The immortal recluse does not know
          this is just a painting:
he keeps hearing the long, screeching cry
          from the tips of the pine trees.

                                        (ch. 29, p. 264)

After Snow—Impromptu

Dawn breaks, snow patches lie on the slopes:
far away, they seem like flocks of sheep
          or maybe geese.
Remember—plodding through spring mud
          to see the budding willows,
in camel-hair robe and sable hat
          crossing the icy river.

                                        (ch. 30, p. 265)

Hearing Loom and Shuttle

Creak, creak, loom and shuttle, hidden beyond the trees;
I wake from dream, and remember
                    journeys on rivers and lakes.
Covering the ground, moonlight, cool,
                    almost like water—
the sounds become the creaking of oars
                    rowing me to Yangchou.

(ch. 30, p. 267)

Late in the Year *K'uei-yu* (1333), Staying at the Temple of the Upper Regions

1.
Getting old, I retire to this little mountain district,
yet the actions of other people still influence my heart.
This cloud-hidden temple where I am lodging
                    is perched up really high—
and still I hear a neighbor's pestle
                    pounding in moonlight.

2.
Beside the lamp, I make myself
                    read through a sacred text;
wind blows through the flimsy blinds,
                    the moon glows through the window.
I sit up late into the night—
                    who keeps me company?
A few branches of flowering plum
                    in a vase of bronze.

3.

At leisure I walk the hidden paths,
                    no thought of seeking spring,
when suddenly I see some orchids,
                    purple sprouts all fresh.
Luckily, it is deep within the woods,
                    the entire day can pass
without their fragrance pulling in
                    some other passer-by.

4.

In the mountains, snow piles high,
                    right to the tips of the eaves;
I sit alone by the shaded lamp late into the night.
If the heart of the plum blossom
                    were not iron-strong,
how could it ever go on living in such awful cold?

(ch. 30, p. 269)

WU CHEN (1280–1354)

WU CHEN is considered one of the "Four Great Masters" of Yüan literati painting, together with Ni Tsan (q.v), Huang Kung-wang (1269–1354), and Wang Meng (1308–85). Little poetry by him survives, but is is clear that he played an important role in the development of the integral poem-painting: a painting which has inscribed upon it in the painter's own calligraphy a poem of the painter's own composition. In such works, poem and painting work toegether to evoke a single experiential world.

Paintings of Fishermen

—Two Poems to the Tune, *The Fisherman*

1.
West of the village, evening rays linger on red leaves
as the moon rises over yellow reeds on the sandbank.
The fisherman moves his paddle,
thinking of home—
his pole, lying in its rack, will catch no more fish today.

2.
Drunk, he leans back in his boat,
                              fishing alone for tortoise;
calmly he enters the sea, and rides his boat
                              out on the tides.
"Let the waves strike,
let's float with the wind!"
He crosses his arms at his chest and lets the paddle go.

(p. 215)

——These poems are *tz'u,* "lyrics." The first is inscribed on the handscroll painting, *Fisherman,* in the John M. Crawford, Jr., collection. Reproduced here as Plate 1.

The Fantastic Rock

From lake-caves the tortoise-heads protrude;
the sun comes out and bakes the tortoise-backs.
Turtles and lizards visit these rocks
coming in search of their own kind.

(p. 207)

Inscribed on a Painting of Bamboo

Flow, flow—he's often near water;
blow, blow—he's comfortable in the hills.
Ah, wonderful! this gentleman:
where on earth is he not at home?

(p. 209)

Poems Inscribed on Paintings of Bamboo

1.
In leaf after leaf we seem to hear the sighing of the wind,
utterly dissolving vulgar dust, purifying thought.
Deep in the night, through dreams wind the songs of River Hsiang,
twenty-five strings playing in brilliant autumn moonlight.

2.
For action, I chant out loud, for quiet, I just think;
the mirror shows my temple hairs one by one turn grey.
In my mind if there be a single anxious thought
I entrust it utterly to slanting branches of bamboo.

3.
Leaning on clouds, hugging rocks, slanting every way,
these frosted knots have not the slightest interest in the world.
If anyone should ask you whose brush it was did this,
simply tell them, "Some old bookworm in a chestnut grove."

(pp. 211–12)

Moonlight Bay

The moonlight ripples, ripples
                on water softly flowing;
as the moon is sinking
                the colors of dawn float up.
I laugh at myself—always rushing,
                I am like the moon:
coming from the east, going towards the west,
                when will I ever rest?

(p. 210)

To the Tune, *Chiu-ch'üan tzu*

Evening Clouds at Dragon Pond
Dragon Pond is located beneath the Shrine of the Dragon King
in front of Three Pagoda Temple, three *li* to the west of the
subprefectural city's T'ung-yüeh Gate. The water in it is agitated
and deep. When there happens to be a drought, prayers are offered
here. At times, there are fightening, windswept waves.

Three Pagoda Dragon Pond,
Thousand-year-old spot below
                the ancient dragon shrine:
how many destructions has it suffered
                yet it still survives,
quiet place, where one lone monk returns.

Dark foliage, a path
        runs straight beneath pine branches;
a tower, stories high,
        glittering green and gold.
Prayers for harvest, prayers for rainfall,
        here do reach the god;
beneath the shrine,
        evening clouds arise.

(pp. 212–13)

——This is one of eight poems depicting scenes near the poet's howetown of Chia-ho in
Chekiang. The poem is a *tz'u*.

[Untitled poem inscribed on a painting]

A level forest stretching far and wide,
a country stream, rippling *waves*.
Over this expanse, the evening sun sinks:
suffering, I travel foreign *land*.
In thatch-roofed inn, I meet the moon again;
the road to my village is indirect and *far*.
At the ferry, after everyone's gone home,
the fishermen make music as they move oars of *wood*.

(see Ni Tsan, p. 91)

[Ni Tsan]

The Taoist scholar Yüan-ch'u once resided in the Temple of the
Purple Void at Chia-ho (Wu Chen's hometown), and he enjoyed
the company of the recluse, Wu Chung-kuei (Wu Chen). He thus
obtained many of Wu's poems and paintings. In the tenth month
of this year, I first made the acquaintance of Yüan-ch'u. He brought
out this painting (i.e., the one on which the above poem was
inscribed) and showed it to me, requesting that I write a poem. I
therefore let my brush loose, following Recluse Wu's rhyme words
and inscribing the poem on the painting. The Recluse dubbed
himself Plum Blossom Man of Tao. The year *hsin-ch'ou,* twenty-
first year of the *chih-cheng* period (1361).

[Ni Tsan poem following rhyme-words of Wu Chen]

Mandarin Duck Lake is at Chia-ho,
lake-water in spring all rippling *waves.*
His home is in the Village of Plum Blossoms;
dreams now wind off to that white cloud *land.*
He moved his brush with purity and freedom,
sang his poem that resonates so *far.*
I wish I could be with the man inside the painting,
watching clouds, leaning on his cane made of palm-*wood.*

(see Ni Tsan, p. 91)

YANG WEI-CHEN (1296–1370)

A LTHOUGH he held a number of minor offices in the Yüan dynasty, and achieved considerable fame for his historiographical essay arguing in favor of the Sung dynasty as the only true claimant to historical legitimacy in the period immediately preceding the Yüan, Yang's greatest accomplishments were in the realms of poetry and calligraphy. As a calligrapher, he was the possessor of one of the most authentically eccentric, expressive styles in the history of the art (see plate 2). As a poet, Yang revives the expansive, free-wheeling *yüeh-fu* tradition best represented in the T'ang dynasty by Li Po (701–62); he is, in fact, one of the most successful practitioners of this style to follow Li. Yang also has a number of poems on acts of filial piety which help lay the groundwork for the important role played by this theme in the writings of such late Ming and early Ch'ing poets as Wu Chia-chi (q.v.) and Ch'ü Ta-chün (1630–96).

Tu-lu Poem

The *Tu-lu Poem* amongst the old Yüeh-fu is a work on the subject
of avenging a wrong done to one's father. T'ai-po in his imitation
of it turned it into a verse on redeeming the nation's shame. When
I was in Wu, I witnessed a case of a man who had left unavenged
a wrong done to his father, and yet was still residing in his father's
house—a supreme degradation of human patterns! I have written
this poem, therefore, so as to inspire men to establish the virtue of
a filial son.

Tu-lu, Tu-lu, evil waters running muddy:
an enemy confronts the clan,
a filial son must liquidate this shame.
The filial son is small of body,
but his courage fills the nine provinces
          of the land.
He grasps his sword, and slices the enemy
          who looked askance at father.
If wrongs to father were not avenged,
          with what face could he visit father's grave?
Let him wash out the enemy's skull
          and make of it a drinking cup!
Let him slice up the enemy's flesh
          and make of it a meal!
Then and only then will he
          be able to hold his head up high.

(p. 13)

——T'ai-po: Li Po (701–62). Tu-lu is apparently a placename, possibly of a stream or
river.

Song of a Dream Journey Over the Vast Sea

East of the eastern ocean
a hundred thousand miles from this land
there is an island called Vast Island,
five hundred miles square.
All around are waves of jasper,
        breakers of jade that rise and fall;
and on it nine peaks like Lo-fu's sacred range.
The weather is like springtime
        throughout all the year;
bejeweled flowers and gemstone trees
        never know the autumns of this world.
There the man-bird frolics with sky-deer,
and chimes of magic stone ring out.
The oranges are big as cauldrons,
the lotus leaves the size of boats;
white phoenixes as large as chickens,
red fish enormous, just like cows!
Blue-eyed immortal youths, black hair
        and purple robes
gather on the island to caper night and day.
The Man of Tao of Iron Cliff,
        constricted by the world's nine continents,
rides the wind and navigates
        the seafoam to the east.
At first all dark, the heavens open:
        the moon seems full of snow—
he dons embroidered cloak and enters
        a tower of yellow gold.
In the tower, the immortals
        lord it over this realm beyond the world.
With jasper mouth-organs they entice
        the cranes from Mt. Kou's peak.

They play with jade sceptres,
shattering coral hooks.
They summon Recluse Yüan,
nobly singing from the western reaches of the sky.
Up a long ladder he climbs
          to pluck seventy-two clusters
                   of green lotus.
He orders the Jade Dragon
          to plow 36,000 acres
                   of the K'un-lun mountain range.
The Yellow River, dark and shallow,
          he sees far down below.
"May the Old Men of this Ocean Mansion
          increase my tallies of long life!"

                                     (pp. 26–27)

Song of the Waterfall at Mount Lu

On the night of the sixteenth day of the eighth month, in autumn
of the year *chia-shen* (Sept. 22, 1344), I dreamed that I traveled to
Mount Lu with the Immortal Traveler, Suan-chai Hsien-k'o. Each
of us wrote a poem. Suan-chai wrote the *Poem of Young Man P'eng*.
I wrote the *Song of the Waterfall*.

The Milky Way's silver river
          suddenly has burst
and spilled as if from a cracked gourd
          below Five Elders' Peak.
I think the Heavenly Weaving Bird
          has woven pure white silk,
white silk which has unfurled from the spool
          to hang free in blue sky!

And so I want to take in hand
    a scissor from Ping-chou
and cut myself a section of this glassy, misty sheen.
But I run into Master Cloud Rock,
a man like the Immortal who clutched the moon!
His throat craved wine, he could not bear
    the nighttime thirst,
so he mounted a whale to drink the ocean.
    drying it down to the mulberry-field bed!
And then it stretched out to a hundred thousand feet
of jade rainbow plunging to the pure abyss below!

(p. 29)

——Suan-chai Hsien-k'o, Master Cloud Rock: Sobriquets of the poet, Kuan Yün-shih (1286–1324), who had died twenty years earlier.

——Yang Wei-chen also inscribed this poem across the top of the hanging scroll painting, *Gazing at a Waterfall* by the mid-fourteenth century painter, Hsieh Po-ch'eng; for this version, Yang composed a different prose introduction dealing with Hsieh's painting. See Laurence Sickman et al., *Chinese Calligraphy and Painting in the Collection of John M. Crawford, Jr.* (New York: Pierpont Morgan Library, 1962), pp. 114–115; and Shen C.Y. Fu et al., *Traces of the Brush* (New Haven: Yale University Art Gallery, 1977), pp. 35 and 194.

The Residence of the Emperors of Ch'en

Deserted city, residence of Ch'en emperors,
age-old palace where southern sovereigns lived.
No garden rocks now fill the winding pool,
but stumps of ancient trees do still remain.
The audience chamber, now a Buddhist shrine:
barefoot monks glide to the gong and bell.
Nor do we know a thousand years from now
what further changes will have taken place.

(p. 32)

The Horseman at the Roadside

Spring breezes waft along the avenue
touching willow branches of bright gold.
Beside the road, a well-appointed horseman,
his knightly aura rivaling the spring!
Amidst bamboo, a delicate flower, a peach,
as ravishing as Lovely Lady Tung!
The knight dismounts, and whispers through the leaves,
suspecting she's a flower-spirit there.

(p. 33)

The Horse-Watering Hole

Below the Great Wall—the watering hole:
water your horse there, and he'll rear back in fear.
Who could have known that the bubbling water
still echoes with the ringing of swords?

(p. 57)

Song of the Merchant's Wife

Floating, floating, your boat sets sail,
a thousand, ten thousand miles.
I wish I could take a pair of golden scissors
and cut off the Yangtze to the west!

(pp. 74–75)

Songs of Lake Tung-t'ing

1.
Sun sets on Tung-t'ing's waves;
a Wu girl floats by in her boat.
The man of Tao plays his iron flute:
wind raises more waves with evening.

2.
The man of Tao—his iron flute plays music:
half enters the Tung-t'ing hills.
And wind from heaven blows the other half
over the white waters of Silver Bay.

(p. 61)

Bamboo Branch Song of West Lake

Before the gate of Little Su
          flowers fill each branch;
along the Bank of Master Su
          young girls serve the wine.
You southern officials and northern inspectors:
          here's where you must come!
There's no place in the entire world
          like West Lake in Chiang-nan.

(p. 62)

Impromptu Inspirations

1.
Willow catkins, white as cotton,
          the fluff has just appeared;
plum blossoms, new and green,
          the pits have still not formed.
A woman serves wine at the counter
          wearing a melon-shaped hat;
a young girl takes a sip of wine,
          lips as red as cherries.

2.
This morning the air is fine for Ch'ing-ming;
along the river, wild flowers open everywhere.
An old farmer earnestly carries flowers to the grave:
two butterflies follow him, flying where he goes.

(p. 63)

Bamboo Branch Song of the Seacoast

Sea-lashed coast outside the gate reaches to the hedge;
the stairs here have a fishy smell,
          the sand-crabs are so fat.
The baby's only two years old—he's never seen his dad:
the man is east of the great sea—when will he return?

(p. 67)

Painting Her Nails

At night they pound the vermilion newt
                and stamens of buttercup;
her ten finger-tips, all transformed
                into red gosling beaks.
A leisurely moment—just one tune
                she plays on the jade lute:
several petals of flowering peach
                float upon the waters.

(p. 83)

NI TSAN (1301–74)

O NE OF the most innovative painters in the history of Chinese art, Ni created the characteristic compositional scheme of a spit of land in the foreground divided from a larger landmass in the background by a body of water receding along a subtle diagonal (see plate 3). His brushwork achieved a degree of sparse dryness unprecedented at the time and profoundly influential in later centuries. Ni's achievement as a poet is not on the same level, although the great Ch'ing scholar, Sung Lo (1634–1713) regarded him as a major name in Yüan poetry. The understated, sparse diction of Ni's verse may be linked with the same qualities in his painting. Legend holds that Ni was a virtual fanatic about cleanliness; he is said to have placed fresh goose feathers at the bottom of his privy after each visit there by a guest.

The Woodpecker

Where is he, the woodpecker?
Perched somewhere high in the trees.
His fragile body works so hard:
all day I hear his sound.
What he works towards is flourishing woods,
with no bugs eating trees away!
Alas! The pack of human beings:
they cannot match the heart of this bird.

(p. 46)

Following the Rhymes of the Six Poems, *Thinking of the Past at Ku-su and Ch'ien-t'ang*

(One poem from the series)

Hsi Shih received the favor of Wu:
this ancient terrace marks the spot.
All that remains is the moon of that time;
the people come no more.
Beside the terrace, the road used by Yüeh troops—
how many times have soldiers raised its dust?

(pp. 50–51)

——Hsi Shih: The most beautiful woman in history, Hsi Shih was sent to the King of
Wu by the King of Yüeh in hopes of so distracting him that he would let up his guard
and make it possible for Yüeh to defeat Wu in their ongoing war. The ruse succeeded.

On the Twentieth Day . . .

On the twentieth day of the first month of the twenty-third year
of the *chih-cheng* period (Feb. 4, 1363), several friends and I
gathered at Chen-sung's White Snow Pavilion. In this spot, the
trees and rocks are strangely beautiful, and the windows bright
and fresh. Moreover, the host loves literature and holds antiquity
in esteem. He is a man of both civil and military talents. We sat at
leisure, with delicacies and wine, and exchanged verses. Taking the
line,

Through the clouds we make out river trees,

by the lesser Hsieh, we divided the words so that each of us had to
write a poem with one of them as the rhyme. I got the word, *pien*
("distinguish," "make out").

The place is calm, dusty worries clear;
after rain, the mountain takes on luster.
Pool pavilion hides a quiet place;
lute and wine express our yearning feelings.
Verdant, these flourishing spring woods,
bringing rest to our weary wings.
On the rock are inscribed words:
moss eats at them, they are hard to read *(pien)*.

(p. 53)

———Lesser Hsieh: Hsieh T'iao (464–99), a poet of the Six Dynasties, so called by contrast
with Hsieh Ling-yün (385–433), the "Greater Hsieh."

Lamenting Noble Scholar Chu

This autumn day a noble man has died;
in delicate frost, the orchid withers.
A flock of geese possess the emerald pond;
the crane's shadow is alone on the terrace.
He must have ridden the chill wind out;
I think it's him, returning in thick fog.
Cedars and pines at evening sigh,
moved by what has passed, they hold
                    a lingering grief.

(p. 100)

Inscribed on a Painting by Myself

On the eastern seacoast lives a sick man
who calls himself mad and deluded.
He writes on walls and paints silk and paper:
surely he is more than insane.

(p. 128)

The Painting, *Solitary Fisherman by a Spring River*

By spring banks waterplants are green
and the river water transparent.
Gazing at the mountains and chanting poems out loud,
this fisherman's mind is not on fish.

(p. 131)

Inscribed on a Painting

Before the Shrine of the Filial Marquis
           rain falls;
beyond the bank of Yen-hua Stream
              the sun sets.
Past traces now—as if they were in dreams;
the spring wind in sorrow shreds the passing clouds.

                                        (pp. 134–35)

On the Fifteenth Day of the Ninth Month of the Year *Kuei-mao* of the *Chih-cheng* Period (Oct. 22, 1363), I Painted This to Send to the Summoned Scholar, Sheng-po, and Inscribed This Poem on It

River bank—the evening tides have started to ebb.
Wind-swept woods—frosty leaves are thinning out.
I lean on my cane; the bramble gate is quiet.
I long for my friend; mountain colors—dim and faint.

                                            (p. 138)

——Sheng-po: Yü K'an, a recluse of the late Yüan to early Ming, himself a painter, poet and book-collector.

——This poem is inscribed on Ni's painting, *Wind Among the Trees on the Stream Bank,* in The John M. Crawford, Jr. collection. Reproduced here as Plate 3.

A Man in Hangchou Spread Word that I Had Died. Chen-chü Heard of This and Was Upset, So I Have Written This To Send Him

Fog obscures the deserted mountain,
               deep in autumn colors;
in the thatched hut, the wine is ready—
               for whom shall I pour it?
Chrysanthemums and maple leaves
               share sadness with me;
the gully stream and wind in the pines
               accompany my lonely chant.
I wash out my ears, unwilling to hear
               what vulgar people say;
in drunken sleep, I no longer play
               the pure tones of my lute.
Far off, I know you are gazing at the moon,
               deep in thoughts of me:
how could I help but write this poem
               to console your troubled heart?

(pp. 219–20)

Following the Rhymes of Yü-chai's Poems on Autumn Feelings

(One poem from a group of three)

You ask when I will go back home—
               there's no itinerary;
autumn light, this traveler's feelings:
               both are chill and clear.

Snow preserving footprints of geese:
        surely an illusion;
a tapestry of tortoise hairs:
        what hope it can be done?
A crumbling house, the owners fled—
        cold will-o'-the-wisps flickering.
An ancient palace, its foundation
        overgrown with weeds.
Listen if you will to the gurgling
        of water in the canal:
water really has no feelings, but seems to have them here.

                                  (pp. 226–27)

Inscribed on the Painting, *River in Autumn*

The Yangtze River, autumn colors
        fathomless, no limit;
as wild geese go flying past,
        water splashes sky.
In the river inlets, all seventy-two,
        this night of bright moonlight,
reed blossoms and maple leaves
        cover the fishing boats.

                                    (p. 329)

To the Retired Scholar Chang

The riverside willows sway their green mist;
their reflections merge with ten thousand miles of sky.
The Retired Scholar from time to time
                is starled from his dream:
before the gate, they beat a drum
                as a salt barge sets sail.

(p. 323)

Waking from a Nap

I wake from a nap, light clouds
                fill the gullyside;
cows and sheep at sunset are coming down the southern slope.
Wealth and status in this floating life
                are really worth nothing at all:
it's just like bustling ants that live inside a single stump.

(p. 351)

Two Poems to the Tune, *Jen-yüeh yüan*

1.

It breaks the heart, don't ask
            the affairs of former dynasties!
Again I climb the Terrace of the Kings of Yüeh.
Here, where partridges sing,
grass turns green in the east wind
and flowers bloom in fading sunlight.

Sadly I whistle to myself;
this ancient kingdom of verdant mountains,
noble trees and rich moss.
The moon of those years—
lingering, lingering pale shadow—
from somewhere comes flying back.

2.

Startled awake, back from a dream
            of those years:
fishermen's songs rise from the southern ford.
Painted folding screen of cloudy peaks,
pool bank of spring grass:
unlimited melting of the soul.

My old home must still be there:
paulownia trees shading the well,
willows concealing the gate.
This body at leisure grows old in vain,
in a solitary boat, listening to the rain,
lamplight flickering from the river village.

                                                        (pp. 408–9)

——These poems are *tz'u.*

Two Poems to the Tune, *Hsiao-t'iao hung*

1.

A river of autumn water, pale, cold mist;
reflections as if in sheer silk.
Before my eyes, sorrow of parting—
              several V's of geese
write words against clear sky.

White duckweed, red smartweed form their patterns;
to the sound of Wu songs, oars are rowed.
A long cry of suffering
startles up the egrets from their sleep.

2.

Mist and water of Five Lakes, this body not gone home;
between heaven and earth, my temples turning grey.
White wine, fresh meat, I invite my close neighbors,
host serving guests.

The affairs of this world rise and fall
              through a lifetime.
A few lodgings in the green mountains,
a single leaf of a fishing boat:
with these for now I'll elude the windblown dust.

(pp. 405–6)

——These poems are *tz'u*.

——An additional poem by Ni Tsan will be found at the end of the section on Wu Chen on p. 56.

II

MING DYNASTY
(1368–1644)

CHANG YÜ (1333–85)

O NE OF the "Four Great Ones of Suchou"—the others being Yang Chi, Hsü Pen, and Kao Ch'i (qq.v.)—Chang Yü is among the freshest voices in early Ming poetry. The serene tone of much of his poetry belies the turmoil of his political life: delicate accommodation to the rebel rule of Chang Shih-ch'eng, besiegement at Suchou, exile twice, and finally suicide by drowning, probably to avoid implication in a conspiracy. Chang was a painter (as were Yang and Hsü); the landscape reproduced in Plate 4 may be the only surviving work by his hand currently in the West. It depicts a scene as tranquil as those evoked by his poems.

The Pavilion for Listening to Fragrance

Brilliant, bright—the flowers of the cold season!
Their subtle fragrance arises in the quiet.
Others are hoping to smell them a few times,
but I prefer to use my ears!
The fragrance sends forth jewel-like songs;
singing them out loud, I feel such joy!
And who says there is no fragrance in sound?
Smelling and hearing are really the same thing.
But best of all would be to end all sound,
and also get rid of fragrance and form.
No smelling, and also no hearing at all—
back to the mystery of the Primal One.

(1/27a)

——An amusing anticipation of Baudelaire (1821–67) and his *Correspondences*, with its
conception of synaesthesia.

In a Book-Box I Found the Lost Manuscript of a Poem Sent to Me by the Late Kao [Ch'i]

Brushing away the dust, I opened the broken box
and suddenly held a friend's poem in my hand.
Touching this paper, I felt he was still alive—
but then remembered his death, how hard it would be to find him.
I recalled when we were in Suchou,
how everyone praised his literary talent.
In conversation, he analyzed profound principles
and sent forth fragrant words from his heart.
At that time, I was staying in the northern quarter
in a quiet studio overlooking a pond.

Burning orchid-lamps, we invited the moon to join us;
drinking wine, we plucked the strings of our lute.
Who would have thought that for another evening of joy
we would have to wait for thousands of years!
Now your wandering spirit is far away in darkness,
and only cold words are left, in your own hand.
The dusty ink still gives off a light fragrance,
the paper is torn, but still has luster.
As I linger over the powerfully brushed characters
I recall your voice, chanting poems out loud.
But I never had a chance to reply to this poem:
your deep feeling for me: I have betrayed it!
I finish reading with a long sigh of grief
and the wind in the forest echoes my sadness.
I wonder: on the day you wrote this poem,
could you have foreseen that I would feel this way?

(1/28b–29a)

——Kao Ch'i (1336–74): A close friend of Chang Yü and the major poet of his time. See
pp. 122ff.

Staying Overnight at T'ien-ning Ch'an Temple

I rush to the office when I'm in the city,
but when my duties are over, I take walks in the hills.
This evening I visit a Ch'en-dynasty temple,
its corridors and halls filled with ancient treasures.
In crumbling niches, gold Buddhas shine;
marvelous paintings cover the high walls.
A broken stele can no longer be read:
cracked, and covered with moss.
The old monk, well acquainted with the Dharma,
sits in meditation, cultivating tranquility.

He shows me a palm-leaf manuscript
and we pass the evening in profound conversation.
Wind-bells sound above the clouds
and dew drips into the pond and the spring.
Our words seem to be in perfect accord:
from this day on, I will leave the world behind.

(1/42b)

The Merchant's Joy

All year long, he never visits his home town:
by nature, he loves to be a traveler!
So he has entrusted his livelihood to the rivers and lakes,
never refusing a distant journey for the sake of profit.
Burning magic money, pouring libations of wine,
                    he prays for good winds at dawn;
he makes friends everywhere he goes, east or west.
In this floating home of his, there's nothing to tie him down,
and his name has never been entered
                    in the tax-collector's books!
On board his huge ship, with its two enormous sweeps,
his major concubine can sing for him,
                    and his minor concubine can dance!
He buys fine wines every day at the wineshops along the river,
and knows nothing of the pain of parting in the ordinary world.
There are many houses of pleasure on both banks of the Yangtze:
a thousand doors, ten thousand gates—
                    he has passed through them all!
What other human is as happy as the merchant:
aside from stormy weather, what problems does he have?

(2/1a)

Song of the Old Oak

No one knows how old this tree is, standing before the mountain;
in profusion, its mass of dark colors reaches to the sky.
The frosty branches and twisted roots
                    are like battling dragons and tigers;
in the huge, drooping canopy sing crickets and cicadas.
Its green leaves, weaving patterns, are full of life,
and the holes in the trunk swarm with colonies of ants.
The upper branches darkly slant across the clouds;
the roots below dig deep into the thick earth.
Beside the tree is an ancient shrine to the local god:
people pour libations of wine, moistening the roots of the tree.
"We only wish that the spirit of this place
                    be provided always with offerings,
so the tree and the people who live nearby
                    will live for many years."
An old man of the village, who has raised sons and grandsons,
says, "This tree has been here for ages;
I remember as a child I'd climb this tree,
and when I look at the roots and branches,
                    they still are just the same!"
It has lived through times of chaos, and seen times of peace;
how many woodcutters have chopped away at it,
                    and yet it never died!
The mountain monks, loving this spot,
                    cut thatch for a retreat,
but the thick greenery of the tree still stands firm,
                    here beside the eaves.
Wait until I come in the sixth month, bringing a cot with me:
I'll lie down, and listen to the south winds in this tree
                    like the roar of ocean waves.

                                        (2/8a–b)

The Retreat of Sun Ching-hsiang

Tired of walking in the red dust
you moved to this quiet river village.
To breed fish, you have built a broad pond;
in love with bamboo, you have transplanted some
                              in front of the gate.
Moonlight touches the covers of your books;
mountain colors enter your wine cup.
As for me, I'm ashamed of being caught up in official duties;
I still haven't found my fields and gardens.

(4/5b)

The Mountain Retreat of a Recluse

Your home is deep in the white clouds:
the green of mountains faces your gate.
The trees are thick, their flowers bear fruit;
the earth is warm, the bamboo has grandchildren!
Monkeys hang from withered pines, snapping the branches;
oxen trudge into the shallow stream, muddying the water.
You say that since you've gone into retirement
you can't bother talking to vulgar people.

(4/6a–b)

Reading the Poetry Collection of Lü Fang-ch'ing

Just one hundred poems in this little book—
but in poetry, quantity is not quality.
Halfway through life, you still live in respectable poverty,
but at least you can work at your five-word lines.
The blandness of your style hides inner richness;
in the level places: suddenly, towering peaks!
Late at night, reading these by lamplight
a man drives off the demon of sleep.

(4/6b)

The Retreat of Liu Kuo-pao

From the day you retired to this home of three paths
you have led your life in the Land of Intoxication.
You say the roads of the world are dangerous:
they can't compare with staying at home!
Shaken by the wind, the pines give a cold sound.
Steamed by the rain, the flowers waft fragrance.
So why are you not completely at peace?
Because you still work hard at your poems.

(4/6b)

The Four Seasons in the Mountains

Spring
Dawn: I half-open the gate;
last night the east wind blew wild.
All the blossoms have fallen from the trees:
the ground is covered with the fragrance of white clouds.

Summer
In the sixth month, deep in the mountains,
the coolness of pine breezes touches my clothes.
I imagine the people far away in the city:
their faces are being struck by fiery dust!

Autumn
I sit alone on a rock by the stream;
the woods are deserted, full of autumn feeling.
Late at night, the mountain moon is white
and dew from the pines drips cool on my clothes.

Winter
The old man of the mountains loves the mountains:
in the mountains he has built his thatched hut.
At night, there's a storm; the snow is so thick
it snaps branches of bamboo outside the window.

(6/2b)

Quatrain

At this remote village, I have no neighbors.
In my thatched house, late at night: rain.
A dog barks somewhere out in the fields.
The cook whispers softly in the kitchen.

(6/3a)

Four Poems On the Ch'ung-wu Festival

(Two poems from the group of four)

The Artemisia tiger
They make a fake tiger, and hope it will seem real,
then hang the ferocious beast outside the door.
If the evil spirits have any brains at all
when they see this thing, they will not be afraid.

The Hundred-Fold Cord
A thousand threads, ten-thousand strands
are tied to the child's arm.
They hope the child will live a good long life,
a year for every inch of cord!

(6/3b)

Notes to the poems on the Ch'ung-wu Festival:
According to the *Ching Ch'u sui-shih chi,* a text compiled by
Tsung Lin (c.550–c.563) of the Liang dynasty which describes
various customs of the Hupei-Hunan-Chianghsi region, "On the
fifth day of the fifth month [of the lunar calendar, i.e., the 'Ch'ung-
wu' or 'Tuan-wu' Festival], people make an image of a tiger out of
artemisia—or cut one out of cloth and then attach some artemisia
leaves—and the women vie in wearing them in their hair."
Presumably the image functions as a charm to drive away evil
influences. The fact that Chang Yü says the tiger-charms are hung
outside the door, rather than worn in people's hair, may be taken as
an indication that he is not following the textual account, but rather
describing the actual custom of his day, which may have changed in
this detail from the period of the text.
According to the *Shih-wu chi-yüan,* an encyclopedia compiled
by Kao Ch'eng (c. 1085) of the Sung dynasty, "In the Han dynasty,

on the fifth day of the fifth month, a vermilion cord with a seal of five colors would be hung at the door as an ornament so as to ward off evil influences. Today we have the hundred-fold cord, which is the descendant of the vermilion cord. Thus the practice began in the Han dynasty and originally involved a door ornament, but people today tie it to the arm, which results from an error in the transmission of the custom."

The same text points out that the fifth day of the fifth month represents nearly the mid-point of summer (in the lunar calendar), a time when, although the *yang* force is at its height, the new *yin* force is starting to grow. It is therefore a time of vulnerability, and the customs described in Chang Yü's poems are intended to afford protection from all negative forces.

Paintings

(Two poems from a group of ten)

1.
I close the book in my hands;
you stop playing the lute on your lap.
We look at each other...until evening falls:
there is a lingering music from the mountains and streams.

2.
His pole and paddle have been with him a long time.
He feels close to the water-birds.
This old man of the river, with his bamboo cape,
he has seen them all: the travelers who come and go.

(6/4a)

The Cliff of the Ancient Tomb

(A poem from a group entitled "Seven Poems on Living in the Mountains: Seeing Off Chou Po-yang")

No one comes to this deserted mountain;
at the foot of the cliff, a tomb from a century ago.
Who is it, then, that always sweeps it clean?
—Swaying, swaying, the white poplar tree.

(6/5a)

Brewing Tea at Moon Pond.

I ask a mountain woman for a light
and build a fire of herbs beside the pond.
How wonderful, the taste of the water here,
with its faint bouquet of fallen petals!

(6/6a)

Looking at Chrysanthemums And Remembering Meng-tsai and Yu-wen

In moonlight, we would enjoy these flowers together;
unless they were in the mountains, we wouldn't bother going.

Now, years after our parting,
I face this hedgeful of autumn alone.

(6/7b)

——Meng-tsai and Yu-wen: Yang Chi (c.1334–c.1383) and Hsü Pen (1335–80), who, together with Chang Yü and Kao Ch'i (1336–74), constituted the Four Great Ones of early Ming poetry. These men were all close friends. See pp. 95ff, 112ff, and 122ff.

——"Hedgeful of autumn:" Derived from T'ao Ch'ien's (365–427) famous line, "I pluck chrysanthemums beneath the eastern hedge." Chrysanthemums are the flower par excellence of autumn.

The Moon Window

(A poem from a group entitled "Twelve Miscellaneous Poems On the Fang Garden")

This house was built beside the emerald bamboo;
its window opens, shaped like a circle!
How is it that the moon was taken from the sky
and moved here, into the wall of this house?

(6/8b)

Painting

(One poem from a set of two)

Slowly I walk the gully path, alone,
leisurely clouds following my bramble cane.
I want to find the source of this stream,
but probably only the monkeys know where it is.

(6/9a)

Spring Night

The night is tranquil, the wind-blown curtain
                 flaps open and closed.
The misty moon in the southern garden
                 is lingering as it crosses the sky.
It's hard for the traveler to fall asleep
                 on such a night as this,
especially when the flowers' fragrance
                 reaches him on his bed.

                                (6/10a)

Butterflies

Spring is here, and everywhere they pursue the sweet fragrance,
flying past the vermilion chamber and the painted walls.
It is the beautiful woman who loves them best of all:
pair by pair, she embroiders their images into her dancing robe.

                                (6/10b)

Summer Night at the Pond Pavillion

With disheveled headcloths, we sit late on the bench,
half drunk as the cool breeze blows on us.
Suddenly, someone completes a beautiful line:
                 we clap our hands,
and the egrets, startled, fly up from the lotus pond.

                                (6/13b)

In a Boat On the Cha River

Bignonia blossoms on both shores, a streamful of water,
an inlet of white sand: here I ride my boat!
In setting sunlight, I follow the south-bound geese
                                    with my eyes,
missing all the beautiful mountains as we pass by.

                                                        (6/14b)

Painting

(One poem from a group of four)

A jade cave, ten thousand flowering peach trees
                                    of immortality,
towers and terraces like those of Ts'ai Ching's family!
The divine elixir is ready, but who needs to take it now?
Let's give it to the mountain boy to feed to the crows.

                                                        (6/18a)

——Ts'ai Ching's family: Ts'ai Ching, a man of the Latter Han dynasty, and his entire
    family joined the immortals on the seventh day of the seventh month.

In the Evening, Walking in the Western Fields

White waters twist and turn among crumbling embankments;
far beyond the forest can be heard an evening rooster.
For my quiet walks, I rarely go east of where I live,
because there are green mountains west of my house.

                                                        (6/18a)

Lamenting for Kao Ch'ing-ch'iu, Chi-ti

1.

In lamplilght, I open your book, and start to weep:
my wife and children, startled, wonder what is wrong.
My friend of the river is dead today,
and I have dug the poems he sent me out of a box.

2.

When I first got the news, it was hard to believe;
with you gone, who can I talk to about poetry?
Your son and daughter are little children:
the thousand poems you have left behind—to whom
should they be entrusted?

3.

What can be said of the meaning of your life?
No salary, no land—how sad it was!
But there is your fame which will never fade,
like the *yüeh-fu* of Han or the poetry of T'ang!

(6/18b)

——Kao Ch'ing-ch'iu (Kao Chi-ti): Kao Ch'i (1336–74), the greatest poet of his time and Chang's close friend.

——*Yüeh-fu:* A type of poetry based on folk songs.

Hearing a Song from My Boat

Where is this beautiful song being sung,
          with its short and long notes?
Shore-wind, sand-rain mingling with the sad sound!
There's no need to hear it at the ends of the earth
          to be deeply moved:
I'm only one day away from home, and it's breaking my heart.

          (6/21b)

To the Innkeeper at Five Rivers, Sun Pen

The inn towers impressively on the bank of the ancient river.
Day after day you see off the ships of high officials from this place.
If I hadn't shared a cup of wine with you in the lamplight,
how would I have realized that the innkeeper was a poet?

          (6/22a)

YANG CHI (C. 1334–C. 1383)

O NE OF the Four Great Ones of Suchou, Yang was a poet and painter both. He was a child prodigy, able to recite the entire *Six Classics!* He is said to have greatly impressed Yang Wei-chen (q.v.) by writing a poem in Yang's own style about his famous iron flute (Yang Wei-chen was known by his nom-de-plume of the Master of the Iron Flute). Yang Chi took office briefly in the rebel government of Chang Shih-ch'eng, probably less out of enthusiastic support for Chang than out of expediency. After being sent into exile as a consequence, Yang eventually was appointed to office under the new Ming dynasty. False political accusations ultimately led to his death at hard labor. Yang's poetry, like that of his associates Chang Yü and Hsü Pen (qq. v.), contrasts dramatically with his difficult life in its predominant tone of serentiy.

Nesting Among Clouds

—Written for Chou Meng-chi

The white clouds are mindless, they never come to rest;
now you have built a "cloud-nest" to live among the clouds!
You built for ten years, until clouds filled the mountain;
then the clouds kept you there, and you have never left.
You made a nest of clouds—but the clouds know nothing of this:
the doors and windows are made of clouds, clouds for beams and
                                                pillars.
In this nest there is nothing at all, except for clouds;
the tables, mats, pillows and mattress—all are made of clouds.
People say you are nesting in a bundle of clouds:
but you're not nesting in the clouds, the clouds are nesting in you!
Who is right? Who is wrong? Who can really say?
Clouds are you, you are clouds—nothing is impossible.
All those generals of Cloud Terrace, with their incomes
                                        of thousands:
like a flash of lightning through ten thousand miles of blue clouds!
Human wealth and nobility are like floating clouds,
how much better to nest in clouds, in the few rooms of this home.

                                                        (pp. 142–43)

——Probably a playful poem of congratulation to a friend on the completion of his private
retreat.

——"All those generals of Cloud Terrace": Emperor Ming of the Latter Han dynasty had
portraits of twenty-eight great generals painted in a building of this name.

A Poem on Passing by Hsin-k'ai Lake at Kao-yu in Light Rain

The remnants of a rainbow fall to the western bank at dawn,
gulls and egrets fly in confusion through the rain.
All day long, the little boat travels inside a painting:
lotus leaves and lotus blossoms, an unbroken fragrance.
In the bow of the boat is an old man
     with a beard a foot long,
piling up water chestnuts, and selling fish.
His son can work the rudder, his daughter sweeps the scull:
what use for them to be brilliant and read lots of books?

(p. 187)

The Studio for Listening to the Snow

Beneath the silent eaves, a tinkling as of jade,
clearer and clearer as night draws on.
The sound of wind is nothing like it,
the dripping of raindrops is not so crisp.
Sitting by the window, I listen without tiring;
as I stir up the fire, my ears are amazed!
If you say it is plum blossoms falling,
no, plum blossoms fall lighter than this.

(p. 262)

A Poem Making Fun of Chi-ti for His Eye Illness

Sleepless, you hear the neighboring temple bell,
the sound seems to brighten your ears!
When you chant poems at night you must avoid gazing
                                        at the moon;
when you walk in the morning you must keep your back
                                        to the wind.
All images seem to appear in a haze,
the mountains are shrouded in fog.
You try going out—and crash into the door;
you must ask the children whether it's night or it's day!

                                                    (p. 264)

——Chi-ti: Kao Ch'i (1336–74), the great early Ming poet, and a friend of Yang Chi. See
   pp. 122ff.

Living in Master Fang's Garden—Ten Poems

(Three poems from the group of ten)

1.

The autumn season comes to the country,
a fresh coolness, as if after rain.
Your bag contains medicines proven to work;
your mat is piled high with the books you have written.
When the wine is warm, you know sadness will diminish.
When flowers open, you will feel your illness cured.
Why should you ever waste your money to buy
mountain fruits or fresh-water fish!

2.

You remove a jade pendant—to exchange for a lute,
and sell a few books to buy wine.
Nights in the pavilion, among the bamboo, listening to the snow;
time spent looking at flowers at the plum blossom hut!
Your daughter has been married to a local farmer,
your son has become a gardener.
The old man next door is impossibly vulgar:
but how can you refuse when he asks you over for a drink?

3.

Your garden hut stands by the green waters.
No tax-collectors ever come here!
For your yearly stipend—a thousand orange trees;
for your autumn wardrobe—half an acre of lotus!
When you drink, you get drunk before all your guests.
The transmission of your poems you leave to the masses.
Because you love the scenery along the stream,
you go off alone in a boat, for a week at a time.

(pp. 270–73)

Living in a Riverside Village—Miscellaneous Impressions—Twenty Poems

(Six poems from the group of twenty)

1.

Three feet of mud in this narrow alley:
no one comes to visit me, hidden in seclusion.
Whistling at the window, the wind keeps me from sleep;
dampening the stove, raindrops make poverty even worse.
On country roads, wild flowers greet the traveler,
on bridges spanning the river, willows see him off.
For now, I must lead this primitive life
and rest this exiled body as best I can.

2.

I planned to get drunk to ease my sadness,
but my sadness just increased when I got drunk!
I've been returned to my home province, but I still seem
                                        to be a traveler;
the older I get, the more I feel like a monk.
Impressions for poems?—flute music carried from the tower
                                        by the wind.
Sounds of chessmen?—from the lamplit boat in the snow.
Don't think this life is unbearable:
the hermit-farmer can take it all.

3.

Reflections in the river: trembling spring trees.
High-water marks: engraved on the evening sand.
Green reeds, three feet of rainwater;
red hibiscus, a hedgeful of blossoms.
Leave your country, and you still think of your country.
Return home, and you go on dreaming of home!
I have never had a desire for rank and salary:
why do I have to be so far from the capital?

4.
Suddenly, warm weather, I change to lighter clothes.
Quietly, I stroll along the green banks.
The birds chirp, as if they had a complaint;
the flowers look saddened, as if lamenting some loss.
I remember the older generations for their integrity,
and stand in awe of the young for their talents.
I feel a natural love for the pleasures of the country:
I've never purposely hidden from the world of reputation!

5.
I've given up poetry—I have no new manuscripts.
I've stopped playing the lute—it's hidden in its box.
Mushrooms are growing in the mortar
     where I used to pound herbs.
Lichens have covered the spade which once dug flower-beds.
The pathway is full of puddles—I'm too lazy to sweep them away.
The garden is overgrown—I'm too tired to pull out the weeds.
And I'm fearful of questions about my past life:
before people have even opened their mouths,
    I start to feel ashamed.

6.
Just a few feet away, a temple from the Six Dynasties,
pines and cedars shading its low walls.
Wild monkeys steal offerings to Buddha,
and mountain birds imitate the way people speak.
The stones here are imbued with spirit—even on clear days
     they are moist.
The stream has a voice—in the utter silence
     it keeps babbling.
My worldly mind has long since become void;
this place is my Jetavana monastery.

(pp. 279–84)

——Jetavana monastery: In Buddhist hagiology, a park near Shravasti in India, donated
 to the congregation of monks by the great donor, Anāthapindika.

Living in the Country at Kou-ch'ü in Autumn—Miscellaneous Impressions—Ten Poems

(Three poems from the group of ten)

1.

This thatched hut, its master returned;
this desolate village, like a foreign country . . .
The trees are cold, crows circle the moon;
the river is chilly, wild geese cry in the frost.
Shadows now depend on lamplight for life;
sadness is forgotten, as long as there is wine!
Tomorrow morning, when I look in the mirror,
how many more white hairs will I have?

2.

Shut in behind the window, a glittering candle;
burning in the censer, the thin smoke of incense.
No wind—it still is not too cold.
It is raining, making the night seem even longer.
Hungry rats shake the food sacks;
dying fireflies fall into the tattered bookbag.
My dream of rivers and oceans, for ten years now—
on a night like this, could I expect to forget it?

3.

This place is near Hua-yang Mountain;
I come and go alone, among its three peaks.
The plants there are fragrant—a thousand species of herbs.
The pine trees are ancient—covered all over with moss.
I'm amazed by monkeys reading over my shoulder!
The door is nudged open by an occasional deer.
East of the walled enclosure are bamboo plants.
I've transplanted some of them to the northern courtyard.

(pp. 285–86)

——Hua-yang Mountain: The Taoist name for Mount Kou-ch'ü, given to it by the great alchemist and thinker, T'ao Hung-ching, who, like Yang Chi, lived there in retirement.

Wu Shan-yang

(One poem from the series, "Thinking of My Friends at Kou-jung Subprefecture")

Mind and environment—you have quieted both.
You close your door when the wind blows from the pines.
For pendants, you knot orchid leaves of purple.
For a cap, you use the skin of mottled bamboo.
You drink little—always drunk before everyone else!
You write a lot—you expunge many of your own poems.
Recently you've been too lazy for mountain climbing,
so you've covered your walls with paintings of autumn hills!

(p. 290)

From Sand River to Ts'ai Rock

(One poem from a group of four)

After my illness, so hard to be a traveler!
At the edge of the sky, alone, just myself.
How many days since I heard the magpie's call?
For a thousand miles, I haven't met a soul.
My dreams are good—an empty kind of happiness;
my poems have gotten better—no cure for poverty!
I'm ashamed to let loose this fishing boat of mine
along the banks of the Five Lakes.

(pp. 298–99)

Meeting My Fellow Countryman, Yü Wu-chung

I pour out wine in a libation to the river god
and prognosticate my future path from the wind.
Here, beyond the grasses of the spring,
I have made the acquaintance of a countryman of mine!
We talk intimately—it is difficult to part.
Our friendship is new—but that just makes closeness easier.
And because you have asked where my ancestors are buried,
fresh tears fall, and dampen my clothes.

(pp. 299–300)

Selling My Official Robe

In the "phoenix ranks" I was granted the Purple Robe,
decorated with embroidered clusters of autumn sunflowers.
On night duty at the Imperial Shrine
                I'd wear it before the crowing of the rooster.
During spring audience at the Inner Palace
                I'd wear it as I sat on horseback.
The dew of those immortal precincts dripped on it:
                it glitters still!
Royal incense perfumed its sleeves: it still smells fragrant!
But here in the mountains I have no more dreams of paradise—
I'll exchange it for money to buy some wine.

(pp. 375–76)

Reviewing the Troops at Kuei-lin
with Military Inspectors Chiang And Chang

On the pennants of blue are bold characters:
    "Wild Cat Imperial Guards."
Linked armor of gold is worn over field coats.
A thousand ships moored for the night—
    the misty river is wide.
Breakfast fires burn in ten thousand stoves—
    the vaporous mountains are high.
On the general's broad swallow-jaws
    whiskers bristle like lances.
The prisoners—emaciated geese!—
    have faces that look like knives.
I'm only sorry that Kao Shih is not here
to ride horses with us to West River
    and review the mustered troops.

(p. 399)

——Kao Shih (?702–65): A famous poet of the T'ang dynasty who was particularly interested in military affairs. Yang Chi uses him to represent Yang's friend, the poet Kao Ch'i, who was also interested in the military.

Walking in the Country Outside
T'ai-yüan on a Spring Day

Teeth of clogs, carriage wheels, the hooves of horses:
everywhere, the green brush has been worn down into paths.
But there's no one here to lament the flowers as their petals fall,
so I have come to listen a while to the calls of the birds.

I love letting my sandals follow each bend of the river;
I want my spirits to rise as high as these mountains!
Now my poem is finished—who will accompany me on the flute?
No, I'll inscribe these words on the vines
        or maybe on the stones.

(pp. 403–4)

Spring Dreams

Spring dreams, more spring dreams:
dreams the same as the waking world.
Even if the wind should blow them away
we'd look at each other and still be in a dream.

(p. 413)

Five-Color

A five-color robe of embroidered silk:
many flowers, and a few sparse branches.
Spring is here, and I'm afraid to put it on:
the butterflies might all land on me!

(p. 414)

A Painting of Bamboo by Ni Yün-lin

In painting bamboo, the spirit must be transmitted;
whoever said it's a matter of being realistic?
Only you comprehended this principle:
you must have been Master Yü-k'o in a former life.

(p. 417)

——Ni Yün-lin: Ni Tsan (1301–74), one of the major painters of the Yüan dynasty. See
pp. 66–75.
——Yü-k'o: Wen T'ung (d. 1079), the greatest master of bamboo painting.

A Noble Scholar Playing the Lute

The river is calm, the moon reflected in its waters.
The mountain is quiet, autumn filling its pavilions.
He plays for a while and then he stops:
music never meant for people to hear.

(p. 418)

Pitch-Ball

(One of a series of ten poems entitled "Ten Poems on the Tuan-yang Festival")

Down, up—a single dot of red:
suddenly it rises above the blue clouds.
In the brisk winds, it comes to earth slowly:
everbody gazes up, face toward the sky.

(pp. 425, 427)

Submitting a Memorial Requesting Permission to Return Home and Care for My Parents

I wish to submit a memorial expressing my feelings:
the feelings are intense, so the language is strong.
I'm afraid the high officials will get angry at something—
here beneath the lamp, I read it through again and again.

(p. 429)

Scenes

(One poem from a group of four)

Eastern neighbor, western neighbor:
        swallows flying.
Tomorrow or the next day,
        spring will be gone.
Much sadness, much illness,
        saying goodbye:
no wine, no money,
        pawning my clothes!

(p. 437)

Spring Days in My Home Town

(One poem from a group of eight)

Thousands of flowers, thousands of petals:
        turned to dust on the ground!

Only the vines are still blossoming, by themselves.
But things must be even worse at my neighbor's house:
the butterflies that flew into his garden
            have come back here again!

(p. 449–50)

Springtime Embroidery

(One poem from a group of four entitled "Paintings of Ladies Engaged in Four Sprintime Occupations")

The wind fills her embroidery loom with willow catkins,
and pairs of purple swallows come flying in.
Now, when she rests her needle, is the moment she really enjoys:
wetting a piece of wool in her mouth,
            she spits it out the window!

(p. 456)

On Seeing a Firefly in My Room

On a rainy night, the house is desolate—
            I've stopped chanting poems.
Now a firefly flies in through some crack,
            as if looking for me!
He must have pitied me for having no candle or lamp,
and entered, within the gauze curtains,
            to illuminate the depths of this night.

(p. 458)

Miscellaneous Impressions of T'an-chou— Nine Poems

(One poem from the group of nine)

Up at the prow, I wash my mouth, dripping water on my robe.,
Petals are flying across the surface of the water—
                    my mouth is perfumed!
As I sit here, I love the dragonflies and butterflies
for bringing so much springtime to the mast of my boat.

(pp. 494, 496)

Describing My Feelings While Living in the Spring Quarters at Chiang-ning

—Four Poems to the Tune *Ch'ing-p'ing-yüeh*
(One poem from the group of four)

Wild singing, drunken dancing,
in the blink of an eye, past and present are gone!
White hairs, just a few thin strands on my head;
I have heard each drop of spring rain in Chiang-nan!
Now I've retired to this three-room hut of thatch:
the "flowing waters of peach blossoms" go bubbling by!
Let's not plant any bamboo outside the window:
I want to be able to look out at the western mountains.

(pp. 507–9)

——"Flowing waters of peach blossoms:" A direct quotation from a famous poem by Li
   Po, *Question and Answer in the Mountains:* "The Flowing waters of peach blossoms go
   off into dark distance..." Yang implies that, like Li Po, he too is living the life of a
   recluse in harmony with nature.

——This poem is a *tz'u*.

Describing My Feelings While Living in Retirement by the Riverside

—Seven Poems to the Tune, *Ch'ing-yü an*
(One poem from the group of seven)

The oriole songs hold me to look at the mountains
                    even longer.
Before I leave, I glance back once again.
Although there is spring beauty everywhere,
the warm breeze, the light vapor,
the pale mist and fine rain
are mostly in the willows by the river.

I know I have no political skill,
nor any ambition to be granted a fief
                    with an official seal big as a dipper.
Who needs millionaire friends from Gold Valley
                    to have a good time?
I'll just find a man willing to pawn his clothes—
so we can get drunk together on Chin-ling wine!

                                        (pp. 521–22)

——This poem is a *tz'u*.

HSÜ PEN (1335–80)

LIKE Chang Yü, Yang Chi, and Kao Ch'i (qq.v.), Hsü was one of the "Four Great Ones of Suchou," and like Chang and Yang, he was also a painter (see Plate 5). These four men were considered to form part of a larger grouping called the "Ten Friends of the Northern Quarter," (i.e., the area outside the north wall of Suchou city). Hsü led a checkered political life, as did all these men in the tumultuous years of late Yüan–early Ming, but he conjured a world of serene detachment in his simple but profound poems.

Five Things Sought For—In the Manner of Han Wo

(Four poems from a group of five)

1.

By nature I love to dress my hair,
combing it carefully, arranging it neatly about my face.
As I hold the mirror in my hand,
a thousand times I gaze at my own image!
But, alas! my hand grows weary of this,
and so I must try to find:
> a mirror-stand.

2.

Yesterday, as I went down to the bridge at the river,
I was stared at by all the passers-by.
The flowers were sparse—I had no place to hide,
and so they all could see my newly made-up face!
Every moment was filled with embarrassment,
and so I must try to find:
> a silken fan.

3.

Time after time, afraid of the chilly spring weather,
I have refused to walk in the garden.
Now the almond blossoms are all on the ground,
and long rains have thickened the moss.
I want to get rid of the fallen petals,
and so I must try to find:
> a feather-broom.

4.

I love the p'i-p'a's music in my heart,
and play its tunes quite nicely with my fingers.
One day, the strings all break,
and there's no way they can be fixed.
I want to play, but I cannot,
so I must try to find:
                    a set of new strings.

                                                        (pp. 83–84)

——Han Wo (fl. 902): A popular poet of the late T'ang dynasty.

——P'i-p'a: A stringed instrument with neck and frets, shaped like a lute. The strings can
   be plucked either with the fingers or with a plectrum.

Ballad of the Ferocious Tiger

Where did this tiger come from?
He has invaded the village of Three Forks!
Yesterday he devoured the eastern neighbor's pig,
today he has eaten the western neighbor's dog!
The animals of the mountain dare not make a sound;
dark winds blow in the poplars and bamboo.
A youth from one family, feeling very brave,
goes off into the mountains, with his bow and arrow.
Late at night, beneath a black moon, he stalks the tiger . . .
and the next day, only his white bones are found,
                    in the wild grass.

                                                        (pp. 89–90)

Ballad of the Merchant

The merchant's boat is piled high with goods;
in the morning, south of the Yangtze,
                    in the evening, back up north.
His livelihood depends upon the wind and the waves,
his name has never been entered in the tax-collector's books.
At the prow of his boat, a shaman sings an invocation to the gods,
lifts a cup of wine, bows twice, and pours a libation to the waves.
"We promise to burn innumerable packets of magic paper money
if only our wealth continues to increase!
May the god desist, and the wind die down,
and our entire family enjoy unlimited blessings!"
The merchant promises himself never to plant fields:
year after year, you must labor for the government!

(p. 91)

A Poem on Buddha's Begging Bowl
—For Hui-ku, His Holiness Ming

The sage and the ordinary man both have bodies
and must use utensils to eat and drink.
When the Buddha had his stone bowl made
it wasn't only to pass on the Teaching!
But it did become a symbol of the light he left
and a tradition developed of handing it down.
And so, later generations of his followers
would fight and squabble over this bowl!

I think that such people go too far:
they should understand the meaning of "raising the flower."

(pp. 147–48)

——The Ch'an (Zen) school of Buddhism traces its origins to the moment when Buddha
"raised a flower and [his disciple] Kāshyapa smiled," because he had understood the
ineffable essence of the Master's teaching.

To the Filial Son, Ts'ui

At Hung-tung Mountain, the war-drums sounded:
the eastern neighbors were killed,
            the western neighbors taken prisoner!
Ts'ui managed to escape, deep into the mountains,
leading his children by the hand, carrying his mother piggy-back!
Any moment the troops would be upon them,
            they couldn't move too slow.
The moon was dark, the ground slippery with frost,
            the mountain steep and treacherous.
The eldest child tugged at Ts'ui's robe,
            the youngest was crying—
but Ts'ui thought only of saving his mother:
            he forced himself to ignore the children.
He deserted them there, among the rocky crags,
cutting off his love for them, knowing they must die!
But next day, some neighbors found them and brought them back,
and the delighted family was together once again.
I know Ts'ui did what he did out of love:
if the gods had not protected these people,
            how could they have survived?
Now the children bow to their parents,
            and the grandchildren to their grandparents:
the family lives together again in a paradise of their own.

(pp. 163–64)

Following the Rhymes of Kao Chi-ti's Poem: "We Had Planned to Travel to Cloud Cliff But Couldn't Because of Rain"

Nothing in our lives to stop us,
and we have not forgotten our love of leisure:
so we planned to sail with a boatful of wine
and stay overnight in a Buddhist temple.
But the season is not always beautiful—
the flowers in the garden have lost their petals.
The wild mountains, beyond the veil of rain:
we want to see them, but they are lost in mist.

(p. 182)

——Kao Chi-ti: Kao Ch'i (1336–74), a close friend of Hsü Pen and the major poet of the
time. See pp. 122–37.

In Harmony with Kao "The Second" Ch'i's Poem: "On Hearing a P'i-p'a Played Next Door"

Springtime of low walls and flowery darkness:
sounds of a p'i-p'a from the neighbor's house!
She plucks faster now—this must be a new tune;
now puts down her plectrum, as if waiting for someone . . .
If I could see her, I think I'd fall in love;
even hearing her music, I feel close to her!
Heart-breaking, the sadness in these notes:
how could words have expressed it so well!

(p. 182)

Hermit Li's Herb Garden Retreat at T'ung-ch'uan

This little residence is far from any village;
the gate opens on waterside bamboo.
Every plant and reed can be used as an herb;
each cloud and bird—material for poems!
In the spring rain, you go off to till the fields;
in setting sunlight, return from seeing patients.
Flowers hide the stream which leads to this place:
only a drunken boat can make it through!

(p. 197)

——Fifteen hundred years before Rimbaud, Pi Cho (d.c.329) is reported to have said, "If
I can fill a boat with several hundred measures of wine, pile up delicacies of all four
seasons at bow and stern, and then go floating around in this drunken boat *(chiu-
ch'uan)* with a wine cup in my right hand and a roasted crab-leg in my left, I will
consider my life a complete success."

To a Hermit in the Mountains

You've lived there long, away from the trappings of office,
your mind at peace, cut off from the world.
In jars: herbs, handed down by your teacher.
In bags: elixir, refined by your own hand.
You whistle out loud beyond the thousand peaks,
walk quietly along a hundred streams.
You resent even the intrusions of woodcutters and shepherds,
so now you want to move still deeper into the clouds.

(p. 204)

Hermit Feng's Residence on the Lake

Your house is near the southern tip of the lake;
the green mountains end at your gate.
The fields are low, often covered by floods;
your neighbors are few, not enough to form a village.
You've lived here a long time—now you know how to farm;
enjoying tranquility, you've come to understand
                    the meaning of Taoist sayings.
Men like you, who've escaped our troubled times:
how many of you are left?

(p. 206)

Saying Goodbye to a Monk from Japan

Thousands of miles away—the Fu-sang Tree,
                    among the faint colors of dawn!
Vast ocean sky, seen by few travelers.
No need to follow the tides with your wooden bowl:
you can fly toward the sun on your golden staff!
You'll go on eating Chinese food as you travel back east,
but you'll put on native clothes again after you reach home.
Your countrymen are sure to ask: "How's the Dharma doing there?"
Just show them the palm-leaf manuscripts you're bringing back
                    with you.

(p. 230)

——Fu-sang Tree: In Chinese mythology, a tree at the easternmost point of the sky, from which the sun rises.

——Palm-leaf manuscripts: Buddhism originally came to China from India. The presence in China of Indian, Sanskrit manuscripts of the original Buddhist scriptures would prove that China was still in touch with the motherland of Buddhism.

The Tomb of the Singing Girl Ch'iung-i

Secluded within the women's quarters—that was sad enough,
but far worse this small mound in the land of underground springs!
The moon is cold—no more mornings at the dressing table.
The place is deserted—this wild goose knows nothing of the
                    autumn.
Her old rooms, among the reeds, are inhabited by monks now.
The new pavilion, beneath the bamboo, awaits passers-by.
With no great name left behind in the local gazetteer,
how will travelers know this is a place
                    where they ought to stop their boats?

                                                    (p. 240)

The Deserted Estate at South Garden

The cassia hall has collapsed,
                    the lotus pond, all withered;
the old paths wander, leading the visitor astray.
There is an archery range, but in the spring breeze
                    who rides his horse here anymore?
There is a stage, but beneath the moon at night
                    only the crows sing there.
Still, the occasional visitor does come to gaze at the flowers,
although no revelers call out for another cup of wine.
So many noble mansions have fallen into ruins:
why is it that I linger at this place alone?

                                                    (p. 242)

The Mountain Residence of Secretary Cheng Ching-ssu

When the Secretary gave up his office,
                and returned to the mountains,
he brought his entire family to live among the clouds.
In this leisurely life, he raises his sons
                to be woodcutters and fishermen;
as he gets older, he depends on monks
                to bring him medicine and tea.
Trees from twin cliffs form a thousand layers of green;
the mists of a hundred mountains
                create multicolored patterns.
From here, it is not too far to Stone Bridge Temple:
as he sits in his house, he hears the echo of the temple bell.

                                      (p. 243)

A Leisurely Stroll

(One poem from a set of two)

Mountain of green trees and orioles everywhere!
I return from watching clouds over the stream.
Human life can never be without some kind of trouble;
it is only when walking in the mountains
                that we really achieve peace.

                                      (p. 258)

——This poem is inscribed on Hsü's painting, *Streams and Mountains*, dated 1372. Reproduced here as Plate 5.

KAO CH'I (1336–74)

SINCE the publication of Frederick W. Mote's excellent book, *The Poet Kao Ch'i* in 1962, Kao has been the best-known Ming poet in the West. Together with Chang Yü, Yang chi, and Hsü Pen (qq.v.), he was one of the "Four Great Ones of Suchou," as well as one of the "Ten Friends of the Northern Quarter." He knew the rebel leader Chang Shih-ch'eng, but managed to avoid service in his government, unlike Yang Chi. Under the new Ming administration, he held a post on the Historical Commission, which had the responsibility of compiling the official history of the Yüan dynasty. Kao appears to have contributed the section on biographies of women. At the age of thirty-eight, Kao was executed on the dubious grounds that an acquaintance of his—the then prefect of Suchou—had used the old site of Chang Shih-ch'eng's palace in Suchou for his own offices, and Kao had written a prose piece commemorating this event. Mote has opined that "the emperor wished to intimidate political dissidents" by executing Kao. Kao is clearly one of the major poets of the entire later period and an important figure in Chinese literary history. For more on Kao Ch'i, see Frederick W. Mote, *The Poet Kao Ch'i* (Princeton: Princeton University Press, 1962).

The Song of the Man of Green Hill

On the river lies Green Hill. I moved to the south of it, and so gave myself the name, "The Man of Green Hill." I have lived here an uneventful life, spending the entire day painstakingly chanting poems. In spare moments, I have written this Song of the Man of Green Hill to express my feelings and to rebut those who mock me for being a "poetry fanatic."

Man of Green Hill,
gaunt and pure,
originally an official of the immortals
          beneath the Pavilion of Five-Color Clouds:
what year was he sent down in exile
          to this world below?
He won't tell people his family or name.
Hiking in sandals? He's tired of distant trips.
Shouldering a hoe? Too lazy to farm!
He owns a sword, but lets it rust,
and books which lie scattered in confusion.
Unwilling to bend his waist
          for five pecks of rice,
unwilling to wag his tongue
          to persuade cities to surrender.
He only enjoys searching for verses,
chanting to himself, with himself exchanging poems.
Through the fields, he drags his cane
          and wears a rope belt:
onlookers don't know who he is,
          they just laugh and mock!
They take him for the crazy scholar of Lu,
the wild man of Ch'u.
But when the Man of Green Hill hears,
          he pays them no heed:
the sounds of chanting leave his lips
          endlessly, humming a steady stream.

Chanting in the morning—he forgets his hunger;
chanting in the evening, to calm his unease.
And as he painstakingly chants,
he goes into a trance as if drunk.
His hair he has no time to comb;
family matters he can't bother to attend.
If baby cries, he feels no compassion.
If guests come, he doesn't even greet them.
He has no fear of running out of food, like Hui,
nor does he admire the full coffers of Mr. Yi.
He feels no shame in wearing coarse garments
nor does he envy flowery hatstrings.
He pays no heed to dragons and tigers
                bitterly fighting
or the Crow and Frog as they hastily run their course.
Along the water's edge alone he sits
or in the woods alone he walks.
He hews out Primal Vapor
and explores the Primal Essence.
So hard for the Creator and ten thousand creatures
                to conceal themselves from him!
Throughout the eight corners of the universe
                sweeps the blade of his mind,
causing that which has no image
                to produce a sound.
Minute! Like shooting a louse, hanging
                from a hair;
Gigantic! As if butchering a whale.
So pure, like sipping immortal nectar;
dangerous, as though steep cliffs were piled high.
Burgeoning, clouds gathering in the sky;
issuing, shoots of plants through frost.
Climbing high to the root of Heaven,
                exploring the moon's caves;
rhinocerous horn illuminating Ox Island Abyss
                where ten thousand monsters appear!

Subtle meanings suddenly comprehended,
      as if by a spirit;
lovely landscapes always competing
      with the mountains and streams.
Stars and rainbows contribute to the luster;
mists and fogs moisten flowery bloom.
Listen to the music—harmonies of Shao;
savor the taste—he's mastered the Great Broth.
There's nothing else here in this world
      that pleases me,
only sounds of metal and stone
      chiming and ringing together.
In my thatched hut beside the river,
      clearing after wind and rain,
I close my door, wake fresh from sleep,
      and finish a new poem.
Beating on a jar, I sing out loud,
not caring if vulgar ears are shocked.
I want to call the old father from Mount Chün
      to bring with him the long flute played by the immortals,
and harmonize with this song of mine,
      playing in the moonlight.
I only fear that suddenly waves will arise,
birds and beasts will howl in fear
      and mountains crumble away.
If God hears this, He'll be angry
and send down a white crane to bring me back,
not leaving me to do my mischief in this world,
but again to tie on my pendant of jade
      and fly to the Jasper Capital!

                                 (pp. 1–6)

——Hui: Yen Hui, Confucius' favorite disciple who nevertheless suffered poverty.

——Mr. Yi: Yi Tun, a legendary millionaire.

——Crow and Frog: These creatures were believed to inhabit the sun and moon respectively.

——Shao: The name of an archaic, classical music long since lost in Kao's day.

——The old father, etc.: According to an old story, he taught a traveling merchant how to play three magic flutes.

In the Mountains, Parting from Master Ning as I Return to West Bank

A quick climb to the Incense Terrace
        to watch the setting sun;
a single tree in the sandbank village
        darkens, dim and faint.
The old monk does not come out
        from the temple in green hills,
only the boom of the temple bell
        escorts the visitor down.

                      (p. 12)

The Well of the King of Wu

They say that once it mirrored palace ladies,
their jade-white hands tugging the rope—
        flowers decked with dew!
Today, the mountain is deserted:
        a monk draws water alone,
one jarful, cold, for flowers to offer Buddha.

                (MST, 8/39a)

Passing By the Battlefield at Feng-k'ou

The road turns back, the desolate mountain parts:
it's like emerging from a frontier pass.
Startled sand flits up on all four sides;
a chill sun dims almost to darkness.
Above are the caws of famished crows,
below, the roots of withered tumbleweeds.
White bones lie strewn before our horses:
who can tell the rich men from the poor?
We do not know which generals they were
who in the past did battle in this place.
I want to question someone on the way,
but villages we pass are all deserted.
We climb a hill and view the ruined encampments;
ghosts rise into clustered clouds of grief.
The 100,000 troops who fought here then,
of those defeated, could any still survive?
That old man, alone, must be here now
to mourn some son or grandson he has lost.
For years now there's been no end to war,
the strong and weak both swallowed up by it.
In the end, who earns fame and merit?
They've been killing people everywhere on earth.
Ashamed I have no plan to end this chaos,
I stand stock still, lamentation in my soul.

(pp. 22–23)

———The Japanese scholar, Iritani Sensuke, has speculated that the battle referred to here
was one between the troops of the Mongol Yüan dynasty and those of the anti-Yüan
rebel, Chang Shih-ch'eng, which took place at Feng-k'ou, north of the city of
Hangchou, in 1356–57.

Seeing Flowers I Remember My Late Daughter, Shu

My second daughter, I loved her so much!
To the age of six we loved and nurtured her.
Holding her, I watched her nibble fruit;
putting her on my lap, I taught her to chant poems.
In the morning she would rise, and imitate
                    elder sister's make-up,
scrambling to the mirror for a peek.
She had a liking for silk and satin
which our family, poor, could not afford.
Alas! For years I was disappointed,
traveling crooked roads in rain and snow!
At evening I'd return to her happy welcome:
my sad feelings would always turn to joy.
Why is it that one morning of illness,
also a time of crisis in the world,
we heard the shocking news and then she died
with no time for medicine to be applied?
In haste we prepared a flimsy coffin,
and escorted her in tears to a distant slope.
Far, far, already hard to find;
pain, pain, still I bitterly grieve.
And I remember last year's spring,
the flowers opened by the pond in the old garden.
She dragged me over beneath the trees
and had me pluck a good branchful!
This year, the flowers bloom again
and I live a traveler by a distant shore.
The rest of the family lives, you alone are dead:
as I watch the flowers tears in vain now fall.
One cup of wine does not comfort me:
evening's curtain flaps in chilly wind.

(pp. 44–46)

——This poem dates from 1367.

Mooring Our Boat at Tan-yang Harbor

Where can we buy wine? We ask
            at the gates of the harbor;
in neighboring boats, flickering lamps at dusk
            and conversation.
Today I begin to sense how far I've come
            from my home town:
here, at this village outside the walls
            of the city of Tan-yang.

(p. 50)

———Tan-yang was located on the Grand Canal between Suchou to the south-east and
Chen-chiang to the north-west. The poet was planning to continue to Nanking by
road.

Along the River, Seeing the Home of Absconded Farmers

The times are good, there's no cruel government:
when did they cast off their home?
The old man next door
            has taken in their hungry dog;
passers-by pluck their lovely flowers.
The woods, deserted, no smoke rises;
the gate, shut, the sun about to set.
Where would they be, out there in the world?
May they soon return and plant new crops.

(pp. 97–98)

Song of the Duck Hunters

Off to hunt ducks,
dawn on the river;
back from hunting ducks,
evening on the pond.
Water chestnuts,
        leaves withering in autumn,
                mist and rain cleared up;
the flock of ducks
        still not landed,
                the decoy-cranes cry out!
The foliage gives low cover
                to bamboo bows all drawn;
the water cold, fields deserted,
                all the ducks so gaunt.
Boats, don't come and scare the ducks!
They eat the bait, forget suspicion,
                fighting for the food!
Beaks snapping,
feathers shining—
the hidden bows all shoot at once,
                the ducks have no idea.

(pp. 129–30)

——Decoy-cranes: Duck-hunters of Chiangsu are said to have trained cranes to act as decoys and attract ducks.

Silkworm Song of Torchlit Fields

In eastern village and western village
        they celebrate New Year's Eve:
towering torches, a thousand of them,
        light the fields all red!
The old people pray with smiles,
        the young folk sing songs:
"We wish for a year good for silkworms
        and also good for wheat."
In bright starlight strange shadows are cast,
        startling the perched crows;
flames from torches burn off the cold,
        giving birth to spring.
Late at night, torches all burned out,
        the people return to their homes;
they all say prognostications
        show a prosperous year ahead.

(MST, 8/6a)

A Walk to the Eastern River Bank

The setting sun illuminates half the river—
this is when I always take walks by myself.
The sunset deepens my depression,
the autumn clarifies the poet's mind.
Birds peck at a rotten willow tree;
insects hang lightly from dying leaves.
Why is it that I still feel homesick,
even though I've finally come home?

(pp. 75–76)

A Spring Day—Remembering Living on the River

A streamful of flowing water,
          half the village in flowers:
my old home, the southern neighbor
          was a fisherman.
I'll always remember his boat coming in
          filled with spring's intoxication,
clouds encaging fading sunlight,
          rain hissing on the sand.

                                                        (p. 137)

Going Out to the Country on a Boat Trip, Sheltering from Rain Beneath a Tree

A bank of spring clouds, rain swelling the stream:
I wish I could borrow a fisherman's coat
          but there's no one else around.
How very kind of the tree in front of the riverside shrine:
it shelters my solitary boat as I sleep through half the day.

                                                        (p. 138)

Moss Below the Stairs

Don't sweep away this green after the rain;
let it fill the tranquil stairway path.
Leave it there to cushion fallen petals
so the spring mud cannot dirty them.

                                                        (p. 141)

Lying at Leisure During Rain

My bed concealed by a folding screen,
        bamboo desk aslant,
I lie and watch the year's new swallows
        arrive at my humble home.
Living at leisure, in my mind
        is not one troublesome thought:
watching rain, my only worry—
        it may damage the apricot bloom.

(p. 142)

Nodding Off

Amidst bamboo, gate pulled shut,
        living like a monk;
white bean-flowers thinning out
        after gusts of rain.
My couch engulfed by steam from tea,
        I happen to nod off
and wake to find the book I was reading
        still clutched tightly in my hand.

(pp. 142–43)

Seeking Out Hermit Hu

I cross a stream, cross another stream,
admire the flowers, admire still more flowers.
In spring breeze, along the river road,
before I know it I have reached your house.

(p. 144)

Where Does My Sadness Come From?

Where does my sadness come from?
As autumn starts, suddenly it appears!
I want to describe it—hard to find the words;
mutely, I'll have to keep it to myself.
Still active, why should I fear age?
Unsettled, how complain of low position?
This is neither the impoverished scholar's lament
nor the sorrow of a man in exile.
If you say I'm longing to go home—
I've never left my home country behind!
If you say, "It's all this seeing off!"
My friends and loved ones are not apart from me.
I wished to say it's like the creeping vine,
but it will not wither in evening dew.
I'd also say it's like the mist or fog,
yet autumn wind can't sweep it away.
It stays so gloomy in my heart and eyes;
comes on fast but leaves me oh so slow!
You may ask, "How long is it
you've suffered from this sadness?"
In the past I lived by West Stream bank,
and still enjoyed the wonders of hill and river.
Now I've returned to the eastern garden,
and sigh with grief that plants and trees die out.
Living in retirement, who pays attention to me?
Only this sadness follows me everywhere.
Most people in the world are happy within,
still not tired of the pleasurable banquet.
But I alone must feel this sadness;
vacillating—what shall I do now?

(pp. 151–53)

Ballad of the Deserted Mansion

In a neighborhood of tinkling jade,
                 a general's mansion:
the halberds in rows have disappeared,
                 the vermilion doors are closed.
A local woman tells passers-by
                 what happened in the past:
her house was snatched away by them
                 so they could enlarge their pool!
This year, the place was requisitioned;
                 the officials own it now,
and every son of that noble house
                 has scattered and gone off.
The kitchen long has burned no smoke,
                 there is no grain or meat;
packs of rats in hunger come,
                 then enter neighbors' homes!
The officials have sealed off the place,
                 and allow no one to live there;
as days and days pass, rains increase
                 the green carpeting of moss.
Twisting corridors, sunk deep in silence,
                 reach to rooms behind;
the painted screens, covered with dust,
                 are dark and lusterless.
The guards, who ordinarily
                 would dare not glance in here,
now enter in from time to time
                 to gather fallen earrings.
In spring wind, how many trees were there
                 with lovely blossoms?
Now they have been transplanted
                 to the homes of wealthy men.

                                 (MST, 8/4a–b)

Ballad of the Neighborhood Shaman

If people in this neighborhood get sick,
    they'll never take a drug;
as soon as His Lordship God arrives
    the demon of sickness leaves.
They run to welcome the old shaman
    who brings the god at night,
when white sheep and red carp in profusion
    are offered up to him.
A man and woman earnestly
    bow before the altar:
"Our family is poor and has no meat,
    oh god, please take no offense!"
The old shaman beats the drum,
    dances now and sings;
paper money swishing, swishing
    in burgeoning dark wind.
The shaman proclaims,
    "Originally, your life was to run out here,
but the god, mindful of your devotion,
    has postponed your death!"
The shaman escorts the god to his horse,
    and walks out of the door;
the family climb up on the roof,
    and cry to the soul to return.

                (MST, 8/5a–b)

Returning to Lotus Village

Once before I loved this quiet place
and vowed that here I'd build myself a house.
How could I know I'd fall in the world's net
and not return here for ten years or more!
After loss and hardship, at least I'm in one piece;
smoke and fire have darkened the old place.
The bramble gate is far down in the alley;
in setting sunlight, willows and elms are sparse.
The old man next door, to celebrate reunion
brings over a basket with a pair of fish.
Concerned, he asks, "Sir, why is it
that your face looks different than before?"
How can he know that one who's been through trouble
has many griefs, and very few his joys!
But poverty and lowliness don't shame me;
my heart is set on living quietly.
"Please, old man, do not make fun of me:
in the end, I'm at the start once more."

(MST, 8/18a–b)

YANG SHIH-CH'I (1365–1444)

HOLDER OF the exalted position of Grand Secretary from 1421 to 1444 under the reigns of no less than four emperors, Yang was a brilliant political tactician. Few officials in Chinese history who rose to such prominence also achieved such a high degree of authority as poets; Yang is a true master of early Ming poetry. It also appears that Yang was a painter, especially fond of doing paintings of bamboo as farewell presents for friends.

On the Hall of Precious Virtue

The cock crows—cock-a-doodle-doo! —the east grows bright;
from every house, people rush out to slave for profit!
They dash to the east, hustle to the west,
                         tumbling over each other:
thousands of dollars? tens of thousands? No amount is enough!
In your noble hall you sit calmly, not doing a thing;
clumps of green trees overhang limpid wavelets.
Wearing colorful clothes, you pour wine
                         for your compassionate father:
elder brothers and younger brothers, all truly happy.
In human life, poverty doesn't matter if the Way is present:
a mountain of yellow gold is no treasure at all.

(vol. 5, 1/28a)

——Colorful clothes: A reference to the well-known tale of Lao Lai Tzu, who, at the age
    of seventy, put on colorful children's clothes and played like a child before his parents
    so that they would feel young again.

Night Rain: A Wall Collapses
—Sent To My Neighbors

A heavy rain crumbles a wall of my house;
I rise at night, grab my clothes, and run!
The wind enters the room, flapping the curtains;
water pours in a stream down the stairs.
The pots beneath the stove still not inundated;
quickly, I run to save the books on my desk.
If only I could be like my eastern and western neighbors:
calmly sleeping, not a thing to worry about.

(vol. 5, 2/6a)

Following the Rhymes of Shao-pao Huang's Poem on Being Moved While Visiting the Farmers

There is a drought, the farmers have a hard time finding food:
what terrible suffering in this district!
They comb the fields for pieces of stubble:
they might as well steam sand for rice!
Now the tax collectors are putting on the pressure,
and the autumn harvest seems more distant than ever.
What are we officials doing about it?
Eating meat, growing old in the capital!

(vol. 5, 2/7b)

——The Shao-pao Huang: Huang Huai (1367–1449), an official who served under the
first five emperors of the Ming dynasty.

——"Steam sand…:" An image taken from the Buddhist text, the *Śūraṅgama Sutra*
(translated from the Sanskrit in 705): "One who wishes to attain samadhi without
cutting off evil is like one who steams sand or stones, hoping it will become rice:
after thousands of kalpas, it will still just be hot sand."

A Group of Officials . . .

A group of officials went on an Imperial Tour with the Emperor
to Dragon Mountain during which they ascended Ox Head
Mountain and visited Buddha Cave Temple. Scholar Hu wrote
some poems about the trip. On that day, I was ill and unable to
participate. Imagining what this superb excursion must have been
like, I have followed the rhymes of Hu's three poems.

(One poem from the group of three)

Beyond the temple, a hidden cliff,
    reached by a path of stones.
On the cliff, an enlightened hermit,
    like Master Tan-hsia.
His mind holds the moon in the waters,
    empty of all dharmas.
He sits facing a cold precipice
    where a single blossom falls.
In the clear night, the sound of the tide
    turns the pages of his palm-leaf book;
at all times, cloud-vapors protect his monk's robe.
From afar, a fleeting glimpse of him: you know
    he's hard to find!
And then—a flutter of returning horsemen,
    surrounding the Imperial carriage.

              (vol. 5, 2/26a–b)

——[Poet's note]:Beyond the temple is a stone cliff where a monk has been living for a long time, practicing Ch'an meditation. The officials who visited the temple were sorry they could not meet him.

——Scholar Hu: Possibly Hu Yen (d. after 1445), a poet and a scholar of calendrical and medical matters.

——Master Tan-hsia: An eccentric Ch'an master of the T'ang dynasty who is said to have burned a Buddha image to demonstrate that it contained no relics of the real Buddha.

Searching for the Ruins of the Pavilion of the Drunken Old Man

A deserted mountain, streams and stones,
    but no one living here.
The pavilion of those years has long since
    turned to dust.

The writings of this famous man
                touched on the movement of the universe:
men of the district who visit here now
                must feel ashamed.
Cold forests, vague beyond the wild mists;
a frost-covered path, twisting and turning
                along the ancient stream...
The scene may have changed, but customs remain the same:
I see the peasants of Ch'u-chou, coming and going
                with their water-jars.

                                                  (vol. 5, 2/29a)

—— The Pavilion of the Drunken Old Man was built by the great Sung-dynasty statesman
and writer, Ou-yang Hsiu (1007–72), when he was Prefect of Ch'u-chou. His delight-
ful prose essay on the pavilion, the *Tsui-weng-t'ing chi*, is a masterpiece of Sung dynasty
literature.

The Palace of Prince Ma
—Now It Is a Buddhist Temple

(One poem from a group of three entitled, "Three Poems on Ch'ang-sha")

In the days of the Prince's glory
the palace halls bustled with life.
Now no singers or dancers can be seen;
there are only the sounds of chanting and bells.

                                                  (vol. 5, 3/1b)

White Stone Slope

(One poem from a group of six entitled, "The Intendant Yao Shan Has Requested Six Poems on Living in the Mountains")

Among the pines—White Stone Slope,
covered with the emerald of moss.
There is a man of pure heart
who comes here alone to look at the tracks of the birds.

(vol. 5, 3/2a–b)

Ten Scenes at the Hsiao Family Stone Ridge
—Written for Hsing-shen

(Three poems from the group of ten)

1. Blue Mud Shoal
It reaches to Gold Fish Dike:
light boats ply back and forth.
The water is so clear you can see the bottom,
the white stones that look like jewels.

2. Liang Family Pool
The river's flow collects and forms a pool,
deep, too deep to fathom.
Sometimes, clouds and fog arise from it,
and people think it hides a dragon's cave.

3. The Natural Stockade at Bamboo Lake
Precipitous, rising beyond the purple clouds,
a circle of stones like teeth of a comb!
Once I met a man here who was a hundred years old;
he told me stories about the days of soldiers and spears.

(vol. 5, 3/4b–5a)

Night Rain Beneath the City Walls of P'i-chou

Toward evening, the weather turns cold
and I moor my boat for the night by the shore.
Lying on my pillow, I can't fall asleep:
rain at night, on the roof of my lonely cabin.

(vol. 5, 3/3a)

A Painting of Water Buffaloes

(One poem from a group of four)

The herdboy returns, none too early—
beside the stream, heavy wind and rain!
Looking behind—a mother's love for her baby:
it is running after her, but can't seem to catch up.

(vol. 5, 3/6a)

Sha-ch'eng, "Sand City"

Overlooking the water, a desolate city
where wind-swept sand gets in your eyes.
Half the people here are refugees,
behind the closed gates of their thatched huts.

(vol. 5, 3/6b)

Sha-ch'eng, "Sand City"

In former years I passed this city
and met an old man from Chiang-nan.
His body was aged, his mind, sad, but at peace:
I wonder if he is still here?

(vol. 18, 60/4b)

Dragon-Tiger Terrace

The tall terrace crumbled long ago,
covered by clumps of brambles and weeds.
It still bears the name of "dragon-tiger,"
but it's oxen and sheep that graze here now.

(vol. 5, 3/7a)

Dawn: Clear Skies

All around my house at midnight: rain,
softly hissing, never really making a sound.
In the morning, I rise, and look out under clear skies:
snow has covered the tops of the green mountains.

(vol. 5, 3/6b)

I Was Received in an Early Audience at Heaven-Gate and Then at Noon I Was Summoned to the Yu-shun Gate. In the Evening I Withdrew, and Improvised This Poem.

The Purple Precincts touch Longevity Mountain
                    to the west;
twice I am summoned to view the Dragon Visage!
I bow down, receive the wise counsel of the Sage,
and then, my sleeves filled with Heaven's fragrance,
                    I emerge through the ninefold gates.
                              (vol. 5, 3/14b)

Red Heart Station

In front of my horse's head, I see Red Heart Station,
thatched roofs up and down, half of them wine shops!
Swaying gently beyond the bridge of vermilion railings,
willows—some branches hanging limp, snapped by the west wind.
                              (vol. 5, 3/17a)

Hsi-li Echoed My Poems, and I Respond to Him, Using the Same Rhymes—Also Sent to Tsung-lien

(One poem from a group of four)

Not sobered up from my muddy Kao-yang drunk,
from time to time, pigs'-feet with a jar of wine!

Half soused, poetic thoughts swell up like springs:
silk scrolls, patterned papers, I'll inscribe them all!

(vol. 5, 3/19a–b)

—— "Kao-yang drunk": A reference to Li Shih-ch'i of the Han dynasty, a former advisor
of Emperor Kao-tsu (before he had become Emperor) who is reported to have said,
"I'm one of your drinking companions from Kao-yang, not some Confucian scholar!"
when the newly enthroned emperor refused to see him.

Libationer Hu Became Ill from Eating Sunflowers. These Poems Are Playfully Presented to Him and Are Also Intended to Thank Him for the Vegetables He Sent Me

(One poem from a set of two)

After the rain, the vegetables from your garden
　　　　　　　　　are wonderful to behold!
But suddenly I hear that you are sick,
　　　　　　　　　lying in your hidden studio.
It must be that you really *have* no "method for calming the mind":
whatever made you cut those sunflowers from their stems?

(vol. 5, 3/19b)

—— [Poet's note]: In a recent poem, Hu claims that he has a "method for calming the
mind."

—— Libationer Hu: Hu Yen (d. after 1445), a poet and a scholar of calendrical and medical
matters.

Ten Miscellaneous Poems Written as a Member of the Imperial Retinue on an Inspection Tour of the Frontier—We Reached Hsüan-fu and Then Returned

(One poem from the group of ten)

Forty *li* through Chü-yung Pass,
twisting ridges, doubled peaks: we wind in and out.
Beside the road, stone-cut inscriptions no one can read:
all of them are from the former dynasty,
                              written in Mongolian!

(vol. 5, 3/24b)

——Hsüan-fu: Located northwest of Peking, in the region of the Great Wall.

Recording a Dream

I fell asleep in the daytime,
                    and dreamed of my home town:
with a bamboo cane, I was visiting my western neighbor.
The old man greeted me with great respect
and invited me to view the magnolias with him.
We had a cup of wine, sang a song,
and before we knew it, the red sun was setting...
Then I awoke, with a feeling of emptiness:
here I was, still floating at the ends of the earth.

(vol. 17, 55/26b–27a)

Inscribed on the Painting, *Stabbing a Tiger*, by Chao Tzu-ang, in the Collection of Scholar Yang

The woman pulls the cart;
the husband pushes from behind.
In the cart is their son,
face as smooth as white jade.
The whole family is moving to the frontier,
                    not afraid of hardship;
it is sunset, the road is desolate:
                    they camp beneath their cart.
Mountains—cold and somber;
forests—swept by sighing breezes.
Suddenly, a dark wind swirls by . . .
and the man falls prey to an evil tiger!
The woman quickly leaps after the tiger,
                    grabs hold of his foot!
She yells to the boy to bring a knife—
                    and slits open the tiger's belly!
Out fall the tiger's guts, and—the husband,
                    as if he has returned!
But still the woman's anger is unappeased:
even the lives of a hundred men could not bring him
                    back to life.
The local officials present a memorial to the throne
                    describing her righteous deed;
now a proclamation-banner flutters brilliantly
                    above her humble house,
and the Imperial Historian has recorded this miracle
                    of a thousand generations.
In human life, wealth and high station pass like birds
                    flying by;
how many people's names are recorded in glory
                    on the tablets of history?

Now, Chao Wu-hsing was magnificent as a poet and painter,
and when he was in the west, he learned the details
of this affair.
The sages of the past worked diligently
to instruct the people;
they strove to make known deeds of virtue,
as moral examples.
The Scholar of Chien-an has the mind of the ancients;
he has treasured this painting and protected it well.
Now he takes it out to show to me, and I sigh in admiration
for the ancient Way.
Brush in hand, I inscribe this poem, like decorating
an official cap
with dog-tail instead of sable!

(vol. 17, 57/22b–23a)

——Chao Tzu-ang, Chao Wu-hsing: Chao Meng-fu (1254–1322), a major painter, callig-
rapher and poet of the Yüan dynasty. (See pp. 21–32)

——Scholar Yang (the "Scholar of Chien-an"): Yang Jung (1371–1440), a poet, and with
Yang Shih-ch'i and Yang Fu (1375–1446), known as one of the "Three Yangs."

Song of the Merchant's Wife

When he trades in tea—it's right nearby,
on the slopes of the green mountains.
But now he trades in pearls, and must seek them afar,
along the coast of the vast sea!
Our family needs so much food and clothing . . .
surging, surging, the waves where the whales play
sadden my heart!

(vol. 17, 57/34b)

Crossing the River

On horseback, I am crossing the river,
but my horse is thirsty, and stops for a drink!
When he's had his fill, there's no need to use the whip:
he leaps ahead, with a great whinny!

(vol. 18, 60/5a)

Sent to All My Nephews and Nieces at Tung-ch'eng

(One poem from a set of two)

I've drawn a salary in the capital for forty years now,
and as I grow old, my every thought is of a safe return.
There are endless beautiful mountains and streams
                    near my hometown:
where, among those pines and catalpas,
                    should be my grave?

(vol. 18, 60/38a–b)

Enclosed with a Letter to My Family—For Shu

Every day I receive the Imperial favor
                    as I attend upon His carriage.
But no matter what I do, I never forget the family!
I send this to you now, Ch'ao-erh, to say,
be diligent in your studies of the *Documents* and *Poems:*
                    don't upset your dad!

(vol. 19, 61/18a)

——Ch'ao-erh would be the childhood nickname of Yang's son, Shu.

A Eulogy on My Own Portrait

The old boy's seventy-three this year,
and keeps on dreaming of returning to the south!
If the Emperor would let me take off my official cap
I'd get myself a fishing pole and fish at Stone Pond!

(vol. 19, 61/40b–41a)

Rhymed Words Sent to My Eldest Son

After holding office in the capital for forty years, I was able to visit
home for only forty days! Friends and relatives—both close and
distant—came from far and near to see me. Day and night, I had
no rest from all the socializing, and so not a word of serious family
talk passed between my son and me. Finally, the evening before
my departure, we did exchange a few words as we drank some
wine, but they did not suffice to express my feelings. After parting,
in the boat, I lay awake thinking of this, and ended up putting my
thoughts in the form of poems—thirty in all—which I wrote out
and sent to my eldest son, Chi. The love of a seventy-five year old
father for his son is fully expressed in these pieces of paper. Chi,
strive to absorb my meaning, do not stray from the path of filial
piety!

(Two poems from the group of thirty)

I.

The false words of the Buddhists and Taoists
                    are a pack of lies!
Anyone who comprehends this truth
                    is a real Confucian scholar.
Stupid people are manipulated by other stupid people:
they make offerings of thousands in cash,
                    and don't get one iota of benefit!

2.

Li Hsü of Ch'ien-chou is an old friend of mine.
Once, when you were drunk, you insulted him to his face!
Two officials who were on the scene told me what happened,
and I could only hang my head, and feel ashamed inside.

(vol. 19, 61/42b–43a, 44b, 46a)

——Most of the thirty poems consist of tedious moralizing. It should be kept in mind
that Yang's son, Chi, was thirty-one years old at the time (see 61/46b)! It does appear,
however, that Yang truly loved his son. According to the official records, Yang died
of grief at the age of seventy-nine when Chi was sent to jail in connection with a
political problem.

Inscribed on a Painting of Bamboo Presented to Lecturer Ch'en Upon His Departure to Resume His Duties at Nanking

(One poem from a set of two)

Even ordinarily, parting is difficult,
and now I must part from a lifelong friend!
The trees are shedding leaves, the weather is cold,
              the year draws to a close,
and one white-haired man says goodbye
              to another white-haired man.

(vol. 19, 62/25b)

——Lecturer Ch'en: Probably Ch'en Ching-tsung (1377–1459), an official and writer.

——It appears that Yang Shih-ch'i was a painter of bamboo and plum blossoms, frequently
making gifts of his pictures to friends departing from Peking. Apparently, none of
these paintings survive today.

The Evening of My Birthday

—To the tune, *P'u-sa-man*

On this day of my birth, I see no visitors:
the family is busy with the celebration!
As evening draws on—
green wine, yellow oranges—
I'm congratulated for being seventy-three.

Candles wish me joy with their flames,
my relatives—branches of the same tree—
                              crowd around,
with golden chrysanthemums.
The little grandchildren
imitate their elder brothers
who kneel before me and present me with poems.

(vol. 19, 62/45a)

——A *tz'u,* or lyric, to a variant of the familiar tune-pattern, *P'u-sa-man.* The common pattern of line-lengths in *P'u-sa-man* is 7-7-5-5/5-5-5-5, where each number represents the number of characters in the respective line. In the present example, the pattern appears to be 4-4-3-4-7/4-4-3-4-4-3.

——Chrysanthemums were traditionally associated with longevity.

HSIEH CHIN (1369–1415)

LIKE Yang Shih-ch'i (q.v.), Hsieh was a Grand Secretary, the most powerful office in early Ming government, but his career provides a cautionary warning as to the fate in store for those lacking Yang Shih-ch'i's prodigious talent for political survival. Arrested and imprisoned by political enemies, Hsieh died in prison, while his entire family was exiled to the far northeast. Hsieh's poetry, like Yang Shih-ch'i's, is unexpectedly fine for such a high official. He was also a calligrapher of repute, and his *Song of Cursive Calligraphy* (see pp. 156–58) is one of the most powerful on this theme in all of later Chinese poetry.

Inscribed on a Painting of Dragons by Ch'en So-weng

Ocean tides curl in anger, swift winds rage,
white-capped waves pile high, jutting mountains of snow!
An old dragon sports among the waves,
                    along with his scaly brethren:
his claws and scales all drip with moisture from the spray.
Since ancient times, who has been most skillful
                    at capturing such scenes?
Only one man attained "spiritual wonder": Ch'en So-weng!
Ah, how many are the transformations in this scroll!
Thunder and rain spring forth from the strokes of his brush.
Inspired, I unroll the picture, and inscribe this for you:
it may not belong to Seng-yu's oeuvre,
                    but it's a treasure of great price!

(4/2b)

——Ch'en So-weng: Ch'en Jung of the Sung dynasty, the greatest master of the art of
dragon painting. A masterpiece of his, dated 1244, is in the Boston Museum of Fine
Arts.

——Seng-yu: Chang Seng-yu (fl. 500–50), one of China's most famous painters.

Song of Cursive Calligraphy

Ten years of my life, spent at the window or beneath the lamp,
practicing calligraphy day and night without a break!
Beside the "ink pond" I've used up an ocean-full of water;
my worn-out brushes, piled high, would make a Mount Omei!

When the spirit moves me, I pour out
                eight hundred gallons of wine,
get drunk, go wild, and let my brush do whatever it will.
Rabbit-hairs in hand, I let the tip loose,
and sweep my way through a million sheets of tinted phoenix paper.
One stroke across,
one stroke down:
a gold spear thrust into the ground, an awl stuck through the wall.
A brilliant rainbow arching across a blue autumn sky,
a waterfall rushing down the stones of a cinnabar cliff.
One dot large,
one dot small:
at midnight, a falling star, dazzling as it follows the moon;
flying through the air, a crossbow pellet, reaching toward the clouds!
A black pearl from the sea, glittering in a vast sky!
As lovely as: a beautiful woman, gathering flowers,
                displaying her new make-up;
as bold as: a courageous soldier, grasping a spear,
                on the battlefield!
As vibrant as: multicolored rocs and purple phoenixes
                trying to out-fly each other;
as swift as: autumn serpents and spring snakes
                darting away...
Forms like those of thick clouds in a million transformations,
postures like those of lightning bolts, flashing
                across a clear sky!
Wild geese flying in formation against the autumn clouds,
dragons doing battle in the surging waters of a spring river!
Don't you recall why Wang Hsi-chih
                was a man who loved to raise geese?
A true artist should have the same ambition:
beneath his brush, gods and spirits must appear!

                                      (4/15a–b)

——Ink-pond: Chang Chih of the Latter Han dynasty, the father of cursive calligraphy
    as an art form, practiced so much that the pond he used to sit beside turned black
    from his discarded ink.

——Wang Hsi-chih (303–79) was the greatest of Chinese calligraphers. He loved to watch the elegant lines of the geese's necks as they swam. From this he derived inspiration for his calligraphy.

——According to Ch'ien Ch'ien-i (1582–1664), *Lieh-ch'ao shih-chi hsiao-chuan* (edition published by Chung-hua shu-chü, Shanghai, 1959, p. 161): "[Hsieh Chin] was good at 'wild cursive' calligraphy [*k'uang-ts'ao*], and he would sweep it forth from his brush like wind and rain!" Hsieh himself describes how, as a young man, he would employ his cursive calligraphy in the service of the first emperor of the Ming dynasty:

"I, Chin, when young, waited upon His August Excellency morning and evening, ready with brush, ink and paper to attend upon His Majesty's pleasure. He particularly loved to compose poems and songs. His brilliant thought would issue forth in godlike poems of great inspiration, like the rumbling of thunder or the flight of lightning. In an instant, these Imperial Creations would reach lengths of thousands of words, all produced in a single, unbroken stream. I would immediately write them down, filling sheets with my cursive calligraphy, the brush barely able to form strokes and dots quickly enough. Then I would present the manuscript to His Majesty, and He would make whatever corrections were necessary in the lines and rhymes, although at times He did not have to change even a single word!" (*Wen-i chi*, 7/5b).

To the Fortuneteller, Hsüeh T'ieh-yai

In a mirror of bronze
      can be seen beauty and ugliness,
but the mirror of books is better,
      where right and wrong are seen,
or the mirror of a man,
      where can be seen the roots of good and evil,
      or the workings of fortune!
Fortuneteller Hsüeh of Ho-tung
      calls himself "Old Master Mirror."
His godlike eyes are clear as autumn waters;
lightning flashes from his three-inch tongue!

He has correctly told:
    that a lost man by the riverside
        would be a high official;
    that a lonely soul on the road
        would be a rich man;
    that one who in former years was a sleepy fellow in Shantung
        was really a dragon, a tiger!
    That one who is now a nobleman of Yen-shan
        is really no great bear!
His words can be counted on to hit the mark:
there will be no discrepancy in the give-and-take of fate!
When he sees a son, he exhorts him to be filial;
when he sees a father, he exhorts him to be compassionate.
When he sees a minister, he exhorts him to be loyal.
The upright will always act properly,
the devious will inevitably slip.
This is how he mirrors the Tao
in accordance with the precepts of the ancients.
This Taoist of the Iron Cliff
        once studied the *Documents* and the *Poems,*
and missed his true calling by accepting the *chin-shih* degree and the
        purple robe.
Then one day, a gentleman of Dragon Gate
        invited him to join his entourage,
and for ten years, he never rose in official rank—
        what a slow career!
Now, among the Five Lakes, we meet, and discuss our lives:
he assures me I will again have an audience at the Golden Courtyard.
He has mirrored my mind, and understood it,
yielding nothing in knowledge to Tzu-ch'ing and T'ang Chü.

We get drunk together, play the flute . . .
        and then I leave,
the sky blue, the moon among the branches of flowering pear.

(4/40b–41a)

——"He has correctly told . . ." Presumably these refer to actual successes of Master Hsüeh, but they cannot be traced today. It is also possible that they are veiled political references of some kind. The phrase "is no great bear" [*fei hsiung-p'i*] may refer to the following story: When King Wen of Chou was about to go hunting, he consulted a diviner who told him what he caught would "not be a dragon, not a *ch'ih*-dragon, not a *hsiung*-bear or a *p'i*-bear [*fei hsiung fei p'i*]. . . ." Instead, he "caught" Lü Shang who was to become his trusted minister. (Recorded in The Yüan dynasty text, *Shih-pa shih lüeh*.) Thus the line may imply that the man in question was appointed to an important government position like Lü Shang. But the more apparent meaning— that the man is really not as outstanding as might be thought—remains plausible.

——"A gentleman of Dragon Gate . . ." This and the following line are difficult to understand, and the translation is tentative.

——"Now, among the Five Lakes . . ." Paraphrase: "Both of us now live in retirement, like the famous minister of old, Fan Li, who disappeared among the Five Lakes. He tells me that I am sure to be recalled to the capital sometime in the future."

——"Tzu-ch'ing and T'ang Chü:" T'ang Chü was a famous fortuneteller of the Warring States period. Tzu-ch'ing was probably a similar figure, but is harder to identify.

A Playful Poem on a Chicken Egg

A hard shape to describe—not circular, not square:
it seems to encompass both Heaven and Earth.
Keep in mind the two levels of white, inside and out,
and, centered within, the single spot of yellow.
Before the division of Primal Chaos—already, an image!
After the split of the Universe—vicissitudes appear.
Nurtured here are wings that will reach for the Milky Way,
or be transformed into the Golden Crow
                that moves with the sun.

(5/14a)

"What Does the Little Boy Love?"

When I was not yet able to speak, I nevertheless understood what others communicated to me. I dreamed that a man presented me with a five-color brush which had on it flowers something like lotus blossoms. When I was four or five, I was already composing poems, but was unable to write them down, and so I often forgot them. The present examples were recorded by my great-uncle, Master Yüan-ching, who had playfully asked me to compose something. These poems have been passed around and have received some degree of praise, and I cannot bear to put them aside, so I am including them here. "The intelligence is not as great as it once was, the moral level falls further everyday from that of the First Heart." Here we can see again how true were these words of Master Han!

1.
"What does the little boy love?"
He loves this room of fragrant plants!
He wants to mount a flying dragon
and fly to heaven, to see the red sun.

2.
People say the sun is in heaven;
I say the sun is in the heart.
Don't you see that when the rooster crows
it clearly responds with the sound of temple bells?

3.
"What does the little boy dream of?"
At night I dreamed of a brush sprouting flowers.
And where were the roots of the flowers?
In the heart of hearts, which is my home!

4.

The Sage has the *Six Classics*
just as Heaven and Earth have sun and moon.
Sun and moon have lasted millions of years
and the *Classics* too will never disappear.

(5/24a–b)

——The story of how these poems came to be written is also recorded in Ch'ien Ch'ien-i, *Lieh-ch'ao shih-chi hsiao-chuan* (p. 161): "When Hsieh was four years old, his great-uncle took him on his lap, and playfully asked him, 'What does the little boy love?' Hsieh immediately responded with four quatrains . . ." Ch'ien goes on to quote #3, with the first line reading, "What does the little boy love?" The dream described in this poem and in the prose introduction is reminiscent of the famous dream of the poet, Chiang Yen (444–505). In this dream, another poet, Kuo P'u (276–324) appeared to Chiang and demanded that he return the five-color writing brush which was actually his (Kuo's). When Chiang did so, he found, upon awaking, that he had lost his powers as a poet. It is clear that both in this famous story and in Hsieh Chin's childhood dream the five-color writing brush represents poetic inspiration, or the muse. Hsieh's dream adds the significant touch of lotus blossoms flowering out of the brush.

——Master Han: Probably Han Yü (768–824), although I have not been able to trace these particular lines.

——The Sage: Confucius.

Things Experienced upon Withdrawal from Court

(One poem from a group of five)

The government wine of Peking is sweeter than honey;
an Imperial Decree is circulated:
       "Enjoy this fine brew!"
Even His Sage Majesty has not yet tasted it
       at a Royal Banquet,
and he sends some to his scholars and ministers,
       truly an Emperor's gift!

(6/1b–2a)

To Hsiao Shih-ying

In nineteen years, we have parted, and met;
now I meet you, part from you again—
           how heavy the feeling!
We brew tea, and sweep the ground
           to share with the moonlight,
face each other, and play our lute
           until the bells of dawn.

                        (6/8a)

Parting from Liu Nan-chou

(One poem from a set of two)

Wait until I too "hang up my carriage"
           and return to the old mountains:
together, we will play the flute in the bright moonlight.
At Egret River and Conch-Shell Bay
           we will make friends with the fishermen,
far better than associating with immortals or gods!

                        (6/11b)

Sandal Mountain

Skimming the waves, deep in the night,
           an immortal passed by here:
his sandal fell off, and remained behind,
           floating on the water.

The years went by, mountains became valleys . . .
                    but it never disappeared:
it changed into a pillar of stone,
                    blocking the flow of the river.

                                                      (6/24b)

In Grief, Lamenting for My Elder Brother, Ts'ang-chiang

(One poem from a group of eight)

I still remember Conch-Shell Slope, west of the River Tzu:
you would grind the ink for me, and I would write poems!
Looking at the mountains, letting the wine flow,
                    talking with our guests,
this was the happiest time in my entire life.

                                                      (6/25a)

A Poem on a Little Pine

A tiny little pine tree, still shorter than the fence,
every branch, every leaf bearing the bitter cold.
Now is the best time to see it, with your head
                    at a comfortable angle:
one day, it will pierce the sky,
                    and you'll have to strain your neck!

                                                      (6/27a)

SHEN CHOU (1427–1509)

SHEN CHOU is one of the greatest painters in Chinese art, a central figure in the Suchou-centered Wu School of literati landscape painting. His achievement in art has been fully appreciated in the West for some time now. But as early as the sixteenth century, the scholar Ho Liang-chün (1506–73) lamented that "some of Shih-t'ien's (Shen Chou's) poems are outstandingly fine, but they have been obscured by his painting and so the world does not praise them." It is clear from other sources that Shen Chou took disciples in poetry as well as in painting. Of the "painter-poets"—that is, men primarily famous as painters but who were also accomplished poets—Shen may well be the most successful in poetry. Ch'ien Ch'ien-i (q.v.), in his authoritative biographies of Ming poets *(Lieh-ch'ao shih-chi hsiao-chuan),* treats Shen Chou as a poet of major significance. For more on Shen Chou see Richard Edwards, *The Field of Stones: A Study of the Art of Shen Chou* (Washington, D.C.: The Freer Gallery, 1962).

To the Tune,
Nan-hsiang-tzu

—Expressing My Feelings

I'm a mad immortal between heaven and earth,
painting pictures, writing poems,
                   but never to sell for cash!
Pictures—in debt! Poems—unpaid taxes!
                   Busy until old age.
What a shame . . .
Friendships, feelings for people, all have led to nothing.

This has been the worst year of all:
waves pounding the thatched walls,
                   river flooding the fields.
I'd better pick up my brush and inkstone
and—say no more!
move my home on board a fishing boat.

                                             (p. 779)

——This poem is a *tz'u*.

Sent in Parting to Yen Kung-su

Your little house stands in a bamboo grove.
Your boat—"Floating Duckweed"—waits by the shore.
It is Autumn—the last leaves have fallen,
                   the wind shakes the trees;
the bamboo curtains are bright in the moonlight.

I ask your age—
               you point to your white hair.
We discuss the Book of Changes under a dim lamp.
Tomorrow, you will leave, to the East, to the West—
winecups in our hands, we gaze at the stars of dawn.

(p. 369)

Consoling Wu Te-cheng on the Death of His Son

In mourning for your second son
you have written six poems
and still not expressed
the depth of your sorrow.
But weeping bitter tears
will bring no relief—
you will find his spirit
everywhere.

Inscribe an epitaph on jade
from the western mountains
for your family's lost treasure,
this pearl
sunk in the ocean.

And the Spring is still beautiful;
old as you are,
you have planted orchids—
watch them sprout
and bear blossoms
in time.

(p. 561)

On the Fifteenth Day of the Seventh Month I Came Home Late from the City

Stayed late in town, sped home in my boat,
afraid the dust had soiled my fisherman's cap.
Home again, I found there had been a storm:
torn leaves hanging from the banana trees.

(pp. 687–88)

To the Tune, *Bamboo at West Lake*

Springtime—and the green willow catkins
are like my love-thoughts, floating in the wind.
At home I have wine, flavored sweet with sugar:
come and have a taste, and you will understand.

(p. 697)

The Taoist Huang Has Died of Alcoholism

Your master died from drinking too much;
now you have followed in his steps.
A mound of dregs will be your grave,
your tombstone inscribed with the "Ode In Praise of Wine."

Unsteady on your feet, you tripped and stumbled,
your face flushed, your liver wasted.
Now you are gone, not even your shadow remains;
there is only your portrait, drawn in my poem.

(p. 340)

Paying a Sick-call to Yao Ts'un-tao in the Rain

I will write you a poem instead of bringing rice.
As I pick up my brush, my mind fills with thoughts.
Everyone in the world today is suffering;
illness is not your fate alone!

Dark vapors arise from all directions;
rain drips in ten thousand trees.

I think of you, head propped on your hand,
saying nothing
watching the clouds.

(p. 408)

Drinking at Night with Yen Kung-mou

The sun is in the West. Fishing boats,
pulled up on the sand, make us think
of distant places.
After the Spring rain,
petals cover the ground
and green bamboo
surrounds the house.
The flame of our candle
startles roosting swallows;
our voices mingle
with the croaking of the frogs.
Wine before us, we stroke our beards,
look at each other, lament
the passing of the years.

(p. 408)

The Bamboo Villa

—Following the Rhymes of T'ao An

Simple food, coarse clothing are all you need—
more content than Tu Fu when he stayed in the West.
Your old wife prays to Buddha at the altar;
your daughter is weaving by the fire.

Chilly clouds scatter leaves from tall trees;
the moon's reflection surges in the cold stream.
No visitors come to the quiet thatched hut—
you get up, light a stick of incense,
            watch the smoke write words in the air.

(p. 560)

Temple of the Ocean of Awakening

—Following the Rhymes of Chao Ta-ts'an

Climbing, climbing the path of stones
            deep into the mountains;
no more villages to be seen,
            only peaks of green.
Facing the gate, grass is growing
            at the foot of a cliff;
along the gully, petals fly
            and fall to the water's heart.
Ten thousand ravines of mist and cloud—
            truly a kingdom of happiness!

Temple bells, Sanskrit chanting
                    through dense forests
                            for hundreds of years...
The old monk brushes moss from the wall,
asks me to commemorate my visit
                    with a poem.

                                        (p. 596)

The Stone Bridge

(One of ten poems on Pao-lin Temple)

South of the bridge—
            a horse-and-carriage road.
North of the bridge—
            the precincts of the temple.
On the bridge—
            a monk, walking,
his shadow startling the fish below.

                                        (p. 667)

The Moon in a Winecup

The moon comes from the blue sky,
falls into my cup of wine.
The wine finished, the moon disappears,
shining as always in the sky.

                                        (p. 679)

A Lady Picking Flowers

Last year we parted as the flowers began to bloom.
Now the flowers bloom again, and you still have not returned.
Purple grief, red sorrow—a hundred thousand kinds,
and the spring wind blows each of them into my hands.

(p. 758)

A Painting of Peach Blossom Spring

Boys and girls crying with hunger, all over the village,
and the tax colllector knocking at every door...
The old man, unable to fall asleep at night,
finds brush and paper, starts work on a painting
     of Peach Blossom Spring.

(p. 748)

[Untitled Poem Inscribed on a Painting by Himself]

White clouds like a scarf enfold the mountain's waist;
stone steps hang in space—a long, narrow path.
Alone, leaning on my cane, I gaze intently at the scene,
and feel like answering the murmuring brook
    with the music of my flute.

(Edwards, *The Field of Stones,* Plate 18A)

——The painting is reproduced here as Plate 6.

——An additional poem by Shen Chou will be found in the section on Wen Cheng-ming
on pp. 221–22.

LI TUNG-YANG (1447–1516)

L I WAS an official who rose to the exalted position of Grand
Secretary, as had Yang Shih-ch'i and Hsieh Chin (qq.v.) before
him. Li's position in the development of Ming literature is as a
forerunner of the so-called Former and Latter Seven Masters who
were to establish emulation of the High T'ang poets as the standard
of literary orthodoxy. Li himself, however, was an admirer of such
a later T'ang poet as Lu T'ung (d. 835), the "Master Jade Stream"
he "imitates" in his important narrative poem, *To Yung-erh* (see pp.
174–76).

To Yung-erh—Imitating a Work by Master Jade Stream

At night I sit, uneasy and unhappy;
I write a poem to present to Yung-erh.
"Yung-erh, where do you come from?
You come from the southeastern frontier.
You tell me you were a Kuang-hsi native;
your prefecture and county you don't recall.
You only know your family name was Li,
and for generations you were shaman-healers.
The household had three head of cattle,
and fields that you could weed and till.
Then one year the Ching-chou barbarians
rebelled and forced the imperial army to come in.
At night, you heard the wild troops arrive:
they had the power of tigers or of wolves.
Your dad was murdered—
his blood and flesh were spattered all around.
Your mom was taken prisoner,
and no one knew if she would survive.
The officials registered handsome young men,
castrated them and sent them off as slaves!
You were only thirteen then,
broad of brow, but gaunt in body.
And you were born with left eye nearly blind,
so luckily you escaped this mutilation.
Then prison boats carried you 'rice-pickers'
by stages until you reached the capital.
Military officials memorialized your names
so civil authorities could give you your assignments.
Now I am dull and lacking in all skill,
yet I received benevolence
        as if I were a duke!

After all, what thing am I
that the Emperor's brush itself
                should mark my name!
In the vermilion throneroom
                I kowtowed in gratitude,
then still in child's hairdo
                you came to be my companion.
We boiled broth to make you food to eat,
stitched cloth so you'd have clothes to wear.
I could not bear to make your tasks too hard,
or punish your faults with the bamboo rod.
When at home, I'd have you at my side;
traveling, I'd have you come along.
And I spoke earnestly to the children,
urging them never to be cruel to you.
I also exhorted the other servants
to support you when you would get sick.
I think of the virtue of the former Emperor:
how could I ever repay it now?
Imperial gifts of living creatures
                were always animals,
but this one's better far than chicken or pig!
And the present Emperor has given two more servants
whose origins were among the Ssu-en barbarians.
Ts'en Liang is eleven years old,
and as for Wu, he's two years less than that.
They see you as their elder brother,
so you can take them as younger brothers now.
You stand in rank like a flock of geese
playing for me flute and ocarina.
They're still small, not ready to take blame;
you are older—teach them to behave!
Yung-erh! Come before me:
I have a worthy lesson for you now.

At crack of dawn, you must rise quite early;
when sun's gone down, you must go to bed quite late.
Basket in hand, sweep out all the halls;
draw well-water to irrigate garden beds.
When guests arrive, serve them tea and fruit;
when they have left, put away the chess board and books.
You have a mouth—don't use it to drink wine;
drunkenness is a crooked path to death.
You have two hands—don't use them to steal;
become a thief at the risk of your own hide.
In human life, no matter high or low,
just ask what company he keeps!
To grow up as an official's servant
beats being a barbarian, Chuang or Li!
Yung-erh! Why are you so dumb?
I tell you these things, and you seem unaware."
He hangs his head, asleep, without a word:
I'm chanting my poem to myself alone.

(MST, 22/17 a–b)

——Master Jade Stream: Lu T'ung (d. 835), an eccentric poet of the mid-T'ang period.

——It would appear that Yung-erh was originally a member of the Chuang or Li tribe,
ethnic groups which lived in the far southwest of China.

Inscribed on the Painting, *Meaning of a Poem by Wang Wei*

Level fields expand into lakes;
summer's second month is full of rain.
On the spit, egrets too damp to fly;
in the woods, orioles hold back—then sing.
Firewood? The villagers borrow from neighbors;
field-lunches brought out in time for noon.

Bramble gates here have no locks:
men leave and return with stick and sandals.
The white gulls and farmers seem to know each other;
they've gotten beyond distinctions of "thou" and "you."

Minister Wang belonged to the poets,
but his talent in painting was also Heaven-sent.
Just consider, Sir, after a hundred generations
there are still so many who imitate his art.
Now I have always loved mountains and valleys;
by chance I've been tied down with sash and cap.
Let me question this old man beneath the pine tree:
"How many others left the world with you?"

(MST, 22/15a–b)

———Wang Wei (701–61): The greatest nature poet of the T'ang dynasty and a major painter as well. By Li Tung-yang's time, it is unlikely that any authentic paintings by Wang were available. Li may have seen a painting by a later painter inspired by a poem of Wang Wei.

The Long Handscroll of Bamboo by Wang Meng-tuan

The Old Man of Nine Dragon Mountain,
    full of inspiration,
grasped in hand a twisting, writhing staff
    of green bamboo.
Wine-drunk, angrily he tossed it
    into a river's flow
and it transformed into a dragon
    hundreds of feet long!

This dragon leapt up, a second dragon followed,
and suddenly, a whole flock of dragons
                    hurtled through the waves!
They dived through sand, drilled through rock,
                    they touched the foggy clouds;
their horns rose, awesome, from their brows
                    as they turned to face each other.
Among these creatures, the smallest of all
                    were known as "young shoot dragons";
their fins and scales they molted then
                    and gained full power and force.
People say that this old man was good at playing games:
the powers of creation he held in the palm of his hand.
Sir, do you not wonder:
                    Where has he gone off to,
                         this Old Man of Nine Dragon Mountain?
—To Nine Dragon Mountain, so full of windswept rain!
On a white wall in deserted hall he has left
                    the shadow of his staff, so cold:
at midnight, when no one is around, it speaks
                    the language of dragons!

(MST, 22/24b)

———Wang Meng-tuan: Wang Fu (1362–1416), one of the greatest painters of bamboo in
the Ming dynasty. A number of extremely long bamboo handscrolls by him survive
today.

A Trip to Yüeh-lu Temple

This precarious peak commands a view
                    of the Ch'u river's shore;
how many twists of the sheep-gut road
                    until you reach this place?

Ten thousand pines and cedars
        where two paths converge;
four mountains-full of wind and rain,
        a single monk, so cold!
Over level sands, pale grasses
        stretch to the horizon;
in setting sunlight, a solitary town
        is visible across the water.
Chi to the north and Hsiang down south
        both are seen from here;
surrounded by songs of partridges
        I lean on the balustrade, alone.

               (MSPT, p. 60)

Song of the Painting, *Catching Fish*

The poor people use snare-nets
        when they go out to fish;
the rich people use seine-nets
        when they go out to fish.
And so poor people make less profit
        than those already rich:
one sweep of the seine pulls in
        dozens of feet of fish!
River flowers embroider the banks,
        river banks so steep;
at such a time, each foot-length of fish
        is worth its weight in gold.
The banks are tall, the snare-nets small,
        they can't haul a big load;
the fishermen's songs are full of grief,
        saddening the heart.

Every family sells its catch
   along the riverbanks:
large boats come and small boats too,
    too many of them to count.
The large boats have the finest fish,
    and make the biggest profit;
the small boats float there, sadly, sadly,
    all day into night.
This traveler, a man of Ch'ang-sha,
    sits thinking of his home;
how could I get to return and sit
    by the riverside to watch?
Buying fish and pouring wine
    to face the brilliant moon:
although I would not drink myself,
    I'd raise my cup for form.
Now I am living to the west
    of Peking's Lakeside Bridge;
a court messenger brings me a fish
    as long as a large chopstick.
My neighbors have never seen such food:
    can I bear to eat it alone?
I lean on the bridge-rail and throw it out
    to swim away in freedom.
The inspiration of my life
    has never come from fish;
examining books and viewing paintings
    is quite enough for me!
I have no family enterprise,
    so what do I know of these things?
My only wish is that all the people
    throughout the land
      share this abundant food.

         (Yoshikawa, pp. 163–64)

Following the Rhymes of Yang T'ing-ho's Poem,
On the Road Back, Accompanying the Imperial Retinue on a Visit to the Tombs of Former Emperors

No more post-stops on the road—
     we enter the capital.
River towns and mountain towns,
     how many we passed through!
We'd meet people, rent a room,
     though we didn't know their names;
on horseback, we would dash off poems
     not knowing where we were.
On sand banks, returning wild geese
     were forced down by the wind;
at stone weirs, fish would dive below
     just as waters cleared.
The jeweled towers must be ahead,
     beneath the vaulted sky:
let not the slightest wisp of cloud
     bedeck the brilliant moon!

(Yoshikawa, pp. 165–66)

——Yang T'ing-ho (1459–1529): A Grand Secretary, one of the highest positions in Ming government, and father of the poet Yang Shen (1488–1559; see pp. 267–80).

CHU YÜN-MING (1461–1527)

CHU IS recognized as the most important calligrapher of the Ming dynasty, and one of the greatest masters in the entire history of the art. His calligraphic achievement runs the gamut from exquisite, small characters written on tiny silk album leaves to some of the boldest, wildest cursive brushwork ever executed. In 1977, works by him played a significant role in the Yale University Art Gallery exhibition of Chinese calligraphy, *Traces of the Brush,* and Shen C. Y. Fu devoted an entire chapter of his accompanying catalogue to an in-depth study of Chu's art. Chu associated with such Suchou Wu School artists as Shen Chou and Wen Cheng-ming (qq.v). His poetry, like theirs, owes much to the expressive diction of T'ang poetry, but possibly even more to the understated depiction of everyday life characterisitc of Sung poetry. For more on Chu Yün-ming, consult Shen C. Y. Fu et al., *Traces of the Brush: Studies in Chinese Calligraphy* (New Haven: Yale University Art Gallery, 1977), Ch. 6, pp. 203–36.

Too Lazy To Write Poetry

I don't understand it myself—
for some time now I've stopped writing poems!
Could I have lost the "brush of Magistrate Chiang?"
Or could the "shuttle of Master Hsieh" have broken my teeth?
Feelings for the moon? As heavy as wine!
Love for the flowers? Overflows like waves!
Spirit of poetry, quickly, come back!
Don't let the spring go by without any poems.

(vol. 1, p. 117)

——The poet Chiang Yen (444–505) dreamed one night that the poet Kuo P'u (276–324) appeared to him and demanded his writing brush back. Chiang gave Kuo a five-color brush. After this, Chiang never recovered his poetic gift.

——Hsieh K'un (280–322) flirted with the woman who lived next door until she threw a shuttle at him and broke his front teeth. When he was made fun of for this, Hsieh proudly asserted, "I still haven't given up chanting poetry!"

Remembering My Late Wife

My books, my sword, the wind-swept curtain:
                    I've lost my Meng Kuang!
Tender feelings—I cannot stop them—soften my hard heart.
Distant mountains: their somber silence
                    quiets this Chang Ch'ang
Flowing waters: their enticing music
                    misled this Master Juan.
White silk, pressed and sewn into skirts,
                    I remember those past days.
Green gauze, a thin blanket,
                    I fear the new frost.

Now I can't bear to see the view
        from Feng Shan Pavilion:
the wild ducks are flying in pairs,
        and landing on the banks of willows.

(vol. 1, p. 119)

——Meng Kuang: The wife of the Latter Han dynasty scholar, Liang Hung. Although she was fond of wearing heavy makeup when they were married, she changed to a more modest type of dress when Liang told her that he wished his wife to dress in a manner suitable for a life of reclusion in the mountains. She is thought of as a model wife.

——Chang Ch'ang: A Han dynasty scholar who loved his wife so much that he would paint in her eyebrows for her.

——Master Juan: Juan Chao of the Latter Han dynasty, who, together with a friend, was searching for herbs in the mountains when two beautiful women led them into a cave, and treated them to a feast. Upon returning home, they found that seven generations had passed. A Chinese Rip Van Winkle story.

The Shrine of General Pien

My skinny horse
        west of the city
                walks in the sunset.

A temple building
        rises, imposing
                protected by flowers.

I dismount,
        enter through the gate
                and quickly bow down in respect:

someone has told me
        that this is the shrine
                of General Pien.

(vol. 1, p. 163)

For Several Years I Have Wanted To Grow a Garden, But Have Never Finished One. This Year It Is Already Halfway Through Summer, and This Has Made Me Despondent.

I always talk of living in the mountains,
but I can't even care for my one acre of land!
A willow grew up here—now I scold children
     for harming it!
Bamboo was planted here—but it too is going to ruin.
How can I trouble to "form the ranks" again and again?
The problem is laziness; I'm not being stingy!
I wonder if the year *hsin-hai*
has any peace in store for Master Chu Yün-ming!

(vol. 1, pp. 240–41)

——[Poet's notes]: Line three—I loved a certain old willow tree, which flourished until one of my boy servants harmed it, to my great regret. Line four—This is because it lost its protective railing.

——*Hsin-hai:* The cyclical name for the year 1491.

Miscellaneous Poems Written in My Studio on an Autumn Day

(Two poems from a series of 15)

1.

A bamboo bed, rattan pillow,
   vines climbing the bookcase—
here I loosen my sash, lie down for a nap
   after the noonday meal.
As the wine gathers strength in me,
   I travel to the land of dreams
and—suddenly—drop the book I was holding in my hand.

2.

The rumble of thunder brings evening rain
cleansing the autumn landscape.
Lying on my bamboo mat, too lazy to get up
   after my dream,
I contemplate the ants, those officials of the kingdom
   beneath the southern branch.

              (vol. 1, pp. 273, 275)

——The kingdom . . .: A reference to a famous tale which exists as a T'ang dynasty short story and as a play by T'ang Hsien-tsu (1550–1616). The hero of the tale falls asleep under the "southern branch" of a tree, and dreams of an entire official career in a distant kingdom. Upon awakening, he finds that there is a colony of ants beneath the tree, and realizes that this was the kingdom he had served in. For T'ang Hsien-tsu, see pp. 338–43.

A Painting of the Butterfly Dream by the Master Artist Li Tsai

I used to dream of Chuang Tzu;
I read every word in his book.
Day and night I thought of meeting him,
"flitting and fluttering" before my eyes!
But Chuang Tzu cannot come back,
the butterfly cannot appear again:
so who put them into this painting?
I see them and feel we're old friends!
If Chuang Tzu could become a butterfly,
why shouldn't a butterfly be able to become me?
The dream of a thousand years, here on this paper—
how do I know it is not my own?

(vol. 1, p. 288)

——The poem is based on the famous story of the Taoist philosopher Chuang Tzu, who dreamed that he was a butterfly, "flitting and fluttering around, happy with himself and doing as he pleased" (Burton Watson, *The Complete Works of Chuang Tzu* [New York and London: Columbia University Press, 1968], p. 49). After waking up, Chuang Tzu could not decide whether he had been Chuang Tzu dreaming he was a butterfly, or was now a butterfly dreaming he was Chuang Tzu.

——Li Tsai was a major painter of the first half of the fifteenth century.

A Fan from Korea

This oriental country, year after year,
        sends its long-journeying ships;
presenting a tribute of wind and moonlight
        they come to China.
I trust you will not view this as some trifling affair:
the world now is a single family.

(vol. 1, p. 291)

A Landscape Painted on a Fan—Echoing a Poem by Wen Cheng-ming

For cover—the tall forest,
    for a floor—the moss.
The stone folk, the tree people will keep you company.
You'll have everything you need if you live in the mountains;
the only problem is—no one is willing to try!

(vol. 1, p. 291)

A Little Landscape

A silent, thatched hut deep among the trees—
but the hermit's tracks are hidden, and hard to trace.
It must be that he has gone off alone, lute in hand,
to play in harmony with the ancient music
    of pine tree and bamboo.

(vol. 1, p. 298)

Forest Birds (A Woman Speaks)

I.
What can I do, I love you so much!
As you leave, I cling to you.
I am to you as the forest bird to its mate:
getting to perch together with you,
    but not to fly with you.

2.

You and I are like birds in a forest,
coming together for a while, then parting again.
When night falls I perch next to you,
but when day breaks, I cannot fly with you.

(vol. 1, pp. 552–53)

Drinking

I sit with my wine—there's no singing or dancing.
I just watch the sky, chanting poems out loud.
The works of the T'ang masters are piled on my desk:
half of them are poems about chaos and separation.

(vol. 2, p. 691)

Improvisations

1.

Old Man Chih-shan has a head of white hair;
he's gotten rid of everything—only craziness is left!
From this day on, he'll spend his time among old friends:
ten years with the poets of Han and Chin,
    ten with the poets of T'ang!

——Old Man Chih-shan: Chu Yün-ming himself.

2.

No robe, no sleeves, my hair uncombed,
I walk around the verandah a hundred times, all by myself.
I walk and walk—to the central courtyard
          where I lie down facing the sky,
and feel like a fish, swimming through the waters of paradise!

3.

Unruly hair, bare feet—busily studying books;
my head unprotected by any cap, my calves by any trousers.
Everyday I drink good wine, and enjoy the company of women—
then I climb into bed, and walk to the Land of the Great Locust
          Tree.

                                              (vol. 2, p. 701)

——The Land . . .: A reference to a man of the T'ang dynasty, Ch'un-yü Fen, who fell
   asleep beneath a locust tree in his backyard, and dreamed of traveling to a country
   hidden within the tree, according to an old tale. The same tale is referred to in
   "Miscellaneous Poems Written in My Studio On An Autumn Day."

Making Fun of the Well at the Inn
Below the Mountain

Feet covered with mud, the smell of meat on their breath:
how many people drawing water, jostling for a good spot
          with their jugs and jars?
Just nearby, on the mountain ahead, are natural cold springs—
What a laugh! These people live here and don't even know.

                                              (vol. 2, p. 710)

Late Spring—Traveling Through the Mountains

My little boat emerges at Heng-t'ang;
the morning air is fresh in the West Mountains.
Here women sweat away at the water-wheels,
while young men take joy rides in palanquins!
Wheat being threshed—pounding sounds from every house;
tea leaves being picked—everyone carries baskets.
The scenery is wonderful here in Wu,
and the farm scenes are the best of all.

(vol. 2, pp. 710–11)

As I Looked at a Lake, My Thoughts Turned to a Certain Friend

On the lake, the autumn wind blows blue ripples:
as I watch them, they become thoughts of you.
But what is the connection between ripples on a lake and you?
I myself don't understand this mystery.

(vol. 2, p. 764)

Poem Inscribed on a Landscape Painting

(One poem from a group of 33)

Clouds are swept into the sunset—a sky beyond the sky.
Standing against the wind—sparse willows,
       their branches blown aslant.
The fisherman throws down his nets to dry on the hillside,
and lies beside them—drunk—to catch some sleep.

(vol. 2, p. 817)

WANG CHIU-SSU (1468–1551)

WANG WAS the eldest of the so-called Former Seven Masters *(ch'ien ch'i tzu)*, the writers who were to dominate literary orthodoxy in the Ming dynasty for decades. He was a close friend of another of the seven, K'ang Hai (q.v.); both men were political allies of the eunuch, Liu Chin (although K'ang's link to him appears to have been tenuous). Liu's fall from power led to Wang's return home to Shensi province. Wang is highly respected as a writer of *san-ch'ü* poetry and drama. Here he is represented by his *shih* poetry, in which he shows himself a master of long narrative poems with a moralizing tendency. His interest in the eccentric T'ang Buddhist poet Han Shan is also worthy of note and indicates how difficult it is to establish a simple dichotomy of stuffy orthodoxy vs. eccentric individualism in Ming poetry.

After Reading the Poems of Master Han Shan

(Two poems from a group of four)

1.

This crazy man has escaped the world,
with his messy hair and bare feet!
His body sleeps among the clouds of Cold Mountain,
his mind is like the moon in an autumn pond!
He enjoys the company of the monk Feng-kan;
sometimes he visits the Cowrie Palace.
He looks up to heaven, and laughs out loud:
an ocean bird crying in the cool shade!
Flourishing his brush, he inscribes mountainsides:
dragons and snakes writhe in the lofty heights!
Handed down for thousands of years,
his fame will never die out.

2.

Floating, floating, the river waters,
naturally forming patterns in the wind.
Beautiful, the jade of Ching Mountain:
carve it, cut it, and it loses its true nature.
Men of talent, striving for fame,
write too much poetry, and damage their souls!
They are like the parrot:
he is able to talk, but he just is not a man!
Where can we find a real recluse
who locks his door to keep out all the dust?

(vol. 1, pp. 78–79)

Miscellaneous Poems on Living in the Woods —In the Manner of Han Shan

(One poem from a group of five)

A total failure—Master Han Shan:
he laughs out loud; when will he ever stop!
He lives in a cave, on a strip of cloud,
and his door faces snow, unmelted for a thousand years.
With tattered sleeves, he dances in the spring wind;
he enjoys the autumn moon, reflected in the pond.
How many hundreds of poems has he written,
letting his genius fly where it will?

(vol. 2, pp. 717–18)

Ballad of Selling a Child

The village woman brings her five-year-old son
to sell to our household for four and a half measures of grain.
I ask her, "Why do you wish to sell your son?"
And she answers me, with repeated sighs:
"My husband is old, sick in bed, and blind in both eyes;
from morning to evening, there's no telling if he'll live or die.
Our five acres near the village are only poor land,
and our two rooms, circled by a wall, are falling apart.
My eldest son is thirteen, and he can push a plow,
but our fields are few, our profit meager, so we don't have enough
        to eat.
Last winter we were late with our tax payments:
the officials came knocking at our door, pressuring us to pay.

Only when a rich family made us a loan did we manage to get
    through,
but thinking back, that only made our life more difficult than before.
My second son, eight years old, knows oxen and sheep,
so the eastern neighbor bought him to care for his herds.
Meanwhile, the rich people demand payment of our debt, as if they
    expected us to pay with our lives.
and my sick husband coughs and wheezes, his stomach completely
    empty.
Come to such a pass, we realized we had no choice at all,
and so I've brought my youngest son here to exchange for grain.
Half this grain will be used to repay the rich folks' loan,
half will be used to make some gruel to feed my poor husband."
When the village woman stopped speaking, she prepared to leave,
but her son tugged at her clothes, crying his mother's name.
The woman, miserable, lingered for awhile,
and borrowed the use of a spare bed, so she could pass the night
    with her son.
When the morning drums beat solemnly, and the roosters cried their
    wild cry,
the woman rose, and hesitated as she watched her son in his sound
    sleep.
Then, stifling her sobs, holding back the tears, she left the city walls
with the grain that would at least alleviate her terrible suffering.
When the boy woke up, he called for his mother, but she was
    nowhere to be seen,
so he walked around the house, crying out loud, unsteady on his
    feet.
Everyone who saw him wept tears at the sight,
everyone who heard him knit his brow.
Alas! The wild tiger does not eat its cub,
and the old ox will lick the calf.
How can we throw away this pearl we hold in the palm of our hand,
cutting away this flesh from our heart!

Please realize:
     The rich grow crueler as their fields increase,
and they buy servants and slaves with their wealth.
Then, one day, they curse them in anger,
whipping them unfeelingly until their blood flows!
Don't they know that all flesh and bone comes from the same womb,
that another's son and my son are of one form?
Alas! Will the four seas and the nine continents ever share the same
     springtime,
so there will be no more people who must sell their daughters and
     sons?

(vol. 1, pp. 95–96)

Song of the Painting of the Long-Life Star

The old man, a slight smile on his lips, rides a grey deer.
A white monkey leads it by the reins, just like a human servant.
A black monkey plucks a branch of red plum blossoms,
and shoulders two baskets woven with threads of blue silk:
in the baskets are rare mushrooms of five colors.
Another monkey, coarse and unbearably ugly,
straddles the deer behind the man, putting on a wild show.
We feel as if the wind blows from the pines,
                         filling our ears with the roar of waves.
In the shadows of the tall trees hangs the spring moon.
Beneath the moon, bats flit back and forth,
three by three, two by two: as if they had been summoned
to greet the colors of spring, and visit the empyrean!
The old man is really the Southern Pole Star:
who has transformed him into paint?
I hang this scroll in the Spring Rain Pavilion of my home,
and I am startled to find paradise within my own four walls!

The South Pole Star will glitter beautifully forever in the sky,
and our great Ming dynasty will reign sovereign,
                 its mandate firm as rock.
May his majesty the August Emperor
                 live a full ten thousand years!

                                         (vol. 1, pp. 114–15)

———This poem is filled with auspicious symbols: the star itself, personified as usual, the deer, the mushrooms, the pine trees, the bats (considered lucky in China), etc. It is apparently intended as a hymn of praise to the Ming dynasty, although its style is much too free for it to be considered an "official" poem.

The Robber of Kuan-shan

(One poem from a group entitled "Ten Miscellaneous Poems About Shensi")

Today I am a farmer in the fields;
yesterday, I was a robber in the hills!
When I recall my former life,
I sigh out loud, and then I laugh out loud!

                                         (vol. 1, p. 203)

Forced Feelings

(One poem from a group of eight)

You think I am happy:
in my heart, I suffer!
A fake smile on my face, I play the p'i-p'a:
but the tune is wild, music never written down.

                                         (vol. 2, p. 707)

For Several Days I Have Not Visited the Garden Pavilion—A Poem Sent to My Pet Crane

Since I parted from you, immortal bird,
I have lived in dust for more than ten days.
You must be perched on your accustomed bamboo;
your voice, I recall, reached high into the clouds.
You still must have a mind to fly ten thousand miles:
how far can it be for you to the Three Mountains?
On a night of flute music and brilliant moonlight
I will come to watch your elegant dance.

(vol. 2, p. 717)

——Three Mountains: The island-mountains of paradise, conceived of as far to the east
in the ocean.

Chanting Poems

I've been chanting poems for forty years:
the ocean of learning has filled my life.
Two or three masters from the Han and Wei,
and several hundred poets of the T'ang!
Stroking my beard, I've polished verses,
feeling proud whenever I get them just right.
Don't you see that in Tu Fu
the feelings are real, the words naturally beautiful?

(vol. 2, p. 726)

Rising from Sleep

I lie beneath my patchwork blanket at the southern window,
comfortable in the natural warmth.
The neighbor's rooster knows the spring dawn;
the windbells at the eaves feel the night wind.
When you possess the Tao, a thousand cash seems valueless.
The mind serene, all worries disappear.
My meal done, there is nothing I must do:
I watch the children playing the games of peace.

(vol. 2, p. 728)

Thunder

Thunder in the southern mountains, the third month of the year:
it shakes the darkness by the window at night.
When I rise in the morning, I hear an old farmer
say, "This is an omen of a good harvest this year!"

(vol. 2, p. 738)

Quiet Sitting

As I get older, I like quiet sitting:
too many worries harm your soul.
My poems are not achieved by slaving at each word;
of all the emotions, serenity is best!
The perfumed steps are covered with flowers;
in blossoming trees: frequent songs of birds.
When the feeling comes, I dance and sing,
completely forgetting my head of white hair.

(vol. 2, p. 757)

——Quiet sitting: A form of non-Buddhist meditation practiced by the Neo-Confucianists.

Recording My Happiness

I'm sound asleep, when a knock at the gate wakes me;
at midnight, they tell me I have a grandson!
The family books say his name should include "wood";
it might be wise to use a word like "root."
Heaven must always have had this in mind;
how can I, a white-haired old man, ever forget this kindness?
In the morning, I get up, and watch the sun
rise in a clear sky;
the green of the southern mountains seems to reach my gate.

(vol. 2, p. 757)

——Lines four and five: In Chinese tradition, each male child of the same generation would be given a name in which one of the characters would be the same, or, if the personal name consisted of only one character, the radical element would be the same for each child. Although the fourth line is partially illegible, it seems to suggest that the grandson's name include the character *ken*, "root," which has the wood radical.

Living in the Woods

—In the Manner of Yao Ho

(One poem from a group of six)

I love the serenity of living in the woods;
every morning I visit the little garden.
As I sit, I call to the boy to shoo-away the deer;
as I lie, I hope no visitors will knock at the gate.
In the late afternoon, the flies get worse;
as the sun sets, the sparrows chirp wildly.
I left a book lying on a bench beneath the eaves:
the wind flips the pages by itself.

(vol. 2, p. 762)

——Yao Ho (fl. c. 831): A T'ang-dynasty poet noted for his intimate landscape poetry.

Ballad of the Fatherless Boy

The fatherless boy, thirteen, walks and weeps.
On the road he meets a man who asks him his story.
He says, "I am of the Wang family at Hu-hsien—
my grandfather was once the Prefect there.
Two years ago, I went east with my father,
thousands of miles of hardship, to visit his in-law.
His in-law—of the Liu family—came from Pa-hsien:
he had borrowed some money, but when the debt was called in
                        he didn't pay it back.
One day, he left his job, and all of us took the boat together
                        toward his home town.

On the way, my father had angry words with him,
                              and became very ill.
Our distant journey took us past Ching-men,
                              through the Yangtze gorges;
as we traveled, my father's illness became much worse.
Liu and his wife were crueler than tigers:
when we reached Ch'ien-chiang, they put us out of the boat!
My father was gasping for breath—I was at his side—
we had no untorn clothing to wear, or any food in our stomachs.
Now, a certain venerable Jen of Kuei-lin
was Supervisor of Education at Ch'ien-chiang, a man of reputation.
An innkeeper ran to tell him about us,
and when Master Jen heard the news, his heart was filled
                              with compassion.
Immediately, he treated my father with herbs,
and gave us food to eat, morning and night.
But, alas! my father still did not recover—
a cold wind scraped the earth, heaven turned black!
Master Jen personally took charge of the funeral:
he had him buried at a beautiful site,
                              and erected a gravestone.
But this was the south, thousands of miles
                              from my home in Ch'in:
the way was long, I was weak—how could I return?
Master Jen took me into his care, gave me lodging
                              at his offices,
and raised me himself, afraid only that he might fail at the task!
He had me write a letter, and printed up copies
which he sent to the capital for distribution to the provinces.
Soon, an uncle of mine came to get me,
and before too long, I was reunited with my mother.
Ah, Master Jen!
He supported me like Heaven and Earth!
How can I ever repay my debt to him?

I wish his grandchildren to be many and wise;
may his house prosper greatly, may he live for thousands of years!"
When the man heard the child's words,
he leaned on his cane, and sighed three times.
In this world, flesh and blood can become enemies;
how often do people sit back and watch
                          while relatives die in ditches!
Consider the deeds of Master Jen of Kuei-lin:
he is a noble phoenix, the equal of the ancients!
I have written this ballad of the fatherless boy
so Master Jen's name will shine in the pages of history.

(vol. 2, pp. 768–70)

——Wang never makes it clear whether he is the "man" in the poem, or indeed, the boy (like the boy, he was "of the Wang family at Hu-hsien"). Perhaps the poem is autobiographical. It is also conceivable that the story is actually an allegory of Wang's political experiences.

T'ANG YIN (1470–1523)

ALONG WITH Shen Chou and Wen Cheng-ming (qq.v.),
T'ang was one of the greatest Ming painters of the Wu School,
and his painting is now well known in the West. A large body of
semi-legendary lore about T'ang has also made him a famous—
indeed, notorious—figure in Chinese popular culture. T'ang was
involved in a scandal when he apparently acquiesced in bribery to
obtain copies of examination questions, and as a consequence any
hope of an official career was nipped in the bud. Nevertheless, his
life in Suchou was far from unpleasant, as he was accepted as an
active member of literati circles there.

Song of Peach Blossom Retreat

At Peach Blossom Bank is Peach Blossom Retreat,
in Peach Blossom Retreat is the Immortal of Peach Blossoms!
The Immortal of Peach Blossoms planted the peach trees:
he plucks the blossoms and sells them for money to buy wine!
When he's sober, he just sits beneath the blossoms.
When he's drunk, he comes to lie beneath the blossoms.
Half sober, half drunk, day after day,
blossoms fall, blossoms bloom, year after year.
I wish only to grow old and die among blossoms and wine;
I have no desire to bow down before men in horse-drawn carriages!
Carriage-dust and horses' hoofs: these are the pleasure of the rich!
Winecups and blossoming branches: these are the karma of the poor!
If you compare the rich and noble with the poor and humble:
the former are on level ground, the latter are in heaven!
If you compare blossoms and wine with horses and carriages:
they get to gallop around, *we* get to relax!
Others may laugh at me for being so crazy;
I laugh at them for not seeing things clearly.
Don't they realize?—The tombs of the great at Five Mounds:
no wine there, no blossoms—they're plowed into fields.

(vol. 1, pp. 106–7)

——In line four from the end, read *tien*, "crazy," for *sao*, "sad," as in *T'ang Po-hu shih tz'u ko fu ch'üan chi* (Hong Kong, n.d.), p. 20.

Inscribed on a Painting of a Fisherman

Punting pole stuck in the reeds,
              he ties up his boat.
Late at night, the moon climbs to the top of the pole.

The old fisherman is dead drunk—call him,
      he won't wake up!—
In the morning he rises, frost-prints
      on the shadow of his raincoat.

(Wilson and Wong, p. 58; vol. 2, p. 424)

Inscribed on a Painting of Bamboo

Fourth watch, the moon sinks, paper window calm.
I sober up from wine, lean head on hand,
      read books for a while.
But pure imagination presses upon me—
      I cannot stop it …
until ten stalks of cold blue-green
      spread their shadows!

(Wilson and Wong, p. 55)

——Both of the above poems are inscribed on paintings by T'ang Yin in the John M. Crawford, Jr. collection: *Drunken Fisherman by a Reed Bank,* and *Ink Bamboo.* The second is reproduced here as Plate 7. For the first, see Wilson and Wong, p. 58.

Inscribed on a Painting

Thatched hut among the pines, door open near a cliff;
under the cliff, rare flowers surround the terrace.
Who knocks on the bramble gate,
           and wakes me from my dream of cranes?
—My friend has come to visit me
        through a thousand miles of moonlight.

(vol. 1, p. 167)

——This Poem is inscribed on a Painting in the Palace Museum, Taipei. It is reproduced in *Ninety Years of Wu School Painting* (Taipei: Palace Museum, 1975), p. 61.

Spring—River—Flower—Moon—Night

(One poem from a set of two)

The fog of night envelops the flowering trees;
the springtime river floats the disc of the moon.
When this happiness comes, the mind cannot be controlled—
the climax of joy is hard to put in words!

(vol. 1, p. 22)

Miscellaneous Feelings

(One poem from a group of ten)

Galloping around, north and south,
                    my head covered with dust.
My robe and shirt, completely tattered,
                    my cap with drooping corners!
Ten thousand falling petals—each of them a resentment;
only when the moonlight fills my winecup do I forget my poverty.
Even for incense and lamps, this Vimalakirti
                    cannot rise from his sickbed;
even cherries and bamboo shoots
                    do not help pass the Grain Rain days.
I look at myself in the mirror—and laugh out loud:
for half my life, I've been a character in a puppet play.

(vol. 1, pp. 93–94, 98)

——Lines five and six: T'ang Yin compares himself to the famed Buddhist layman, Vimalakirti. He feels too ill to rise from his sickbed even to light the incense and lamps of worship. In the Buddist classic, *Vimalakirti Sutra,* Vimalakirti is depicted as lying in his sickbed when he is visited by the bodhisattva Manjushri. The "cherries and bamboo shoots" would appear in the market late in the third lunar month; these were the so-called "Grain Rain" days.

On a Painting of a Woman Shown Half-Length

1.

Nature has endowed her with complete charm—
what a shame that her beauty is cut off at the waist!
We must blame the painter for his limited vision:
just when he got to the really moving part—
　　　　　　　　　　he stopped painting!

2.

Who used his masterful brush to paint this romantic beauty?
Only—he painted down to the romantic place, and then he stopped!
I remember in former years, I once saw this face:
where the peach blossoms were deep, above a short wall.

　　　　　　　　　　　　　　　　　(vol. I, pp. 118–19)

──One is reminded of the western painter known as The Master of the Female Half-Lengths (cf. Max J. Friedlander, *Early Netherlandish Painting*)!

──An alternate version of the second poem is attributed to the early Ming Poet, Yang Chi (c.1334–c.1383) in the addenda to his *Mei-an chi* (*pu-i*, 3b).

Inscribed on a Painting

(One poem from a group of four)

At the country inn, thousands of peach trees
　　　　　　　　　are heavy with blossoms:
the best spring scenes are west of the painted bridge.
The hermit has been inspired to search for flowers:
as he sits on horseback, his poem is finished—
　　　　　　　　　but he has lost his way!

　　　　　　　　　　　　　　　　　(vol. I, p. 147)

A Rainstorm Has Dragged On for Ten Days Now, and There Is No Fire in the Kitchen. Moistening My Inkstone and Chewing on My Brush, I've Lived in Isolation Like a Monk—and Completed Eight Quatrains to Express My Feelings.

1.

Ten days of wind and rain, depressing darkness!
A family of eight—wife and children—all complaining of hunger.
Surely old Heaven is playing games with me:
no one has come for days to buy the poems I write on fans.

2.

My calligraphy, painting, poems, and prose—none of them
                                        are any good,
but somehow I've managed to make a living from them!
How could I dare look down at even a little bit of money, or rice?
At least they will get this gentleman here through another day
                                        of poverty.

3.

I clasp my knees, all comfortable with a book:
no thick clothes to wear, no fish to eat.
Other people laugh at me for being so dull at planning my life,
but dullness *lies* in planning life—I'm really quite happy!

4.

A plain plank gate in a red hibiscus hedge,
geese and ducks for neighbors—I live here with my wife
                                        and children.
It's hard to describe the natural happiness of the life we lead—
but there's been no kitchen fire for three days now,
                        and yet we don't feel hungry!

5.
I enjoyed the greatest fame in the capital;
now, clothes hanging loose, I've retired to my old thatched hut.
Don't laugh that there isn't enough room here
                              for the point of an awl:
thousands of miles of mountains and streams
                              are born from my brush!

6.
With my blue shirt and white hair, old and a little crazy,
making my living from brush and inkstone,
                              so hard to get anything to eat!
People these days don't even want the rice fields by the lake:
who will ever come to buy the mountains in my paintings!

7.
In this distant village, the sound of wind-swept rain
                              mingles with the cries of roosters;
nothing for the breakfast fires in the kitchen—
                              I'm ashamed before my wife.
I planned to paint a new scroll of ink bamboo to sell,
but in town now, bamboo shoots are going cheap as mud!

8.
Being a scholar—what a dumb way to try to make a living.
Your livelihood depends on your brush and your inkstone.
The days are gone when students would come with gifts of wine,
or you could expect to pay for fish with the poems
                              that you wrote.

(vol. 1, pp. 171–72; vol. 2, pp. 404–5)

Inscribed on a Painting

(One poem from a group of three)

The places I go, leaning on my bramble cane,
                    searching for poems,
are mostly bridges, or country temples—
where yellow leaves bury your sandals, and no one else comes,
or flowers on bean hedges turn a whole stream red.

(vol. 2, p. 384)

———This poem, in a slightly different version, figures in an extremely interesting anecdote
related in Yü Pien, *I-lao-t'ang shih-hua* (preface dated 1547, in Ting Fu-pao, ed., *Li-tai
shih-hua hsü-pien, shang*/5b):

> I once visited T'ang Tzu-wei (T'ang Yin) at his residence, Peach Blossom Retreat,
> in the western part of the city (Suchou). Tzu-wei painted a small landscape, and
> inscribed on it this quatrain:

> > The places I go, leaning on my bramble cane,
> >   searching for poems,
> >   are mostly bridges or *among green trees,*
> >   where *red* leaves bury your *shins,*
> >   and no one else comes,
> >   or *wild pear* flowers *fall in a streamful of wind!*

> (Italics represent passages which differ from the version in T'ang's collected
> works)

> I said, "This is a fine poem, but I wonder if the character *ching* ("shins") is not
> unstable in a level-tone position?" Tzu-wei asked me what precedent I was basing
> myself on, and I replied, "Old Tu (Tu Fu) has this couplet: 'There are no yam
> shoots, the mountains are buried in snow,/ no matter how I pull on my jacket it
> won't cover my *shins.*'" Tzu-wei promptly said, "I was wrong!" and changed the
> line to read, "Where red leaves bury your sandals (*hsieh*), and no one else comes."
> Ah! Such was Tzu-wei's openness to good advice—the opposite of those who
> insist on defending their errors!

All characters, for the purposes of versification, were considered either level-tone or
deflected-tone words. *Ching* ("shins") is proved by the Tu Fu example to be properly
a deflected-tone word in poetry (the Tu Fu couplet comes from the second poem in
the famous group entitled *Seven Songs on Living in T'ung-ku Subprefecture in the Ch'ien-
yüan Period*). Recognizing his mistake, T'ang immediately substitutes an appropriate
level-tone word, *hsieh* ("sandals," "shoes"). The anecdote provides an invaluable
account of the kind of discussions about poetics which formed an important part of
the scholar-officials' conversations.

Poems Inscribed on Paintings

(Four poems from a group of forty)

1.

The wind sighs in the reeds—autumn on the rustic shore.
His raincoat covered with raindrops, he returns alone in his boat.
Do not hate this place for its wind and its waves:
there are wind and waves everywhere, and everywhere, sadness.

2.

Pines and cedars, a hundred feet of green, clinging to the earth.
The hermit's robe is ragged, his hair, spotted with grey.
The desolate mountain is silent—no human voices here!
Among the wolves and tigers, he reads the *Tao te ching*.

3.

Among red leaves and green mountains, white clouds fly.
White-shinned horses prance on beams of setting sunlight.
This scene—here before my eyes—is beautiful,
                    but so hard to put in a poem!
I just can't get the words right, it's driving me out of my mind!

4.

The mountain pavilion is silent—few people visit me here.
The bramble gate is patched with mud, my clothes are patched with
                    leaves.
I never rise from my bamboo bench—my hair is white as snow;
I no longer have a mind to ask for the secret of Zen.

                                        (vol. 2, pp. 387–90)

Inscribed on a Painting

(One poem from a group of four)

On the mountain, old trees, still green in autumn.
Below the mountain, a fishing boat, moored in shallow waters.
A flute, alone in the moonlight, heard by no one else:
he plays it by himself, for himself to hear.

(vol. 2, p. 423)

On The Butterflies

Soft greens, deep reds, really fresh colors;
flying here, flying there, they ride before the wind!
Sometimes, they fly down to the riverside,
following the flower-merchant as he gets into his boat.

(vol. 2, p. 424)

The Scene at Heaven Gate

Paradise on earth—that's the city of Suchou!
And the liveliest spot there is Heaven Gate.
Blue-green sleeves—three thousand beautiful women!—
     ascend and descend the towers;
yellow gold—worth hundreds of thousands!—moves east and west
     on the canal.
The market never stops doing business, even in the middle of night.
People speak dialects from all four directions,
     no two of them alike.
If you asked a painter to do a picture of this place,
he'd surely say it was much too hard to paint.

                  (vol. 2, p. 442)

——Heaven Gate (Ch'ang-men) was the northwestern gate of the city of Suchou, famous
 as the liveliest spot in town. T'ang Yin's Suchou residence was very close by.

WEN CHENG-MING (1470–1559)

W EN WAS the successor of Shen Chou (q.v.) as the central figure in the Wu School of Suchou. Like Shen, he is recognized today as a great master in the history of Chinese painting, and his works are familiar in the West. In 1976, the University of Michigan Museum of Art initiated a "one-man show" of his art, which was subsequently shown at Asia House Gallery in New York. With this degree of attention paid to his painting, Wen's poetry has not been fully appreciated, and yet he is unquestionably one of the most serious poets among the painters, especially in his moving cycle of poems written on consecutive New Years, the most extensive exploration of this theme in Chinese literature. For more on Wen Cheng-ming, see Richard Edwards et al., *The Art of Wen Cheng-ming* (Ann Arbor: The University of Michigan Museum of Art, 1976).

The Ch'ung-i Temple: Miscellaneous Poems

1.

This little courtyard—the wind is pure,
    the orange trees are blossoming,
the shadows of the walls turn as the sun crosses the sky.
After the afternoon nap, the feeling that books
    have lost their flavor;
quietly, I lean against the railing, and sip my bitter tea.

2.

Floating threads of spider webs hang,
    never swept away:
slowly, green shadows cluster on the courtyard stairs.
The yard is cool, there are few monks,
    all sounds have died out;
but from time to time I hear knocking at the gate:
    such is my solitude.

3.

In the sixth month, outside the gate,
    it's hot as an oven.
But deep within the temple halls,
    I know nothing of the heat.
In the evening cool, after my bath,
    I think of going home,
but stand a while longer to feel the wind from the pines.

4.

A fine breeze blows through the temple halls,
    touches my robe;
beyond the railing, the rains of the plum season fall.
Here there is a tranquil monk to engage in conversation—
he breaks off a palm-frond to use as his chowry.

5.
The day drags on, as long as a year!
Feeling bored, I put aside my books for a while.
No horses ever reach this place, beneath the pines—
I'll have to play this game of *go* against myself.

6.
Tea bowls, incense burning—a good feeling here!
The day is long, the people, gone, the temple is closed.
Suddenly, high in the eaves, a cool wind blows,
bringing the songs of cicadas to mingle with my reading.

7.
Around the temple, pines and cedars—
    nearly a hundred trees.
The bright color of a single flower penetrates the green.
The cool evening breeze fans it where it grows
    beside the pond,
wafting its gentle fragrance across the water.

8.
At the lacquered table—my recent calligraphy
    flows effortlessly;
time and again I wield my brush at the solitude
    of my window.
But I am sorry to find that too much of a good thing
    can become a burden,
as I sweat away, brushing fans of calligraphy for people!

9.
These long verandahs seem to be washed clean
    of dust and noise;
whitewashed walls encircle monks' quarters
    with roofs of turquoise tile.
I walk along slowly, chanting poems to myself as I go,
and the evening breeze blows the plantain leaves
    into confused patterns.

(pp. 76–77)

My Son's One-Year Test: Improvised

(One poem from a set of two)

Smiling, we set the testing tray before the hall:
they say the boy's life can be foreseen
    by the things he grabs today!
As for me—I've already lost my footing,
    and I have no further hope.
Let me open the books of divination
    and see what lies ahead for my son.

(p. 83)

What It's Like Living in My Studio Late in Spring

(One poem from a set of two)

The quiet courtyard fills with greenery:
more than half of spring gone, a time of boundless thoughts.
A fine drizzle brings in the Cold Food Festival,
a slight breeze floats the *hai-t'ang* petals to earth.
But my love for the flowers has diminished with illness;
the day has grown longer, now that I don't read books.
What thing keeps me company, here on my pillow?
A stick of incense, the smoke curling around the screen.

(p. 92)

Staying Overnight at Spirit-Source Temple

At night I follow bell and chant
            here, to this spiritual source.
Smiling, I take off my sash
            and lie down for a sleep in the deserted hall.
I'll engage the monks in conversation—
            many are old acquaintances;
or sit in meditation—perhaps this is my karma?
Stately, noble: the pines and junipers
            sway the mountain moon;
high, imposing: the towers and terraces
            hold the evening mists.
My dusty verses—how many years ago did they reach this place?

(Inscribed on the wall is a poem of mine.)

I try to read them with my portable lamp
            but they're already fading away.

                                                                        (p. 94)

Inscribed on a Painting: Cultivating Leisure

(One poem from a set of two)

Volumes of books, tea and incense:
            all his worries disappear!
He returns from a dream,
            lying on his pillow at noon,
                        wind from the bamboos through the window.
Busy myself, I see this scene and feel ashamed:
how could I ever live as calmly
            as the man in the painting?

                                                                        (p. 108)

——It is assumed that the character *hsien* in the title is a misprint for *t'i*, "inscribed.")

Lines Written on New Year's Day
—In the Manner of Liu Hou-ts'un
[Liu K'o-chuang (1187–1269)]

(One poem from a set of two)

There was no reason to expect sadness
    to visit my little studio.
May I ask, who escorted sadness here,
    who introduced it?
But no, it's just that the old year
    never took its sadness away—
it's not that the new year
    brought in a new supply.

(p. 109)

Painting a Picture, *The Tranquil Boat*—
Sent to Ko Ju-ching

The little boat, tied up at the dock,
    its scull not working now:
it is just like the tranquil man,
    far from the noise of the world.
—Green shade filling the path,
    he rises from his nap
and sits watching the river swelling
    with spring tides.

(p. 114)

On First Returning from Taking the Examinations: Feelings at Cloud-Stop Pavilion

For two months, the dust of the capital
    has darkened my traveler's robe—
today at Cloud-Stop I'll relax my expression for a while!
How can the road compare with home?
My lute, my books must be waiting for me!
I'm already past my prime, and white hairs are appearing:
dare I betray these enlightened times
    and inquire about the green mountains?
But for now, I'll ignore the hundred affairs,
    and enjoy a good sleep
in this season of yellow flowers, and rain that falls and falls.

(p. 205)

While It Was Raining . . .

While it was raining, I was going through my bookbaskets when I
came upon a poem sent to me by Mr. Shih-t'ien (Shen Chou) in
the year *ting-mao* (1507). It reads:

For a long time we've been apart—
    I've often thought of you.
Imagine my joy at meeting you
    at this city by the river.
To know what you're doing
    I depend on words from the heart;
it's hard for old men to expect to meet
    years in the future.

The forest blossoms fall to the ground,
     blown to powder by the wind.
The eaves-drops stop their sound,
     the rain scatters its threads.
Tomorrow our solitary tracks
     will diverge again: north and south.
I will have the wind seal this poem
     behind the wall.

At the end, the poem was dated, "eleventh day of the fifth month."
Now this day is also the eleventh day of the fifth month, and the
year is *ting-ch'ou* (1517): exactly ten years to the day! And he has
been dead for eight years now. I have therefore followed his rhyme-
words so as to express my sadness.

1.

Where among the blue clouds
     can I send my distant thoughts?
Events of the past—only the months and years remember.
His free spirit, a dream of past and present;
his remaining ink, a date between the living and the dead.
I remember you with feeling—
     your life cannot be brought back;
as for me, my thinning hair is completely white.
I want to chant your lines about those days
     at the river city—
but with blurry eyes, and tears of sad rain
     I can't get through the poem.

2.

As flowers fall at the river city, memories come to me;
at the Temple of Two Princesses I write of my old friend.
The noble one is no more, that Wang Wei among men!
And this Hsiang Hsiu grieves in vain to hear the long flute.
The fine grasses hold the mist—
      feelings throb like a pulse.
A cool breeze blows the rain—
      tears fall like threads.
For ten years, I have not walked the road to Hsi-chou:
how can I bear to open the box and read his old poem?

(pp. 212–13)

——Hsiang Hsiu (Tzu-ch'i), passing by the home of his deceased friend, the great poet
Hsi K'ang, heard someone playing the flute and remembering his friend, wrote the
prose-poem *(fu)*, "Thinking of Old Times."

Written While Sick

(One poem from a group of four)

A single illness has lasted three months,
attacking me as the new year comes in.
Everyone whispers that I'm already dead;
as far as I'm concerned, I've had enough of life.
Nearly all my hair has fallen out;
my ears are going bad—at times they buzz inside.
What puts me at ease is good medicine—
beside this, what else should I strive for?

(pp. 240–41)

Mooring My Boat on The Ssu River and Watching the Moon

I stop my boat on the pure Ssu,
    my feelings are unbounded.
At night I look out from my reed cabin
    and watch the moon.
One vast ether opens its expanse:
    a treasury of jade!
Light glimmers on the mirror-surface:
    a thousand slithering snakes of gold!
The blue void, reflected upside down
    with mountains of flowing blue-green;
like white stones, piled in craggy shapes,
    the waves kick up their flowery foam.
Sobering up from my wine, I seem to be sitting
    in the middle of the sky:
where can I find the raft that will float me to the stars?

                                           (pp. 242–43)

Hearing a Flute on the River Chi

The mountains cannot block this dreamlike song
    of flowering plum;
playing away my homesickness—the springtime in this flute!
The night waters have no waves,
    the crescent moon is out:
how many others are sleepless on the River Chi tonight?

                                           (pp. 246–47)

Improvised on Horseback To Say Good-bye to Those Who Are Seeing Me Off—Ten Poems

1.

Beneath the Shrine of the Three Loyal Ones
      the sunset light is clear:
how many times, my feelings at this station
      as I said good-bye to friends!
Today, all of you are saying good-bye to me:
you probably are feeling what I felt back then.

2.

In the past when I saw friends off
      I'd think of going home myself—
my homesick thoughts would fly a thousand miles
      every day and night.
Looking back, the last three years,
      how many partings here?
The only difference is that now
      tears need not dampen my robe.

3.

Wishing to try retirement, I requested release from duty;
my white robes have not been stained by a single speck of dust.
You gentlemen have plenty of real feeling:
coming to see off, not an official,
      but a retired man of leisure!

4.

This man of leisure for twenty years
      has been a robber of empty reputation:
dare I claim that in the past
      I had no real desire for this life?
For "patching His Majesty's robe" and
      "inscribing on the bell" there are many worthy officials:
such glory was not intended for a mere student like me!

5.
I remove my court gown and part from the Emperor's precincts
to make my way through Five Lakes' misty waters
     in a little boat!
Friends, don't look upon me as a man becoming an immortal:
I was old and sick, without ability, and simply had to quit!

6.
All of you are seeing me off, east of the Emperor's city;
sitting on horseback, we pass wine cups,
     braving the north winds.
Do not complain that the willows are so withered
     it's hard to pluck a good branch:
there is plenty of springtime spirit
     right here in these cups of wine!

7.
The wine of parting flowed and flowed,
     flooding the fork in the road!
Now the drinking is done, and we have no choice
     but to go our ways, east and west.
There is only the setting sunlight which stays with me:
full of feeling, it follows my horse's hoofs all the way down the road.

8.
Floating clouds and worldly affairs:
     both are insubstantial.
Once out of the city gates,
     all my worries cease.
There are only my feelings for friends left behind
     which will not go away:
along the southern bank of Twin Canals
     I keep looking back.

9.

I sit on horseback at Twin Bridges,
      the sun about to set.
Dust and sand blow like fog, hiding my baggage carts.
From here, my tracks will be lost in Chiang-nan,
      south of the Yangtze River,
and I'll only see green mountains, never a grain of sand!

10.

For three years I sadly listened
      to the bells of Eternal Joy Palace—
my soul in dream would flit about to the east of Five Lakes.
Now, suddenly, I find myself here in this little boat:
I open my eyes, but still feel I'm dreaming that old dream!

                              (pp. 292–94)

Recording My Happiness Upon Returning Home

Green trees form shade, the path is covered with moss,
my garden and house are undamaged as I return home.
This wise dynasty has a place for us lazy scholars;
our enlightened ruler has never cast off untalented men like me.
These woods and gullies—surely here I can live out my old age;
the mists and clouds will always protect
      the terrace for reading books.
On the east shore of Stone Lake, the road to Heng-t'ang:
how many wild flowers have opened to greet my arrival?

                                    (p. 301)

Walking to the Temple of Precious Light

Cloth socks, straw sandals, robe of coarse cloth,
wine jug, book of poems—and a boy trailing behind!
White-haired, I laugh at myself: I once served at court!
Walking along, who pities me, this old Han-lin official!
I'm happy to hear that my five acres of rice
         have all ripened now;
but it's too bad the chrysanthemums are late for the Double Ninth.
Pine tree forests, valley of bamboo—a place to enjoy myself:
and from time to time, a mountain monk will ask me for a little
        poem.

(p. 304)

"Evening Bell from a Misty Temple"

(One of the traditional Eight Views of the Hsiao and Hsiang Rivers)

The sun sets, the pagoda is darkened.
A distant bell sounds from the misty ridge:
there must be a man who is not asleep,
coldly awakened to the deepest insight.

(p. 306)

New Year's Eve

The drinking is done, the lamps extinguished,
        the night—a vast emptiness.
Moved by things, I remember events of ten years ago.
At gatherings I have seen my friends grow fewer and fewer,
and I start to feel the younger people are the sages of today.
At this river city, there is a slight chill,
        the plum blossoms are early.
On the plains, the frost is clear,
        the trees somber without leaves.
My skin and bones are weakened now, and my spirits exhausted:
again, white hairs and all, I await the New Year.

(p. 319)

The Year Hsin-hai (1551), New Year's Eve: Keeping Watch

I sit here with affection for the lingering year—
        useless emotion!—
in the room at night, candles burning, waiting for the dawn.
I am not so much saddened at being old,
        without my friends;
I am only shamed by the brightness of younger people!
As the New Year comes in, with a smile
        I watch the new calendar replace the old;
sleepless, I grow weary of hearing short and long watch-drums.
The incense burns out, the wine turns cold,
        the people fall asleep—
suddenly, the first crow of the dawn rooster is heard.

(p. 330)

The Year I-mao (1555), New Year's Eve

Laughing, before the lamps, we pour each other
       New Year's drinks:
in the mirror, fleeting time has passed another cycle.
Human life is limited from the start—a hundred years:
thousands of things have happened in mine, I regret none of them.
Remaining hardships? No need to send them off
       in the "fire carriage";
Ailments? Blown away by every firecracker!
Yesterday has gone, and tomorrow is with us:
the spring winds turn the calendar back to the first page.

(p. 347)

——The "fire carriage" was undoubtedly a local custom, probably intended to take with
    it the residual bad luck, etc., of the old year.

The Year Chi-wei (1559), New Year's Day

Working my way through life's karma,
       I've reached the age of ninety:
old, sick, gone to ruin—but still in one piece!
In human life, how many make it to their eighties or nineties?
In one life, I've seen five generations: great
       and great-great grandchildren!
Let's just say tomorrow will be like yesterday;
who would claim that an "added year" is the same
       as "one year less?"
One after the other, the plum blossoms
       fill my eyes with spring;
how can we allow sadness here, around the wine jar?

(pp. 352–53)

LI MENG-YANG (1473–1529)

A FOLLOWER of Li Tung-yang (q.v.) and one of the central figures among the Former Seven Masters, Li Meng-yang was a thoroughgoing classicist in the sense that he upheld the orthodox position (indeed, he was a primary articulator of it) that poets should model their work on the High T'ang masters, especially Tu Fu (712–770). Li himself succeeds almost too well: certain of his poems are stylistically virtually indistinguishable from High T'ang poetry, as is the case with others among the Former and Latter Seven Masters, but his is a Pyrrhic victory, as he has won his orthodox credentials at the expense of a truly personal style of his own. Li is at his best in some of his stunning poems inspired by paintings, for example, the *Song of Lin Liang's Painting, "Two Horned Falcons"* (see pp. 232–35), which nevertheless are ultimately derived from Tu Fu's works in this mode.

Seeing Off Commander In Chief Li to Yün-chung

Yellow winds blow in from the north,
           clouds turn dark and ugly;
stout men of Yün-chou province
           blow their bugles at night.
The general, sword across his lap,
           sits waiting for the dawn;
Ho-kan Mountain trembles, the moon
           moves down the sky.
At their troughs, the horses whinny;
           the soldiers eat their fill.
In the past, their clothes were tattered—
           now they wear broidered coats.
Cantering along the sands,
           they shoot the wild hawk;
where autumn grasses blanket earth,
           the Khan flees fast away.

                                         (MSPT, p. 72)

Song of Lin Liang's Painting, *Two Horned Falcons*

Over the last century,
           when it comes to painting birds
there has been Lü Chi of late
           and earlier, Pien Ching-chao.
These two masters worked at likeness,
           they did not work at feeling:
licking their brushes, focusing their eyes,
           distinguishing each feather.

Now Lin Liang *writes* his birds,
       he only uses ink:
unroll the silk, and half the surface
       is windswept by dark clouds!
Waterfowl and land birds—
       each done marvelously;
hang them up and the entire room
       takes on a vibrancy.
Up a deserted mountain, among ancient trees
       and a river's angry waves,
two falcons suddenly appear
       perched high on frosted cliffs.
Tensing bones, preening feathers,
       full of dynamism:
from all four walls, in the sixth month of the year
       autumn squalls arise!
One falcon peers straight down,
       eyeballs never moving;
immediately we sense those eyes of his
       never miss a hair!
The other falcon lowers his head
       and is about to swoop:
soon, we feel, he'll shake his pinions
       in the soughing wind.
The silken fabric may be fading
but this killer instinct will never disappear!
Horns perched above so awesomely,
       talons, fists of iron!
Almost like two sad barbarians,
       eyeballs popping out!
When northerly winds blow up the sand,
       and autumn grasses wither,
if only I could take them on my arm
       and mount an iron-clad steed!

The evil birds amidst the grasses
            they would all strike and kill
and under ten thousand miles of cloudless sky
            their feathers and blood spatter round.
I have heard tell, Emperor Hui-tsung of Sung
was also skilled at limning these hawks.
Later he lost the throne, of course,
and starved, a prisoner in Five Kingdoms.
Thus I know that painting is the art of a petty man:
work at likeness or work at feeling—
            both give empty fame.
And hunting and riding out on horseback
            are also trivial pursuits:
"Without, he engaged in promiscuous birding"
            says the classic book.
But the present sovereign, noble and dignified,
            has stopped such wanderings;
Every day he repairs to the Palace of Literary Brilliance
            for lectures on the classics.
And so at South Sea and West Lake
            the imperial avenues are deserted;
the masters of hunting and keepers of the game
            are all poor, down and out.
Lü Chi, white-haired,
            sits beside a brazier of gold:
at sunset he comes home,
            without a penny for wine.
In ancient times, the highest wisdom
            did not prize mere things;
who dared then to parade before the king
            decadent arts and skills?

Oh Liang! Oh Liang!
     May your paintings in future
         not be worth much money:
thus preventing later generations
     from doting on art and the chase!
                      (MSPT, p. 75, and MST, 29/15a–b)

——Lin Liang (mid to late 15th c.), Lü Chi (late 15th c.), Pien Ching-chao (Pien Wen-chin, first half 15th c.): three of the major bird painters of the Ming dynasty.

——Emperor Hui-tsung (r. 1101–25): The last emperor of the northern Sung dynasty, a great bird painter but considered a weak ruler.

Spring Vista from the Tower of Illuminated Distance

In the court of examinations
     they've opened a new tower:
cloudy spring day, I stand up here alone.
Along the willows, a thousand warships cluster;
among the flowers, ten thousand homes are thrown.
Wind-driven rain—the river's roar is strong;
troops with arms—the ground below looks cold.
Heart-breaking, sand geese to the north:
they rise in flocks, fly off toward Ch'ang-an.
                    (MSPT, p.76, MST, 29/16b-17a)

Wild Wind

The mountains ring, the wild wind comes,
the River Han also sighs and sighs.
Moonlight bubbles, smell of fish and dragons!
Clouds team up, jackals, tigers prowl!
My family are startled by the season;
sleepless, I think of ancient times.
The traces of heroes of ten thousand generations
in this river city at night lie quiet, cold.

(MSPT, p. 77)

Crossing the Frontier

Yellow sand, white reeds
                stretch far, so sad and sere;
at Kokonor and Silver Province
                there spreads a killer air!
These frontier passes, it is true,
                once knew Ch'in months and days,
but the Nimble General of Han
                was the greatest who fought here.
Travelers who come and go
                lead horses to drinking holes;
all who journey through this place
                have arrows at their waists.
Morning—we set out from Magic Province
                and gaze still farther west:
what we thought were Ho-lan's thousand peaks
                are only clouds and vapors.

(MSPT, p. 77)

——The Nimble General: Ho Ch'ü-ping (d. 117 b.c.).

Autumn Vista

The Yellow River winds along
            the frontier walls of Han;
autumn winds upon the river,
            flocks and flocks of geese!
Travelers pass over trenches
            pursuing the wild horse;
generals with quivered arrows
            shoot the Heavenly Wolf!
Yellow dust at the ancient ferry—
            the transports lose their way;
silver moonlight beams through the void
            and chills the battlefield!
They say that up here in the north
            are many brave stratagems:
but where today are we to find
            a man like Kuo Fen-yang!

                            (MSPT, p. 77)

——Heavenly Wolf: The star, Sirius.

——Kuo Fen-yang: Kuo Tzu-i, a great T'ang-dynasty general who helped maintain T'ang supremacy during the An Lu-shan rebellion in the mid-eighth century.

An Oriole at Dawn

Sweet and lovely, dimly in my dream,
a warbling oriole, west of my emerald tree . . .
I rise, the sun is glowing red,
and he has moved to sing in another tree.

                            (MSPT, p. 80)

Mooring at Hsia-k'ou at Night

—In Parting from a Friend

Outside the Terrace of Yellow Cranes,
              the sun about to set;
in the trees of Han-yang City
              confusion of cawing crows!
A lonely boat is moored for the night—
              the eastbound traveler
is deeply grieved that the Yangtze River
              does not flow back west.

(MSPT, p. 80)

WANG T'ING-HSIANG (1474–1544)

WANG WAS one of the Former Seven Masters of Ming literature. He served in a number of offices, some of a military nature, including acting as a kind of security officer for the emperor himself during a visit to a remote ancestral tomb. When a new imperial ancestral temple burned down in 1541, Wang was dismissed because of the emperor's view that he (along with others) had failed to report on what the emperor assumed to be misconduct on the part of various lower officials leading to heaven's negative reaction (i.e., the fire). Wang was a Neo-Confucian thinker of some stature, but seems also to have had some interest in Buddhism, unless his poem on a wall painting by the Che School painter, Wu Wei (1459–1508) is interpreted as being ironic in tone, rather than imbued with Ch'an-Zen paradox, as it appears to be (see p. 243). The same poem calls attention to the interest on the part of orthodox poets like Wang in the paintings, not of the literati Wu School, but of the professional Che School.

Climbing to the Top of the City Walls at Kan-yü

The ocean air is heavy in autumn;
the west wind pummels the islands, cold!
Past and present?—both water, flowing by.
Between heaven and earth, I lean here on this railing.
Clouds rise, as far as the towers of paradise;
mists return, following the brilliant phoenix.
Foggy waves hide thousands of miles:
which way is the capital?

(vol. 2, p. 602)

On New Year's Day of the Year Kuei-ssu (1533), Releasing Live Creatures

Live fish—someone's New Year's gift to me;
soon, they will be dry fish from the river!
But I can't bear to cut them into a thousand slivers,
and I pity their "cry from the dried-out carriage rut."
So I toss them into the pond, and they swim back and forth:
now they have water to keep them wet.
In thunder and rain, they will leap to the sky
and turn into dragons, spitting pearls!

(vol. 2, p.654)

——"Releasing Live Creatures" (*fang-sheng*) is a traditional practice in many Buddhist countries. Often, fish will be purchased for the sole purpose of releasing them in ponds. The point is to gain merit by showing compassion toward living things.

——"Cry from . . . rut": A reference to the well-known story of Chuang Tzu's encounter with a fish in need of water. See Burton Watson, *The Complete Works of Chuang Tzu* (New York and London: Columbia University Press, 1968), p. 295.

Written in the Office Precincts

The precincts at day, quiet leisure of spring:
I give myself to the solitude, linger at my meals.
Gazing at flowers, I lean against the tree;
listening to birds, walk by the fragrant pond.
The courtyard is warm, a gathering place for the bees;
the stairs under a clear sky—enriched by creeping vines.
Good feelings come from every spot:
it's easy to write new poems.

(vol. 2, p. 658)

Songs of Chiang-nan

(Two poems from a group of twelve)

1.

I pluck *heng*-herbs at the Chin-ling riverside,
walking back and forth on the Shih-ch'eng road.
If I didn't ask the people who live here in Chiang-nan,
how could I learn the names of Chiang-nan plants?

2.
I am a man of Chiang-nan,
and I know how to play Chiang-nan music.
My zither has ornaments of gold,
and a plectrum-guard of white jade.

(vol. 2, pp. 825–27)

The Flowering Tree

The flowering tree does not spare itself:
it lets the creepers wrap themselves around.
Years pass, the creepers grow . . .
now you see creepers—you can't see the tree.

(vol. 2, p. 829)

Song Of the Wanderer

May all your tears, wanderer,
fall into the Yangtze at its western source.
Then the river will flow to the east,
bringing them here to my home.

(vol. 2, p. 837)

Miscellaneous Poems on Spirit-Valley Temple

(Two poems from a group of four)

1. The Pagoda of Master Chih
This pagoda penetrates the clouds;
its steps of stone go straight up, like a wall!
Terrified, I refuse to climb:
if only I had wings to lift me toward the sky!

2. A Wall Painting by Wu Wei

An old monk perches at the tip of a tree—
but this is only external *samadhi*!
Master Wu's brush is imbued with spirit,
but even he can't paint the Buddha-Nature!

(vol. 2, pp. 837–38)

——Wu Wei (1459–1508): A major painter of the so-called Che School, known primarily for his figure paintings. A monk "perched at the tip of a tree" seems an unlikely subject; perhaps Wu's painting actually depicted the Nest Father (Ch'ao-fu), a legendary recluse who did in fact live high in a tree. A painting of him by Wu Wei is in the Tokugawa Art Museum, Japan. For a reproduction, see Suzuki Kei, *Mindai kaiga shi kenkyū: Seppa* (Tokyo: Tōkyō daigaku Tōyō bunka kenkyū-jo, 1968), fig. 94 on p. 172.

Song of Wu-ch'eng

(One poem from a set of two)

Don't ask about the Six Dynasties at the Sui Palace:
Jewel Maiden and Jade Flower have long since vanished like smoke!
Today, there are only the lakeside willows
which still move like dancers in the spring wind.

(vol. 2, p. 859)

Traveling by Boat

(One poem from a set of two)

At Arrow Rapids, the water splashes foam;
wild islets, high gorges—darkened, as if by clouds!
Wind-swept, we shoot along, sideways, lost in a haze of green;
half a day in the middle of the river, following the birds as they fly.

(vol. 2, p. 865)

Miscellaneous Poems Written in the Snow

(One poem from a group of ten)

Thousands of mountains, tens of thousands of mountains,
                    not a trace to be seen.
The sky above, the earth below: one enormous cloud.
The recluse cannot distinguish the morning from the evening.
He wonders if this is the Unity, before the split
                    of Yin and Yang.

(vol. 2, pp. 897, 900)

K'ANG HAI (1475–1541)

O NE OF the Former Seven Masters, K'ang is better known for his plays and *san-ch'ü* than for his *shih* poetry. K'ang was embroiled in political intrigues of various sorts, and may have been a partial ally of the eunuch, Liu Chin. His plays often are political allegories or satires, and his important *shih* poem, *Dreaming of Master Chung-lu* (pp. 247–48), may also have a political dimension. Recent scholarship suggests that K'ang's ancestors may have been of Central Asian origin.

Listening to the Rain

All night long, I couldn't fall asleep,
lying in bed, listening to the autumn rains.
The rain, it seemed, just wouldn't stop,
and my mind could not find peace.
Last year in autumn—eighth month of the year—
heavy rains fell just as the grains were ripe.
The entire harvest turned black with rot,
and even the house collapsed!
Those rains lasted for an entire month:
cliffs crumbled for hundreds of miles.
We wondered, what could the Divinity have in mind?
Does he intend to transplant the ocean?
My life has been one long frustration;
for a decade now, I've worked at farming.
If my fields do not yield a harvest,
the whole family will go hungry.
How can we make our tax payments?
I should have gone in for woodcutting,
                    gathering timber for pillars and beams!
—My old wife says to me,
"Just sit down for now, and don't be upset.
When human affairs cannot be determined,
how can you expect to comprehend Heaven's ways?
Short, long—there are fixed periods;
good harvests and bad—we take them as they come!
By the bed is some fine wine,
its fragrance filling the pitcher.
Why don't you just pour some for yourself:
it will help you in your years of decline."
I lie down, drunk, and it is noon:
soon, snores will sound out like thunder.

(pp. 425–26)

Dreaming of Master Chung-lu

Massive rains darken the marshes and slopes;
my carriage cannot move ahead.
I linger awhile, gazing at the northern wilds:
clouds and mists spread out everywhere.
Turning around, I go back home
where the chrysanthemums by the hedge are brilliant and beautiful.
The season is about to change:
wine cup in hand, I chant the *Great Mystery*.
As I become intoxicated, my body relaxes,
and I dream of visiting the Ninefold Flowery Heaven:
the immortal, Master Chung-lu,
bows down to me, and presents me with a book.
He says, "This is the work of Master Kuang-ch'eng;
can you fathom the fish-trap of its words?
Recall that in the past, Wei Po-yang
vowed that his bones would become those of an immortal.
But I pursued the pleasures of worldly people
and ended up miserable at Wu-t'ing Stream.
With my allotted life soon to be spent,
perhaps my fate did have this in store!
So now I thought of drinking from the spatula of elixir,
turning back old age, and seeking longevity!"
His words done, he grasps my hand,
smiling pleasantly, showing me great warmth.
From his sleeve, he produces two pills
which glitter with a light as of the morning sun.
On these he sprinkles some pine dew,
and each of us swallows one of the pills.
Suddenly, my insides feel pure and fresh,
and my spirit utterly transformed.
"I am living below T'ai-po Mountain,
and you reside at the peak of Mount T'ai—
gathering mushrooms and magic herbs,

imbibing jade and lotus from the well.
Let us meet if only for an instant,
riding cranes as we flutter away.
Master Red Pine will be our escort,
the Jade Maiden wait on us as we dine.
Amazing—beyond the ten thousand phenomena,
how can the world's net hold us back now?"

(pp. 454–55)

——An elaborate Taoist fantasy probably intended as an expression of friendship and admiration for the poet, Li K'ai-hsien (1502–68), otherwise known as Chung-lu (see pp. 281–304). The *Great Mystery*, or *T'ai-hsüan ching*, was a philosophical text modeled after the *I ching* and written by the Han scholar, Yang Hsiung (53 B.C.–A.D. 18). Master Kuang-ch'eng is described by Chuang Tzu as a Taoist master and immortal who once instructed the Yellow Emperor. It is also Chuang Tzu who develops the metaphor of the fish-trap, which he compares to words: just as a fish-trap exists only to catch fish, and is discarded once the fish are caught, words exist only to convey meaning. Wei Po-yang was a Taoist alchemist, c.140. An important text attributed to him on alchemy still survives. Red Pine and Jade Maiden are two of the best-known legendary Taoist immortals.

It is not impossible that the poem also has a level of political meaning, but this would probably be difficult to recover today.

Sitting by Myself

In my village, another year has gone floating by;
is there any place where we do not lament the passing seasons?
The songs of the birds echo in the valley,
    sounds scattered in fragments.
The dew-streaked chrysanthemums invade the steps,
    their shadows perfectly round.
When I am free of illness, I watch the emerald waters;
deeply moved, I lie all day in the grey mist.
At sunset, the herdboy's flute seems to match my mood:
I strain some wine, and invite my neighbor
    to share this mysterious joy.

(pp. 498–99)

Ten Poems on Almond Blossoms

(One poem from the group of ten)

When I have chanted my new poems
        I write them on the wall:
now that I'm old, every day I go crazy over spring!
Lord of Heaven, if you want to gratify my heart,
please lend me another 100,000 springtime scenes!

(p. 513)

PIEN KUNG (1476–1532)

PIEN WAS one of the Former Seven Masters. He held a succession of political posts, and opposed the eunuch, Liu Chin, who was politically linked to two other Masters, Wang Chiu-ssu and K'ang Hai (qq.v.), both of whom were natives of the same part of Shensi province as Liu. (It is therefore apparent that the Masters did not necessarily constitute a political clique.) As a poet, Pien was interested in the *yüeh-fu* tradition of social commentary in the form of relatively long poems with many lines of uneven length. This tradition was revived in the T'ang dynasty by Tu Fu and Po Chü-i (772–846). Pien's *Song of the Transport Workers* (p. 251) exists in no less than three metrically different versions.

Song of the Transport Workers—Seeing Off Fang Wen-yü on His Way to His Post as Inspector of Transportation

Boatmen,
how late you've come!
"When dry winds blow hard on the river
the spring waves can't be crossed."
Boatmen,
how late you've come!
"The canal has sluice-gates,
the river has rapids!
Breaking our poles, fraying our ropes—always miserable!
By night, guarding against insects and rats,
by day, watching for leaks . . .
the official register clearly records each bushel and peck
of grain!
The government worries only that the granaries might run low;
they don't realize that south of the Huai River
people are eating each other!
The government knows only of the sufferings of soldiers;
who pities us boatmen, our strength all used up!"
Boatmen—do not lament!
Now an emissary from the Minister of Agriculture
appears on the horizon!

(p. 59)

Song of the Woodcutter of the Sea

The old woodcutter of the sea
lives on an island in the sea.

He says he cannot live as well
        as the woodcutter of the mountain.
The woodcutter of the mountain chops down trees,
        and takes them home as firewood:
in coldest winter, his house is full of springtime warmth.
The woodcutter of the sea hauls up branches of coral in his net—
even if you wished to burn them in the brazier
        they wouldn't catch on fire!
So everyday he sits with his family, their bellies empty;
who would claim he eats as well
        as the woodcutter of the mountain?
—Now the glorious Emperor holds a New Year's celebration;
he opens wide the palace gates to feast his noble guests.
Imperial messengers seek out rare treasures in all four directions.
The woodcutter of the sea has food to eat,
        the woodcutter of the mountain goes hungry!

           (p. 101)

Song of the Boat-Pullers

Upstream, against the wind, they pull hundreds of feet of rope:
these official barges seem to be climbing the sky!
Bamboo-whipped behind, yelled at in front—the overseers
        are so cruel!—
they strain at the ropes; who would dare to loosen his grip?
People like to hear the pullers sing their boat-pullers' songs.
Little do they know that these are mostly sounds of lamentation.
When will this muddy flow turn to yellow dust?
Then the pullers will be free of the sorrow of charging waves!

           (p. 101)

On the Sixteenth Day I Visit the Temple Again

After ten days I come here again,
climbing, gazing—even more peaceful than before.
The old monks boil lichens for me,
sit with their guest on the mountain top.
From a dark cave—clouds and fog arise.
On a sunny slope—cows and horses graze.
I sigh—I left the city too late
and missed the chrysanthemums this autumn.

(pp. 190–91)

At the Lake—Remembering My Dead Son, Yü

Years ago, to the winding banks of this lake in spring
I brought my son to play.
The flowers greeted his jade-white skin with smiles;
the clouds floated beside his patterned robe.
He explored the bamboo on the shore across,
and took out a boat to search for fish.
Now I come alone, grieving in my heart;
the misty moon at evening holds my sorrow.

(p. 203)

On Hearing That San-p'ing's Newly Brewed Chrysanthemum Wine Is Ready to Drink— Investigating with a Poem

I love wine but have no wine to drink.
You'd think I'd be sober but I'm crazier than before!
Now I hear your new brew is ready,
its color superior to the yellow of chrysanthemums!
A moonlit night—shadows calm in the tower.
A frosty sky—ocean breezes blow cool.
When will I ride off on horseback
and pour as much as I want
          of that "fragrance in the jug!"

(p. 208)

The First Day of Spring

With my many illnesses I meet the spring,
          too lazy to pick up a brush!
At peace, I rest under a thatched roof,
          the blinds hanging down.
A good friend has been kind enough to send fish and wine;
the old farmers are not unhappy to age another year.
On and on—the snowy clouds reflect on the water;
brilliant sun—a ray of light slants suddenly past the eaves.
Cup in hand, I smile to myself as I get completely drunk;
an official, a hermit: how many other men
          can be both of these at once?

(p. 231)

New Year's Day—Following the Rhymes of Inspector Luan-chiang

Lying on my pillow, I am startled to see
            a new year come in again.
From my bed I hear the sounds of hooves and wheels
            in the street.
My cup holds no thick wine—I am too ill to drink it.
My house is surrounded by green mountains—do not think
            that I am poor!
Toward evening, the clouds seem to play with their colors;
plums and willows, in their element, vie in spring beauty.
My door is closed, but I enjoy this rich seclusion:
too lazy to follow those who travel
            east, west, north, south.

                                 (p. 232)

Walking Outside the City Walls on the Day of the Cold Food Festival

At Lai Family Village, the spring is beautiful:
the sun setting over a deserted hill,
            mist rising against a clear sky.
Willow branches, so gentle, their green still young;
flower buds everywhere, red and elegant.
On paths through the fields—dishes of offerings
            for the festival;
beyond a low wall—children playing on swings.
This place, where I rode my bamboo horse happily
            as a child,
I pass again, hair turned white, lost in thought.

                                 (p. 233)

Paintings

1.
The morning sun climbs the eastern peak.
The mountain hermit is still fast asleep.
There are no locks at the entrance to the cave,
only white clouds which seal it forever.

2.
Done playing the lute, but still full of feeling,
I rise and climb the terrace on the river.
The waters are deserted—autumn for thousands of miles,
and not a single boat to be seen.

(pp. 387–88)

Paintings of Various Subjects by Fang Jih-sheng: Baby Chicks Following Their Mother

These baby chicks do not leave their mother;
if they were parted, they would chirp endlessly.
Why is it that scholar-officials
year after year travel to the ends of the earth?

(p. 388)

Inscribed on an Album Leaf Painted by Dr. Lin

On the river, the spring tides are calm.
In the boat, a day seems like a year.
No need to grow feathers or wings—
do nothing, and be an immortal!

(pp. 390–91)

Mooring at K'ou-ch'üeh—Sent to Dr. Lin

1.
Apricot trees form a grove,
          bamboo guards the wall.
Beside the river, clouds float softly in the daylight.
This garden must be the home of Dr. Lin:
the traveler catches the scent of herbs
          as he passes by.

2.
This year of famine, old and young suffer many strange diseases,
but the immortal of Chi River gives wonderful prescriptions!
No need to meet him and ask his name:
everyone in town calls him "King of the Doctors!"

(pp. 413–14)

HO CHING-MING (1483–1521)

TOGETHER WITH Li Meng-yang (q.v.), Ho was one of the two most important Former Seven Masters, and it seems probable that he was in actual accomplishment the finest single poet of both groups of seven (Former and Latter). He was a master of shorter and longer forms both, in "ancient-tyle verse *(ku-shih)*" and "regulated verse *(lü-shih)*." Like others of the orthodox writers, he particularly excelled in long, expansive poems about paintings, as in his "Song of the Painting, *River and Mountains,* by Wu Wei" (pp. 262–64). The orthodox writers in general seem to have been particularly interested in Wu Wei and other painters of the professional or academic Che School, an interest that points to an intriguing paradox: Wu Wei was in fact a highly eccentric painter, although his brushwork as such is derived from the Sung academic style. Similarly, Ho Ching-ming at his best could infuse his poems, founded though they may be on High T'ang models (such as Tu Fu's poems on paintings) with dynamic energy and life.

Ballad of Yi River

A cold wind at evening
        whipped up Yi River's waves;
Chien-li struck his lute-strings
        and Master Ching K'o sang.
In white robes of mourning, weeping tears,
        they sacrificed to the road-god;
then, at sunset, he mounted his carriage
        and left, not one glance back!
In the hall of the King of Ch'in
        they unrolled the map;
Ch'in Wu-yang turned pale, afraid,
        he dared not say a word.
Hand grasping the dagger, Ching K'o then
        struck only the pillar of bronze:
the enterprise already failed,
        how useless his curse so bold!
Yes, alas, Prince Tan of Yen,
        with plans so feeble, was destined to expire;
T'ien Kuang may have slit his own throat—
        what point was there in that?
And what a shame that to no end
        they pushed General Fan to suicide.

(MSPT, p. 89)

——This poem is based on the historian Ssu-ma Ch'ien's (145–c. 90 B.C.) famous account
of a failed assassination attempt on the King of Ch'in (later to become First Emperor
of the Ch'in dynasty) by a certain Ching K'o. See Burton Watson's translation of the
account in Cyril Birch, ed., *Anthology of Chinese Literature* (New York: Grove Press,
1965), pp. 106–18.

Rainy Night

The courtyard, quiet—
        I hear sparse rain;
trees stand tall—
        they catch winds from far places.
Autumn sounds join the cicadas' voices;
cold colors tinge the paulownia trees.
From my short bed, in lonely lamplight—
barbarian pipes echoing in ten thousand wells.
At heaven's edge, this traveler
tonight is remembering his home at River-East.

(MSPT, p. 93)

Ch'ang-an

White clouds, I cannot see their end,
leaning emptily on the tower's balustrade.
At midnight, a wild goose flies by:
the place he is coming from is Ch'ang-an.

(MSPT, p. 97)

Bamboo Branch Song

Above the twelve mountains autumn grasses fade;
cold mist, chilly moon—I pass through Ch'ü-t'ang Gorge.
A traveler in a solitary boat
        upon this river of green maples:

I haven't heard the gibbons cry
        but my heart breaks anyway.

(MSPT, p. 97)

——According to a well-known folksong, when the traveler down the Yangtze River
gorges hears three cries of the gibbons, his heart is broken.

Seeing Off Han Ju-ch'ing as He Returns to the Land Within the Passes

Sacred Mt. Hua, terrace of clouds,
        10,000 miles of feeling;
noble autumn, sun descending,
        gazing toward the city of Ch'in.
The Yellow River, a single thread,
        leading toward the sea;
you are moving on the palm
        of the hand of an immortal.

(MSPT, p. 97)

Presented to Wang Wen-hsi

The traveler will rise at midnight
when the moon has sunk and stars still shine.
As dawn comes, he will leave the city gates;
toward sunset, reach the long river's bank.
At the edge of grass, alone he will set sail,
as birds begin to scatter in the mist.
He'll untie the hawser, and quickly move out
as evening light fragments on the waves.

(MST, 30/12b)

Ballad of the Government Granary Clerk

Spiked thorns all over, and a thirty-foot wall;
towering entrance with iron bolts,
                    double doors sealed shut.
The minor clerk of the granary
                    with grey whiskers and green shirt
writes out ten columns of vermilion characters
                    on the wood-plank board.
Standing in front of an official banner,
                    all day he reads out loud;
with clipped tallies, people form lines,
                    and listen to the numbers being called.
The rich families get plenty of grain,
                    piles of it like hills;
their big carriages go creaking off,
                    taking two oxen to pull.
A hungry man from the countryside
                    stands beneath the wall:
he too wants to come forward for grain
                    but the clerk just curses at him.
                                    (MST, 30/13b)

Song of the Painting, *River and Mountains,* by Wu Wei

Wu Wei grew old and died,
                    he's no longer to be seen;
in vain do scholars of painting in our world
                    sigh in admiration!

I look at this handscroll,
                    Painting of River and Mountains:
exalted floating, vision
                    that approaches the Void!
I imagine that when he moistened his brush
                    and touched it to the silk,
wine-drunk, with the brushstrokes
                    his spiritual bones stuck out.
Over ten thousand miles of blue sky,
                    oceans and mountains move,
in the empty room in broad daylight
                    clouds and fog float forth.
Land-spits crumble, banks collapse,
                    swallowed by ranges of waves;
islands and islets cast reflections
                    churning up whirlpools below.
Along the river, ten thousand boats
                    all set out at once;
in midstream—whistling, whistling—
                    wind whips up their sails!
Crashing waves and thundering tides—
                    this can't keep up for long;
fishermen and boatmen, each of them
                    anxiously looks back.
Parting geese—from afar
                    this seems the Seven Marshes;
falling blossoms—one might mistake it for
                    the entrance to Peach Blossom Spring.
Among misty peaks, old and hoary,
                    are limned two old men:
their faces, hair, clothes, and caps
                    all quite coarse and ugly.
Stones and forests, sand and grass
                    filled with dots and washes:
as I unfold the painting
                    I hold paradise in my hands!

I remember how in the *hung-chih* years (1488–1505)
Wei's art was in a class by itself.
He found patrons of ten thousand carriages,
and was summoned to the houses of nobles.
The rich and powerful of the capital
                    lionized this man,
though when they were dissatisfied
                    they often cursed at him.
It's always been this way—the gifted
                    ignore their own well-being;
and so in misfortune and poverty
                    his life came to an end.
Alas! Master Wu will never paint again;
after his death, his works have become quite rare.
A fragment of mountain, a leftover stream—
                    each sheet costs a fortune;
you could not buy a single one
                    for even a hundred in cash.
The present scroll has been transmitted
                    between the heavens and earth:
looking at it, Master Wu! I see your real face.

                                        (MST, 30/13b–14a)

——Wu Wei (1459–1508): One of the major Che School painters of the Ming dynasty.

Fish in a Painting

A huge fish, bold and noble,
                    stands up like a man,
slicing waves, treading ripples.
                    in brisk wind-blown currents.

Watching him from the side,
        two carp, quite full of spirit:
quick and nimble, showing, hiding,
        following the waves!
In the main hall, fins and flippers
        move in the vast darkness;
only after sitting long
        do I realize it's a picture.
Dark sky over ten thousand miles
        sweeps the silken surface:
the force of the brush in just a few feet of space
        has created a vast cosmos.
At the Gate of Yü and Heaven's Pond
        among the clouds and fog,
in broad daylight rumbling thunder
        is heard beneath the earth.
What man had the power to move this marvel here?
Wine-drunk, I gaze at it
        and my whole expression changes:
I only fear that these three fish
        may turn into three dragons!

                (MST, 30/14b–15a)

Ch'en-hsi County

Early we set out from Ch'en-hsi ferry;
how pleasant to boat on the pure stream!
Mountain towns lean out with whitewashed walls;
river stops gleam with vermilion towers.
Rain drives down, sandbanks crumble off;
weather chills, land spits break the surface.
Barbaric accents get stranger as we go:
on and on, homesickness grows in me.

                (MST, 30/16a)

Night of the Fourteenth

At water's edge, clouds float up:
lonely city in sunset dark!
On ten thousand mountains, autumn leaves fall;
I sit alone, here beside a lamp.
Beneath white dew, river reeds droop;
in western winds, cicadas chirp.
Passes, mountains, the moon tonight:
a flute plays with mournful sound.

                                                            (MST, 30/16b)

Alone I Stand

Alone I stand, facing the flowers' shade;
in the darkness, gazing at the river isle.
All I see is mist above the sand;
I do not see rain falling through the mist.

                                                            (MST, 30/20b–21a)

YANG SHEN (1488–1559)

YANG SHEN was beyond a doubt one of the most truly individual figures in Ming culture. His father was the Grand Secretary, Yang T'ing-ho (1459–1529), for a period the most powerful official in China. In 1524, when the emperor wished to promote his late father retroactively to full imperial status, Yang Shen, along with many others, memorialized against this measure and was publically beaten and sent into distant exile in remote western Yünnan as a consequence. While there—and he remained in exile for thirty-five years—he wrote his fascinating journals on Yünnan province. Yang's *shih* poetry and poetic criticism are of high caliber, but he excelled in *tz'u* and *ch'ü* as well. His *tz'u* and *ch'ü* are represented here, as they are among the freshest, most expressive poems in these genres from the later period. (Poems which are *ch'ü* are so identified; the others are all *tz'u*.) Yang's wife, Huang E (1498–1569)— represented here by one of her *shih* poems, although her *tz'u* and *ch'ü* are also superb—was herself possibly the finest woman poet of the Ming dynasty.

To the Tune, *Ch'ing-p'ing yüeh*

Little boat—untie the line:
spring fills Chiang-nan banks!
Lamps shine down the avenues, halfway through the first month;
on the road, the year turns once again.

I've leaned on every balustrade, shadow aslant;
the traveler turns back his glance at heaven's edge.
Color of the grass south of Sha-shih Bridge,
blossoms of plum in Chang-t'ai Temple.

(p. 5)

——This poem is a *tz'u*, as are all the poems by Yang Shen, except those identified as *ch'ü*.

To the Tune, *Flowers in the Rain*

—Spring Chill

Cold penetrates to the river's shore,
                        at the edge of sand;
warmth is in the hearts of flowers,
                        and under leaves.
Brushed with snow—tower and terrace;
they take in lamps from the courtyard.
Toward evening the red gate is closed tight.

A banner hangs beside the green plaque,
                        low, brushing ground;
dancing sleeves and tiny shoes
                        she's not put on tonight.

Fingers cold on metal blades—
incense warming blue-green blanket—
too lazy to cut out
    good-luck words for spring.

(p. 6)

To the Tune, *Chao-chün's Sorrow*

Outside the tower, the east wind's early to arrive,
dying the willow catkins yellow.
Low they hang to brush the jade balustrade,
fearful of spring cold.

This is a season that tires one out:
noon sleep thicker than drunkenness!
My lovely dream—who woke me up?
The oriole, with one cry.

(p. 17)

To the Tune, *Chiang ch'eng tzu*

The spring here in Tien-nan
    is like spring at Brocade River:
waters ripple with fish,
willows knit moth-brows.
A thousand trees of pear blossom,
and under blossom, cushion-soft grass.
Clear sky and warm breeze are richer than wine,
infusing coquettes' eyes,
intoxicating travelers.

Pliant threads, weak catkins
                soft in the red dust;
jealous of this fragrant time,
they tire the traveler out.
Crying birds startle my heart:
why do they keep calling, "Go back home!"
It's not that I don't want to, but I simply cannot now;
sad, I gaze afar,
tears moistening my robe.

                                                (p. 32)

To the Tune, *Heavenly Immortal*

I remember those years when we shared the joy of love,
that tiny little pond, hidden in the courtyard!
We were close and intimate, we never were apart,
meeting beneath flowers,
meeting beneath willows—
a song sung at a feast among curtains of gold!

But in a moment happiness turned to desolation;
frightening off the mandarin ducks,
                how cruel the wind-blown waves!
As I ponder I realize there's no one I can blame—
she was wrong,
I was wrong,
for all our good relationship bad feelings did arise.

                                              (p. 42)

To the Tune, *Heavenly Immortal*

Waves wash off the peach blossoms,
            wind twirls catkins down:
can spring colors possibly be allowed to stay?
Our four eyes stare at each other;
            our resentments are concealed.
Gold Tooth Road,
Gold Horse Road—
places for broken-hearted goodbyes.

The brown sparrow and the dragonfly
            can't perch on the same tree.
The purple swallow and the shrike
            fly off in opposite directions.
A new resentment starts again just as in the past:
she is wrong,
I am wrong,
in lonely inn beneath wild mountains
            we grieve at setting sun.

(p. 49)

To the Tune, *Moon Over West River*

I've brewed myself a whole bunch of trouble,
and all because of feelings of love!
The spring dream in this house of passion
               never really formed:
I wasted days and evenings
               of "rain-and-cloud."

The swallow—what does he know
               of my feelings?
It's the oriole who seems to call her name!
To get rid of this passion
               I can talk about the Void—
or turn within to look at my own heart.

                                  (p. 47)

To the Tune, *The Southerner*

The moon is the companion
               of the Goddess of Wu Mountain;
the flowers are the neighbors of her lover,
               Sung Yü;
they are as far apart as if the stars were in between!
"Had I known at the beginning the bitterness of parting
I would never have loved you!"

                                  (p. 53)

——Sung Yü: Famous *fu* (prose-poem) poet of doubtful historicity. One work attributed
    to him describes an erotic encounter with the Goddess of Wu Mountain.

To the Tune, *Spring in Tien Is Fine*

1.
Spring in Tien is fine!
The splendid scenes entice the traveler.
Gather blue-greens in the eastern fields—
　　　　　　　the wind blows languidly;
pluck fragrance at the southern shore—
　　　　　　　the water ripples clear.
Could I ever forget the Tien spring!

2.
Spring in Tien is fine!
The blossoms there all yield to the mandala tree.
Along the lake-fronts thousands
　　　　　　　are reflected in the water;
west of the town, ten miles out,
　　　　　　　heat bakes their colored mist.
Could I ever forget Tien flowers!

3.
Spring in Tien is fine!
Blue-green sleeves gently brush the clouds.
Elegant, subtle—coiffures that should be painted;
melifluous southern accents
　　　　　　　more beautiful than song.
Could I ever forget Tien women!

4.
Spring in Tien is fine!
Most I remember the lakeside pavilion.
Fishing fires—night stars illuminating islands;
wine banners—windswept shadows rippling
                        the eastward flow.
Some day together we will come again.

(pp. 56–57)

——Yang Shen is actually using the old tune-pattern, *I Chiang-nan* ("Remembering
Chiang-nan") but has renamed it, *Tien ch'un hao* ("Spring in Tien is fine"), so that he
can use it to describe his experience in Tien, or Yünnan in the far southwest of China.

To the Tune, *Partridge Sky*

Just as I joy at noble autumn—
                crisp air now so fresh—
I grieve that the mid-autumn moon
                knows how to wound my soul.
The wine wears off—memories
                of twenty years ago;
startled awake—in exile, three thousand miles away!

Maple leaf bank,
chrysanthemum ford;
I should go buy a bottle of the finest Ah-ning Spring!
The puppets on the curtained stage
                have always been unreal;
the dream of Han-tan on the pillow—was it ever true?

(pp. 57–58)

——Ah-ning Spring: A type of wine.

——Han-tan: A reference to the famous tale of a man who dreamed an entire lifetime
while waiting for his gruel to be prepared.

To the Tune, *Song of the Plum Blossom at the River Town*

—Staying Overnight at Rivergate

Waterclock drips heavy,
rain drips heavy,
drop after drop on deserted steps
                breaking the traveler's heart.
I huddle under thin blanket,
huddle under thin blanket,
my sick bones invaded by cold,
how can I help but grieve?

In the quiet I hear my gaunt horse
                whinny from the stable;
my Szechwan boy is fast asleep,
                the country roosters, mum.
Travel is hard,
travel is hard,
my white hair is fading:
when will my saddle ever end its trip?

(p. 108)

Four Poems from the Sequence, *Singing of the Moon*

—At a party I heard someone sing the lyrics. If any line proved to have a flaw, I corrected it.

To the Tune-set, *Eight-Tone Kan-chou in the Immortal Lü Mode*

1. To the Tune, Chieh san ch'eng
I love the spring moon,
        rippling flower-shadows in confusion!
Even with a thousand cash
        such a moment would be hard to buy.
Just as it reaches the willow-tips
        the heavenly road is calm;
earlier than anyone it marks the dusk.
It shines on song and music in tower and terrace;
        the sounds seem fainter now.
It glitters on the swing hanging in the courtyard
        sinking to silence with the night.
Penetrating fragrant paths,
truly it is spring color troubling men
so that good dreams are hard to form.

2. To the Tune, Yu hu-lu
I love the summer moon,
        golden cake among the clouds!
It faces one with red make-up,
        at the mirror above lotus pond.
For night excursions,
        who need carry a silver candle now?
Above the dark wall, the fireflies
        illuminate themselves.

3. To the Tune, Chieh san ch'eng
I love the autumn moon,
              best of all four seasons!
With mid-autumn, it is specially crystalline.
Its pure brilliance and fragrant haze
              inspire the beautiful one.
Crickets chant louder,
magpies are startled.
The silver plate—its color ripples
              lotus-blossom white.
The golden grain—its fragrance floats,
              purity of the cassia.
Cold light glitters;
truly it is the seven treasures, diaphanous
transmitting illumination beyond and within.

4. To the Tune, Yu hu-lu
I love the winter moon,
              bright and crisp at the tip of plum trees,
vying in beauty with Feng I's six-fold blossoms.
The jade round and jeweled powder
              illuminate each other,
summoning the poet from his dream of paradise.

(pp. 160–61)

——These poems are all *ch'ü* ("airs," "arias").

——Feng I: At times, he is presented as a river god, at others, as a sky god. His "blossoms"
here are snowflakes, as is the "jeweled powder."

To The Tune, *Child at Play*

Last night in dream so clear I saw her;
on waking—just a pillow and blanket, cold.
Wizard Pi could never shrink
              the land that lies between us;

Nü-wa the goddess could never patch
       the heaven of our parting!
My longing—grief of separation—
       do you know how deep?
My frustration and my sorrow, piled ten thousand-fold!
My farewell tears and the waterclock
       drip together;
my anguished heart and incense flames
       together burn.

                                                 (p. 164)

——This poem is a *ch'ü*.

——Wizard Pi: Pi Ch'ang-fang, a Han-dynasty magician capable of traveling thousands
of miles in an instant.

——Nü-wa: The goddess said to have patched the sky in ancient times.

To the Tune, *Yellow Oriole*

—Expressing My Feelings in the Rain

Threads of rain weave lambent light;
I love green moss embroidering white walls!
Beyond mandarin-duck embankment,
              emerald waves swell.
Fresh bamboo wafts its coolness,
hidden flowers, perfume.
Cloud-corridors, water-pavilions
            are worth a look around.
We fill our golden cups,
bodies light and free,
every place is home!

                                      (pp. 169, 171)

——This poem is a *ch'ü*.

To the Tune, *Stopping My Horse To Listen*

I raise my winecup to the flowers
and mistake an oriole for a cuckoo's song.
Far in the sky—returning geese;
in setting sunlight—returning heart!
Down distant waters—returning boat.
Fifth night watch, a dream of returning
            through the mountain clouds—
one cry from the neighbor's rooster
            calls me back, awake.
Somewhere in this sad neighborhood—cold strings,
strings that always play the song,
            Longing to Return.

(p. 200)

——This poem is a *ch'ü*.

To the Tune, *Yellow Oriole*

—Echoing a Poem by Chang Yüeh-wu in Which Each Line Uses
the Word, *Ch'ou* ("sorrow")

Willows weave spring sorrow,
brow knit in sorrow, I lean from painted tower.
Red sorrow, green sadness—on each branch wither flowers;
the old sorrow not yet gone,
new sorrow comes as well.
How many sunsets have I passsed in sorrow?
The hook of sorrow hangs above:
let me ask the moon about this sorrow.
In sorrow I watch the southern clouds withdraw.

(p. 220)

——This poem is a *ch'ü*.

To the Tune, *New Moon*

The new-born moon gives little light;
now it is covered by floating clouds.
Incense dies, candle gutters, people quiet down;
the night is vast and deep,
it is so hard to sleep,
outside the window, rain beats banana leaves.

(pp. 223–24)

——This poem is a *ch'ü*.

This last poem is by HUANG E (1498–1569),
the wife of Yang Shen:

[Title Lost]

Pearl-teardrops roll and gather,
              water in the inkstone;
broken-hearted, how can I write
              broken-hearted poems?
Ever since that distant day
              when we last held hands
right to this time I've been too lazy
              to paint in my eyebrows.

There is no medicine that can cure
              my grief through the long nights;
I do have money, but can't buy back
              the time when we were young!
Earnestly I entrust my message to the mountain birds:
soon, fly down, south of the river,
              urge him to return!

(p. 432)

——This poem is in the *Shih* form.
——Certain poems by Yang Shen have also been attributed to his wife, Huang E.

LI K'AI-HSIEN (1502–68)

L IKE YANG SHEN an individualist writer hard to contain within any category, Li was friends with such orthodox poets as K'ang Hai and Wang Chiu-ssu (qq.v.), and even coauthored a book on *ch'ü* with Wang, but was far more innovative and idiosyncratic than they. After becoming involved in the affair of the fire in the imperial ancestral temple in 1541 (like Wang T'ing-hsiang, q.v.), Li went into retirement and devoted himself to his extensive writings in all the available poetic forms, drama, and painting criticism.

A Trip to a Mountain Village

I break off a branch, and prod my lazy donkey;
the bags are torn—my books fall out on the road.
Hungry, haggard—two village servants
with shirts so short they don't reach their pants!
Dry and hot, exactly noon,
as we struggle along the dusty road.
One servant is still quite strong,
but the other has no strength left.
The strong man sings mountain songs;
the tired man just sighs out loud.
Suddenly, the road ends, and a wood appears;
they say we have reached the mountain village.
Earthen walls supporting thatched roofs:
lanes and alleys, here, against the cliffs!
When it is learned that distant travelers have arrived,
the farmers happily welcome us.
To go with the millet, a chicken must be killed—
but the chicken has flown into the neighbor's courtyard!
A jug is opened, and thick wine poured out;
wild vegetables are cut, and brought in a basket.
Drunk and sated, I lie on a rope-bed,
and dream at once that I have traveled to paradise.
When I wake: the mountain moon is high;
I rise and walk where my steps take me.
The night air seems fresher than ever;
suddenly, I realize my cares have disappeared.
If I didn't fear burdening my host,
I'd stay here for a month, and not go home!

(pp. 2–3)

Compassion for the Farmers

The wheat has been quickly harvested,
but the early leaves of millet have not appeared.

(There is a proverb, "From the wheat threshing-floor you should
see sprouting millet.")

They'll make it through the summer without suffering,
but the sun's intensity will prevent an autumn harvest.
Unable to meet their tax payments,
they'll flee as refugees; no one can stop them!
The poor will sell their own sons and daughters;
the rich will sell their horses and cattle.
Who will relieve their misery for them?
Will this chronic illness ever be cured?
When the people are impoverished, robbers arise,
spears and shields among the tiny windows!
From ancient times, this has been clear;
the gentleman can only feel hidden sorrow.
I wish to tell the shepherd of this flock:
Quickly, send word to the Emperor!

(p. 3)

A Record of a Past Affair

There was a certain assistant minister
who was in power while I lived in the capital.
When I left my position, his career was at its height;
but he devoted himself to all kinds of schemes and plots.
Late at night, he would go out begging;
he'd take bribes, afraid of future poverty.
In many ways, he took the crooked path,
not caring if people mocked him as he went.

But one day, his actions became public;
he was openly criticized and attacked.
His servants and secretaries ran away;
he was banished to the frontier.
Not only did he lose his salary and position,
but his reputation was ruined.
His mind started to deteriorate, his plans all went awry.
His face grew lined with worry, his speech,
                                                hesitant and slow.
The local people felt, before too long,
                                    he would lose his health
                                                in that distant place.
So they sent letters, pleading with the authorities:
May Heaven's mercy touch him soon!
They dared not hope he would be summoned back,
only that his exile might be closer to the capital,
with some coarse liquid to quench his thirst,
and rough food to fill his stomach.
While the people's request was still in the air,
he managed to pass the capital exam.
But the whole story repeated itself;
he lost his position and got what he deserved!
He returned to his native place, unable to advance;
it was hard to meet old friends again.
Now the actor stepped down from the stage,
and wiped off all his makeup.
For the first time, his true face could be seen:
ashamed, he shaved off all his hair.
His ugly visage remained the same as before;
it was too late for true repentance.
There have always been warnings against illicit deeds:
there cannot be private interests in government.

                                                                        (p. 3)

——Li is undoubtedly describing an actual case of his time, but without certain knowledge
   of the case, this translation must remain tentative. Nevertheless, it is of interest to
   see here a kind of Ming-dynasty "Watergate."

The Prosperous Villager

His family roots are in the mountains,
their traditional profession, in the fields.
Only once a year does he visit the nearest town;
he's lived half his life, and never been to the county seat.
He rides his mare to a vegetarian feast,
or clubs the fatted ox for the village festival.
When it is dry, one rainfall suffices—
talk, laughter, singing of songs!
At the most, he gathers a hundred pecks of wheat,
but he scoffs at a man with ten thousand households.
When the grain has been stored in the granary,
in a loud voice he reckons each measure.
He has never even seen an almanac,
so how does he know his springs and autumns?
When the flowers open, it's time for the spring planting;
when the flowers fall, it's time for the autumn harvest.
Before each cycle ends, the moon is like a plate;
after it begins, the moon is like a hook.
There is no other plan hatching in his mind;
beyond his personal comfort, he wishes nothing more.
Now I have been an official,
and I have seen much evil plotting.
If I could end my days among the fields,
this old man would be my companion.

(p. 4)

The Night of the First Full Moon

I was burning incense, paying respects to my mother,
when a friend came to visit.
He said he had walked down four main avenues,
and there was not a single lantern to be enjoyed!
Last year, on this night of the Lantern Festival,
the special lanterns glittered everywhere.
A fragrant breeze covered the earth,
and a jewel-like moon shone in the sky.
Elegant ladies and handsome men
walked in groups or in couples.
They kept company until the morning bells,
laughing, singing, clapping their hands.
But this year, the authorities, afraid the wind
                                    might start a fire,
have put up notices: "No Celebrating Allowed."
Ever since the terrible harvest,
robbers and thieves have been causing trouble.
This is the Festival again,
but our joy is much less than in the past.
Done with his story, the visitor left,
and I was moved to distant thoughts.

(p. 4)

A Parable

There was a man who studied the art of disappearing.
Before he had mastered the technique, he boasted to his wife:
"Tell me, can you see my body now?"
The wife laughed, "My eyes have not been taken by a ghost!
Your face is right in front of mine, just inches away;
it's not as though you're at the neighbor's or behind a fence!
Since you have a body, why should't I be able to see it,
unless you were clever enough to pull off some trick!"
The man was outraged at his wife's frank words;
he kicked her, slapped her, and cursed her out.
Then he asked the same thing of his concubine, and she pretended
        to be amazed:
she looked all around behind her, then stared straight ahead.
Lying, she said, "Master, what art is this!
Your body is hidden away—I only hear your voice!"
The man, delighted, went to town, and stole something from a
        shop.
At first the shopkeeper was too startled to move—then he became
        furious,
and gave the man a worse beating than the man had given his wife,
screaming and cursing with a voice like a thunderclap.
As for the "master of invisibility," he yelled too: "Go ahead, beat
        me up,
but if you want to *see* my body, you'll have a hard time!"
Now I once lived in the capital, where I became stuck-in-the-mud.
I was afraid to visit the ministers and high officials.
I was rejected, sent away—but still I didn't change . . .
Until I escaped, and held my old fishing rod again.

(pp. 23–24)

——In his ability to turn defeat into apparent victory, Li's "master of invisibility" fore-
shadows Lu Hsün's great creation, Ah Q.

When I Recovered from an Illness After Returning Home To Live in Retirement, I Was Invited by My Friends to Join a Song-Lyric Club

(Two poems to the same rhymes)

1.

While an official, I never wrote lyrics:
I was too busy dashing off to court all the time.
When I retired, it's not that I didn't want to,
but I could hardly sit up straight, I was so sick.
Now autumn is here, and I am stronger;
guests visit me for evening parties.
But who will sing these new works of mine?
I must trouble the women maestros!

2.

All my friends can write them,
but as for me, what do I know?
Still, I've had the chairmanship thrust upon me;
I'm ashamed of my inadequacy for this post!
There are many sad songs, like *Tree of Jade,*
and slangy tunes, like *Bamboo Branch.*
We improvise songs in northern and southern style,
and give them to the singers right here on the mats!

(p. 39)

———In these poems, Li describes the "Song-Lyric Club" (*tz'u-she*) to which he belonged.
He and his friends would write lyrics which would then be performed on the spot
by "singing girls." *Tree of Jade* and *Bamboo Branch* were famous songs of the past for
which poets wrote the lyrics.

Earthquake

(One poem from a group of ten, all to the same rhymes)

The earthquake covered Shansi and Shensi;
millions of people died or were hurt.
Homes were flattened to the ground,
and skeletons could be seen lying everywhere.
The prognostication? "Too much *Yin.*"
Perhaps this is an omen of some fault in government.
Three lifelong friends of mine
in one night fell to the dust.

(p. 50)

——[Poet's notes to lines 5, 6, and 8, respectively:] The prognostication says, "An earth-quake occurs when there is an excess of *Yin.*"

Local officials submitted a memorial, saying, "The land here is usually quiet, but now it has moved: this is because we officials have not been doing our duty."

Yang Shou-li, the Secretary; Han Pang-ch'i, the Investigator; and Ma Li, the *Kuang-lu-ch'ing* ("Lord of the Imperial Banquets"): taken by surprise, they were all crushed to death.

——Yang Shou-li (1484–1555), Han Pang-ch'i (1479–1555), and Ma Li (1474–1555) all died in the quake. Han Pang-ch'i had earlier memorialized to the effect that another earthquake was a sign of inadequacy in government, in accordance with the Confucian idea that the moral state of human society exerts an influence upon nature. See *Ming-jen chuan-chi tzu-liao so-yin* (Taipei, 1965–66), p. 893.

On the Cold Food Festival, Entertaining at the Southern Estate—the Guests Were Li Chiu-ho, Ma Nan-yeh, Wei Tung-kao, Li Hu-ch'uan, Huang K'ung-ts'un, Li Lung-t'ang, and Hu Hu-shan

Singing, dancing—handsome actors entertain;
guests have been invited to the courtyard.
The singers' mats hold the setting sun;
the dancers' sleeves flap in the east wind.
Lakeside willows—this smoky mist is hard to prohibit!
Flowering peach—a fire burning red by itself!
Village women come to ride the swing;
when they're done kicking, their hair is a mess!

(p. 69)

——The "Cold Food Festival" was reckoned as occurring one hundred and some-odd days after the winter solstice. It was, in essence, a spring festival. The wit of lines five and six in the present poem is based upon the practice of prohibiting any kind of fire for cooking during the festival. The swinging of the penultimate line was a game performed by women and associated with this festival. In other cultures too—for example, in India—swinging by women has connotations of fertility and even eroticism. As such, it is a theme in Indian painting (cf. W. G. Archer, *Indian Miniatures* [Greenwich, Connecticut, 1960], plate 92), forming a striking parallel to the use of swinging to symbolize the second (or the third) month of the lunar year in two series of twelve paintings each by the late-Ming painter, Wu Pin. (See *Wan-Ming pien-hsing chu-i hua-chia tso-p'in chan* [Taipei: National Palace Museum, 1977], plates 030–3 and 031–2.)

——The last line of the poem contains the verb, *ts'u*, "to kick," which is here interpreted as referring to the swinging, but which may actually refer to another game connected with the Cold Food Festival and frequently mentioned by Li K'ai-hsien together with swinging: *ts'u-chü*, or "kick-ball." This game is played to this day in Japan (where it is called *kemari*) as a ritual to usher in the spring.

Watching the Swinging

To the east touching Hui-chün, to the north, the Yellow River,
there is a village called Ta-kou-yai. On the day of the Ch'ing-ming
Festival, they set up several high frames for swings, and the women
and girls from the neighboring villages happily gather there. I
happened to be passing by on some other business, and I was
moved to write these poems.

(One poem from a set of two)

The colorful frames are erected beside the Yellow River;
the women laugh and sing.
Their bodies are as light as a passing bird,
their hands are as nimble as a shuttle on the loom.
In the villages, few fires burn;
on the swings, many techniques!
A passer-by suddenly feels a chill of fear:
could his career be as precarious as this?

(p. 92)

—— [Poet's note to line five:] This refers to the fact that many of the people have fled as
refugees—it's not only because of the prohibition against cooking fires for the Cold
Food Festival.

—— Ch'ing-ming Festival: Starting two days after the Cold Food Festival, this is the
spring festival *par excellence,* and is also characterized, among other things, by the
playing of such ritual games as swinging. (See notes to previous poem.)

Early Summer: At the Riverside, Seeing Off Li Chiu-ho as He Returns to Yeh with the Books I Lent Him

(One poem from a group of three)

Not a day goes by without someone borrowing books from me,
because I have such a fine collection!
Do you think it's only a matter of three cart-loads?
There are over ten thousand volumes!
Now a wise prince, a man of great learning,
has sent a representative, eager to borrow.
The books are on their way; may I trouble you
to correct any misprints as you copy the texts?

(p. 70)

——Li was indeed known for his fine book collection.

Commiserating with the Poor

Hiss, hiss—the north wind blows,
knocking people down in the streets.
They have pants which don't even cover their shins;
and they have no food at all; only dust fills their jars.
In the warm houses, what do they know of winter?
The flowery rooms have a springtime of their own!
Those dandies with their fancy pants of silk:
there's not much you can say to them about the poor.

(p. 74)

Sent to the Master Physician, "Almond Orchard" Shih

"Almond Orchard" Shih has been famous as a doctor for a long time in the Ts'ao and P'u regions. Recently, I learned about him from a poem sent to me by Ch'en Yüeh-shan. Not a day goes by without sick people requesting his services, but he has been declining on the grounds of his own illness with increasing frequency each year, so he can devote himself to planting almond trees. Ch'en has already written a poem for him, and I don't want to be the only one to ignore him, so I've written one of my own.

Master Shih's medical fame, because of Master Ch'en,
has now reached here, to me.
In the mountains he walks, collecting herbs,
then sits in the market, with gourds of them to sell.
He has loved almond trees for over ten years,
and has planted a grove of several hundred.
As for me, my one illness is my craze for chess:
tell me, can your arts cure this?

(p. 75)

In the Second Month of Summer, Taking My Family to the Villages East of the City

Feeling constricted by the dusty city,
we take a trip to the eastern villages.
The Three Sprouts have not yet matured,
though the harvest of the Two Wheats has begun.
The great gates are locked all night;
the silk-reels go on spinning all day.

Though I feel the happiness of traveling with my family,
it is sad to see the sufferings of the village lanes.

(p. 81)

——[Poet's notes to lines three and five:] The Three Sprouts are grain, millet, and rice.
　　The people live in fear of robbers, debt-collectors, and tax officials.
——Two wheats: This phrase can mean wheat and barley, or simply "wheat."

Sent to the Painter, Lu Hsiao-feng

Your art has brought you great respect;
your skill has been applied to portraiture.
Now you close the door and decline visitors,
a man of leisure in the noisy city.
Along the roads, the sound of weeping:
the villagers are poor to the bone.
May I trouble you to take your magic brush
and paint me a picture of refugees?

(p. 81)

Wei-ch'i Chess

Dusting off the board, I sit down happily to play.
Putting aside my brush, I'm too lazy to write poems.
When the spirit moves me, I invite a friend for a game;
lost in thought, we linger over every move.
Vertical and horizontal formations: this is how to pass the day.
Victory, defeat: can take place in an instant!
The path of a career is like the paths of this game:
you yourself don't recognize the critical moments.

(p. 87)

——Li K'ai-hsien was himself known as a fine chess master.

A Poem Expressing My Wife's Response to One I Sent Her

Why must you play chess with your friends all day?
And write so many poems that your brush is worn out?
We have so many fields, and they're so hard to care for!
So many books, they're a constant nuisance!
But don't be upset that you're in your fifties, and have no son:
it's all right with me if you spread your favors
                among the concubines!
The courtyard trees share equally in the gardener's care,
and their long branches blossom, glittering
                in the sunlight.

(p. 12)

A Poem About Fan the Fourth

Your smiling cheeks, burning clouds,
                or drunken green-peach blossoms!
I'm so dazzled, I take you for a banished immortal.
You can hold your own with my poet-friends,
                inscribing beautiful lines;
you are grief for the painter, striving to capture you
                with his brush!
Your jadelike body can barely support
                your white jade jewels;
your feet—gold lotus!—look beautiful
                below the saffron-blossom robe.
A hundred years of happiness, an ocean of springtimes—
who cares if frosty white is touching my hair!

(p. 121)

—— This is one of a series of poems on the poet's concubines.

Recording a Weird Happening

—The Winter of the Year, *Kuei-hai* (1563)

The River Mang has always been clear—not a trace of mud;
the Bay of Ma is at its upper reaches.
Why is it that this river, clear for a thousand ages,
should one day suddenly turn muddy?
And it has started to smell of some strange gas;
the old flavor is completely gone!
There must be some reason for this calamity;
my sadness is hard to put in words.

(p. 108)

———The character *mang*(?) is not to be found in the dictionaries; it is here assumed that it is pronounced the same as its right-hand component, *mang* ("blind"), and is used solely as the name of this particular river. One is tempted to speculate about the possibility that some form of pre-industrial pollution was involved.

Thanking Doctor Jen

My daughter was extremely beautiful—but she suffered from *lei-li.* When I heard that the specialist in external medicine, Jen Mien-shan, could cure this ailment, I sent a letter to him by messenger, which reached him at Ch'ing-ch'üan prefecture. Upon arrival, he treated the *lei-li,* and it disappeared at his touch! But because of a complicating fever, my daughter died. It was Fate! When the doctor left, I thanked him with this poem, which was only the proper thing to do. I have always tried to cultivate tranquility, and forget worldly cares, but in this affair I could hardly avoid extreme suffering. If I were to have a son now, perhaps that would alleviate my grief. I may be old, but I must strive to this end.

Master Jen has long been famous
　　　　for treating external ailments.
I send him a letter by messenger,
　　　　and immediately he responds.
The *lei-li* completely vanishes—
　　　　a beautiful daughter again!
But her bones are steamed with fever,
　　　　and she loses her life.
People say you can doctor an illness,
　　　　but you cannot doctor fate!
I thought I had transcended emotion,
　　　　but oh! the emotion now!
I loved this daughter as if she were a son—
　　　　now she is lost;
only a son would be consolation
　　　　for my sorrowful life.

(p. 141)

——*Lei-li* (Japanese, *ruireki*): Defined as "scrofula" in the dictionaries, but Nathan Sivin, in a private communication, has expressed doubt as to the presence of this disease in traditional China. At any rate, some form of glandular swelling in the neck is involved.

On My Birthday—Sick

On the day I was born, many visitors came to see me.
This year, I lie on my sickbed, like Ssu-ma Hsiang-ju, the poet!
With a stomach-ache, I must bear hunger, and eat very little.
My whole body weak, I always think of sleeping,
　　　　and close the doors early.

When I wake from dreams, for no reason,
        I throb with grief;
my mind wanders, I think I'm still asleep,
        in a total daze . . .
Select your prescriptions, mix your drugs:
        they just keep you sick—
my medicines must be the cliffs like screen-paintings,
        and the little villages.

                               (p. 142)

——Ssu-ma Hsiang-ju (179–117 B.C.); A great master of the *fu*, or expository prose-poem.

Pleasures Among the Fields During the Four Seasons

(Three poems from a group of one hundred to the same rhymes)

I.
I've decided to study agriculture,
        and to market herbs;
I've put away my books of strategy
        and my literary classics.
The garden is filled with bright flowers,
        glittering in the sun;
both banks are covered with dark willows,
        combed by the wind.
Plenty of rain—millet and hemp
        are everywhere among the fields;
late in spring, medicinal herbs
        grow by the courtyard steps.
Before the gate is a huge rock, good for sitting on:
the old men say that it is a star
        which fell from the sky.

                               (p. 155)

2.

I've followed the billowing dust as a traveler too long;
beautiful places I've been to before—I seem to see them
                for the first time now.
Floating up from the brazier—threads of incense;
beckoning beside the bridge—a blue wine-shop banner.
I've given up the company of ministers, left the ocean
                of officialdom;
now I meet drunken friends, and visit Buddhist halls.
At night I sit and meditate, without going to sleep,
when a sound as of thunder is heard: a star,
                falling from the sky!

(p. 160)

——[Poet's note to the last line:] On the night of the sixth day of the last month of winter,
    there was a falling star. Its light illuminated the sky, and it made a resonant noise like
    thunder as it passed from the southeast directly northwest.

3.

The men plow, and know everything about "late" and "early";
the women weave, and separate the "warp" from the "weft."
We roast yams over crackling pine-cone fires,
eat fresh green vegetables, spiced with ocean salt.
A neighbor borrows a painting to cover a hole in his wall:
I enter his house and for a moment I think I'm back home!
In this village, we feel as if we were all one family;
beneath the cliffs our homes are built,
                clustered like stars in the night sky.

(pp. 163–64)

Meeting Trappers on the Road in Heavy Snow

The trappers have collected their rabbit traps,
but the way home is hard to find.

Swirling in fog, bejeweled flowers confuse them;
swaying in the wind, jade trees slant across the road.
The chariot of the Spring Emperor has been turned back;
the blossoms of late springtime are troubled.
Soaked with snow, the wine-shop banner hangs limp.
They must ask people they meet, "Where can we get a drink?"

(pp. 182–83)

Describing My Feelings Upon Encountering Snow

(One poem from a group of three)

Crossing the ridge, the woodcutter loses his way.
Roosting in the forest, the bird can't find his nest.
The path of an official career is even more precarious:
I vow never to leave my thatched hut!

(p. 191)

On Snow

(One poem from a set of two)

Jade trees from the rear courtyard of the empire of Ch'en,
jeweled flowers from the shrines of Yang-chou:
such magnificent sights belong only to rich households—
what are they doing here at a poor man's home?

(p. 191)

The Night of the Seventeenth

A full moon on the night of the seventeenth:
this is the first time it has happened in years.
There is a drought now, no clouds in the sky:
I can see each hair on the rabbit!

(p. 219)

——The Chinese, like the ancient Mexicans, saw a rabbit in the moon.

Staying Overnight on the Banks of Embroidered River

Fishermen's fires glitter and fade,
mountains appear, then disappear behind the clouds.
The moon rises, a wind starts to blow:
each of these changes lasts only an instant.

(p. 219)

Impromptu Poems

(Six poems from a group of thirty-four to the same rhymes)

1.
To drink, no fine wines, to eat, no fish:
suddenly I hear the fishermen have returned,
                    and their nets are full.
I want to visit the Land of Intoxication—
                    where can it be found?
Where a wine-shop banner flutters in the breeze,
                    with a single line of words.

2.

In my house is my book collection, filled with book-worms.
One word can lead to enlightenment—
                    then ten thousand words seem empty.
I start to realize that too many words
                    can damage understanding of the Way:
how can they compare with the "fasting of the mind"
                    when no books are read?

——In the *Chuang Tzu,* in response to a question about the "fasting of the mind,"
"Confucius" says, "Make your will one! Don't listen with your ears, listen with your
mind. No, don't listen with your mind, but listen with your spirit"—as translated in
Burton Watson, *The Complete Works of Chuang Tzu* (New York and London: Columbia
University Press, 1968), pp. 57–8.

3.

All morning long I correct my books, changing *"lu"* to *"yü,"*
but doubts are dispelled only when the mind is void.
The door swings open—the south wind enters
and scatters the books all over the floor.

——*"Lu"* and *"yü"* are two characters which look similar and so are easily confused.

4.

Sitting by the riverside with a torn net—
                    it's useless to long for fish!
The moon illuminates my little boat, which is completely empty.
I'd better change profession, and become a merchant
who travels the rivers, buying and selling books.

5.

Beside the river—waterbirds, in the river—fish,
and a favorable wind, blowing my boat lightly,
                    as if I were sailing the sky.
In the midst of happiness, the boat springs
                    an unexpected leak:
ruining my books, old and new—what a terrible shame!

6.

Write in a lively style, as fish swim in the water;
in the midst of substance, put in something light.
The ancients wrote books without using any theory:
writers of today can't write a thing
            unless they *have* a theory.

(pp. 241–43)

—— [Poet's note to last line:] According to a saying, "In ancient times there were no 'men
of letters'; the *Six Classics* were written without 'literary theory.' "

Gazing at Ch'ang-po Mountain

I met this lovely scene once before, on horseback,
but then I was constrained by official duties.
Now I have retired, and nothing holds me back:
I've earned the chance to look carefully
            at the eastern mountains.

(p. 247)

Drunk, Climbing to the Peak of Iron Tomb on Wei Mountain

Grasping my flying cane, several feet of wood,
in an instant I am among the white clouds.
But my drunken eyes are hazy—I don't know where I am,
I think I'm going down the mountain when I'm really going up!

(p. 247)

Songs of the Frontier

(Two poems from a group of one hundred)

1.
The crack soldiers get no sleep:
practicing archery, drilling in units,
                    they prepare for any emergency.
But our spies return, and the news they bring is good:
"The barbarians are fighting each other; they won't invade our land."

2.
Flying sand darkens the air, the moon is a dull yellow;
buffeted by wind, confused by clouds,
                    the wild geese can't fly.
For a thousand miles, smoke has stopped rising
                    from people's houses;
in the deserted cities, ghost-fires roam
                    with blue flames.

                                        (pp. 249–50)

HSÜ CHUNG-HSING (1517–78)

H SÜ was one of the Latter Seven Masters of Ming literature,
and also earned a reputation as a bold and compassionate
official. While serving as Prefect in 1557, for example, he was called
upon to display military prowess as well as civil wisdom in a cam-
paign against a local bandit whose depredations had forced refugees
to flood into the city. Hsü saw to it that the refugees entered the
city in orderly fashion and then led a successful ambush against the
bandits. His poetry is characteristic of the orthodox Ming poets in
that it maintains a high level of polished competence, but only rarely
achieves anything higher.

Song of Catching Tigers

(One poem from a set of two)

How brave the peasant who lives beside the lake:
with his bare hands, in the mountains,
    he captured two tigers!
The martial arts of Pien Chuang-tzu
    seem insignificant now—
how can we get this man to saddle up,
    and ride, swift as the wind,
westward with soldiers and drums
    to beat the barbarian slaves!

                 (pp. 135–36)

——Pien Chuang-tzu: A famous strongman of the Spring and Autumn period. According
to the biography of Ch'en Chen in the *Shih chi*, Pien wanted to kill a tiger, but was
advised that if he waited until two tigers fought each other over an ox they both
wanted to eat, one of the tigers would kill the other, and become wounded itself in
the process, so it would be a simple matter to earn a reputation for killing two tigers
while in fact only killing one weakened tiger! Pien successfully followed this advice.

The Cane of Ch'iung Bamboo

The immortal with his bamboo cane
journeys far past Lin-ch'iung.
If he hangs the cane on the wall, a windstorm will blow,
and the cane turn into a dragon.

                 (p 150)

——Ch'iung, Lin-ch'iung: A place in Szechwan famous for its bamboo canes.

Following the Rhymes of Magistrate Liu's Poems on Entertaining Two Assistant Premiers at Pine-Snow Temple

(One poem from a set of two)

The trees are ancient, thick with patterns of moss;
the mountains, autumnal: dark colors increase.
Penetrating the clouds, a bell announces guests;
perched on a rock, a bird watches a monk.

(p. 150)

Thanking Prince Chen-chi for Giving Me a Bronze Seal Engraved with Diagrams of the Five Sacred Mountains

(One poem from a set of two)

This metal is engraved with Shang-style markings:
you certainly get credit for the greatest marvel
            on earth!
Some future year, I'll wear it, as I enter deep
            into the mountains:
at the peak of Heaven's Eye, I'll stamp it
            on the white clouds.

(pp. 184–85)

——Prince Chen-chi: I.e., Chu To-cheng (1541–89), a descendant in the sixth generation of a son of the founder and first emperor of the Ming dynasty. He has given the poet a truly remarkable object, a bronze seal on which are engraved magic diagrams of the Five Sacred Mountains of China. These diagrams were not maps in the ordinary sense, but highly stylized designs intended to reveal "secret passages for man to reach the spirits who dwell up among the mountains." Laszlo Legeza, *Tao Magic: The Chinese Art Of the Occult* (New York: Pantheon Books, 1975), p. 32. For examples of these diagrams, see Legeza, plates 6–15.

Traveling by Boat at Shun-ch'ang

I travel far in a little boat,
the green mountains following behind.
The radiance of the woods shimmers blue-green colors;
the water's surface is clear as glass.
As I lie on my pillow, clouds enter the cabin;
I open the door—vines hang before my eyes!
Bring on the dangers of the rapids—
with our master boatmen, I feel secure.

(pp. 205–6)

Inquiring About the Health of Li Te-hua

(One poem from a set of two)

Who would have thought that a disease of the ordinary world
could touch you, an exiled immortal!
You love writing poetry, but don't care for your health;
so immersed in books, it has harmed your constitution.
Leaning against a tree, you must be whistling to yourself;
who is there to sit and talk to?
I wish I could come to you on a pair of wings:
we'd shout wildly, and get drunk for ten weeks!

(p. 259)

At Dawn, Climbing the Heavenly Pillar Peak of Mysterious Mountain

(One poem from a group of four)

I shake my robe—and mists disperse, leaving clear autumn sky:
from the topmost peak, I can see ten thousand miles
                    into empty distance.
This magic mountain must have flown toward the ocean:
how could the Hanging Gardens have grown here in the sky?
The Bright Spirit beams down its rays
                    to Yellow Gold Hall;
the Southern Dipper hangs high above
                    the Palace of the Red Emperor.
Carefully count the peaks: there are thirty-six;
every morning, they seem to clap their hands for joy
                    like the giant tortoise of paradise.

(p. 364)

——Mysterious Mountain (*Hsüan yüeh*) was a name given to the Wu-tang Mountains in Hupei during the *chia-ching* period (1522–66). Earlier in the *yung-lo* period (1403–24), palace buildings had been erected there (referred to in lines five and six of the poem).

——The Hanging Gardens: The Chinese myth places these in the magic K'un-lun Mountains far to the west. The conceit seems to be that the Wu-tang mountains actually are the K'un-lun Mountains, which flew eastward as far as Hupei!

——"The giant tortoise . . .:" A mythical ocean creature on whose huge back the three mountain-islands of paradise were said to be supported.

HSÜ WEI (1521–93)

A GIANT of Ming cultural history, Hsü is one of the most original painters and calligraphers of the period, creating an utterly individualistic, expressive style of quirky brushwork which would exercise far-reaching influence on later generations of eccentric painters. His plays are also famous, and his poetry provided inspiration for the burgeoning of poetic creativity in late Ming which centered around Yüan Hung-tao (q.v.), whose rediscovery of Hsü's poetry is reminiscent of Mendelssohn's of the music of Bach. Hsü happens to have been a most unstable individual; having attempted suicide by smashing his testicles in 1565 (he was pretending insanity at the time), he murdered his third wife and was put into prison, sentenced to death. He was, however, released after seven years.

I Tried To Exchange Two Paintings For Some Grain But Failed

In my family there are two famous paintings
which we have treasured and taken everywhere with us.
But one morning, we found ourselves without a thing to eat
so I took out the pictures to barter for grain.
It's not that these masterpieces were not precious to me
but the pangs of hunger are hard to bear!
If I lived alone, I could manage,
but a family of eight!—what else could I do?
History tells of a young man
who exchanged a horse for a beautiful woman.
But in saving people from a calamity like fire
how can you think only of pleasing yourself?
I remembered a man I knew, rich as the millionaire of I-shih,
but now he too had nothing to spare.
He wrote me a letter telling me—
he was ashamed to say it, and felt many regrets,
but the present and the past are two different things:
how could he collect such treasures anymore?
He hoped I would understand his situation;
prosperity and decline indeed depend on fate.
So I poured out some wine to console myself,
to drive away my sadness and disappointment.
I unrolled the paintings and hung them on the bare walls
trying to forget my hunger as I gazed at them.

(pp. 257–58)

A Buddhist Monk Cut and Burned His Own Flesh to Make The Rains Stop—A Man From His Native Place Asked Me to Write a Poem to Send to Him

The sky extends upwards for ninety thousand miles.
When it wants to be clear it is clear,
            when it wants to rain it rains.
For the rain god and the sun god
            it's as easy as herding sheep:
they receive their orders and carry them out;
            who would presume to complain?
So what kind of man is this Buddhist monk,
daring to set up an altar with banners and drums?
With his cracking whip he stands up to Heaven
and cries out to Hsi-ho to bring back the chariot of the sun!
The immortal Chang in broad daylight
            flew up into the sky—
now this monk has a chance to do even better than that!
All he does is to burn a bit of incense
            on an inch of his flesh
and the ocean calls the clouds back to the kingdom of water.
The local alchemists are all impressed by what the monk has done,
and the magistrate gives him a piece of red silk.
But still, this man, virtuous as King Ashoka,
            must bear the pain with his own body
while the farmers all bow down to the Inspector of Fields.

                                                            (pp. 406–7)

——This poem provides a rare example of a member of the scholar-official class taking
   interest in the practices of folk religion.

A Painting of People Strolling Through a Pine Forest

In ten thousand pine trees
        sounds the low roar of the wind
like Master Hu Pa playing his zither once more.
People stroll in and out among the trees
as if they were fish
        appearing above the water
                then disappearing again.

(p. 765)

——Hsün Tzu (born 312 B.C.): "In ancient times, when Hu Pa played the zither, the fish in the streams came forth to listen," trans. Burton Watson, *Basic Writings of Hsün Tzu*, p. 19. See Watson, *Basic Writings of Mo Tzu, Hsün Tzu, and Han Fei Tzu* (New York and London: Columbia University Press, 1967).

On the Road Through the Wu-i Mountains— Making Fun of Chia-tse for Falling Off His Horse

Shen is very sick these days, he's fading away.
Now he rides his horse up the mountain,
        afraid of the winding path.
Suddenly—why can't I see him up on the horse?
Oh, there he is, his whole body covered with mud!

(p. 806)

——Shen Chia-tse: Shen Ming-ch'en, like Hsü Wei, a poet in the employ of Hu Tsung-hsien, commander-in chief of the southeastern armies.

From Chekiang I Went to Hsin-an and Climbed
Even-with-the-Clouds Mountain. On the Way Back
There Were Many Beautiful Sights at the Inns
Where I Stayed and Yet I Could Not Write One
Word of Poetry. When I Got Back to the Main Road
I Wrote These Four Lines to Make Fun of Myself.

I tethered my horse beside the plum blossoms
        and found wine to drink—
streams and mountains in the distance
        set off the flag of the wine shop.
Why is it whenever I come to a place
        which should be put in a poem
I cannot turn out a single word of poetry?

(p. 807)

To Hsü Shih-t'ing

I hear that the peonies are magnificent
        in the famous gardens now
and that rich families will be enjoying them
        until spring is almost gone.
What a shame! I too am a man who loves to look at flowers
but I am much too busy, watering my vegetable patch!

(pp. 807–8)

Songs of Yen-ching

—It is said that the dragon-ox has evil eyes which terrify people.

(Two poems from a set of seven)

1.

In the northwestern pond there is a dragon-ox.
People say it arches up, then disappears again.
Do you want to see how different it is
                from other water creatures?
Just watch for its eyes—two white globes
                above the surface of the pond.

2.

Where does the dragon-ox display its imposing form,
fierce eyes making your belly tremble?
I asked someone who claims he saw it many years ago,
but he only caught a glimpse of the beast
                as it slithered through the fog.

(pp. 813–14)

Returning from the Seventy-Two Mountains

—Written on a temple wall

Five bolts of hanging silk,
        jade dragons on the run!
The Seventy-Two Mountains
        were carved by a demon's chisel.

I've fallen into the water, fallen off my donkey,
        and I don't care at all:
people have always risked their lives
        for a single taste of blowfish!

(p. 859)

A Mushroom Gatherer Deep in the Mountains Among the White Clouds

The white clouds beyond the sky—
        this must be your home.
Both cheeks slightly red, a diet of cinnabar!
But don't expect any magic mushrooms
        to give you immortality;
you're wasting your time, digging with your spade,
        damaging the purple mist.

(p. 860)

Inscribed on Paintings for the People of Hangchow

1.
The puppets which perform before the curtains
        are already an illusion.
A painting of puppets has moved still further
        from reality.
But just consider that the sky
        is also a vast curtain:
then which of us is not an actor on this stage?

——[Poet's note:] This poem is on a painting of wooden puppets on a curtained stage.

2.

In one place, flying clubs,
  in another, men on stilts—
clanging of gongs, booming of drums
  bring the children running.
Men and women with nothing better to do
  also gather like clouds,
and the painter takes the trouble
  to capture it all with brush and color.

—— [Poet's note:] This poem is on jugglers performing with "meteor clubs" and men on
high stilts.

(pp. 867–68)

I Once Did a Bamboo Painting for Somebody—
Now He Wants Me To Do Another. I Have Written
This To Answer Him.

This bamboo I painted a long time ago.
Now you want me to do another?—Impossible!
When the sparrow grows old
  it becomes a clam in the sea.
You ask it to turn back into a sparrow,
  but how can it fly again?

(p. 881)

—— According to the *Monthly Ordinances (Yüeh ling)* of the classic *Book of Rites,* "In the
last month of autumn, the sparrow enters the great ocean to become a clam."

Lotus

(One poem from a group of nine)

Fifth day of the fifth month,
          sun beating down,
I snap my fan back and forth
          but can't drive off the heat.
I want to call for a little boat
          and go off to Yeh Stream:
lotus leaves, lotus blossoms, ten miles of wind.

(p. 885)

Two Fish by a Willow Embankment

—Written on a painting

A row of willow trees, almost green for the spring,
and two fish, lively, ready to jump.
Maybe they will jump, and land in my inkstone—
          it happens all the time;
I'm only afraid that they might splash ink on my clothes.

(pp. 914–15)

A Kite

(One poem from a group of 25)

A man who lives by the sea tells of a young boy who, preparing to
eat some candy, tied the string of his kite around his waist.

Suddenly, a great wind started to blow, sweeping the kite off toward the sea. The boy fell to his death. When his body was recovered, the candy was found still clutched in his hand.
(The kite speaks:)
When the wind is gentle
    and I want to rise
        I cannot rise.

When the wind is strong
    and I want to land
        I cannot land.

Can I cross the ocean?—Depend on me
        to make it by myself;

What a shame that I have carried a boy—
        as he ate some candy—
           to his death.

(p. 921)

Rock Among Bamboo

—Inscribed on a painting

A single rock, vast
    among the wild bamboo:
if Mi Fu saw it
    no one could stop him from bowing down.
If it were possible
    to take it away in an ox-cart
we could sell it to some rich man
    for five hundred dollars.

(p. 1853)

——Mi Fu (1051–1107) was a great painter and calligrapher, as well as being a connoisseur of fine garden rocks.

Inscribed On a Painting

Thunder, rain falling, falling,
              thick blue-green colors:
in the shade of an old pine tree
              the mynah chatters.
I ask him, "Why do you like to talk
              like a human?
I prefer to listen—in the mountains—
              to the language of birds."

(pp. 1880–81)

TSUNG CH'EN (1525–60)

L IKE Hsü Chung-hsing (q.v.), Tsung was one of the Latter
Seven Masters of Ming literature. Indeed, Hsü was a close
friend of his, spending much time with him at a mountain retreat
near Fuchou, and after Tsung's death of tuberculosis, Hsü had a
shrine erected there in Tsung's memory. Tsung died in office in
Fukien province, where he had successfully defended the city of
Fuchou against marauding Japanese pirates. Tsung's poetry, like
Hsü's, is consistent with the orthodox program of writing in emu-
lation of High T'ang poetry, although Tsung brings in effective
references to contemporary events and has a refreshingly direct touch
in his shorter poems.

Song of Chiang-nan

(One poem from a group of four)

On the spring river, you depart;
in the spring chambers, I grieve:
my heart is like the river water,
day and night, touching your boat.

(p. 113)

Song of Meeting

One day I met you,
today I part from you.
We met in the clouds of ten thousand mountains;
we part in a thousand mountains of snow.

(p. 115)

Song of Selling Flowers

People who buy flowers in Ch'ang-an
pay millions for just a few stems.
Beside the road there is a hungry man:
they don't give him a single cent.

(p. 120)

Drinking at the Cave Mouth

In front of Hua-yang cave, autumns pass like sleet;
inside Hua-yang cave, time goes by like lightning.
I heard of this place, deeper and deeper among the cold clouds,
and the single opening, thin as a string, in the stone cliff.
When I arrived, I gave a great shout—
                              and the cliff opened wide!
A green-eyed immortal appeared to me at night.
I stayed there three days without stepping out,
and we swallowed ten million peach blossom petals!

(p. 224)

——A poem replete with Taoist religious imagery. Caves were regarded as seats of spiritual
power, where immortals lived. Peach blossoms (as well as other flowers and herbs)
were imbibed in special preparations in the hope of attaining longevity.

——Hua-yang cave, located at Mao Shan Mountain near Nanking, is associated with the
great Mao Shan school of Taoism. According to the *Lung-ch'eng lu,* a text attributed
to Liu Tsung-yüan (773–819) but probably by someone else, "The Mao Shan Taoist
Wu Ch'o was gathering herbs at the mouth of Hua-yang cave when he saw a little
boy holding three pearls in his hand and playing among the pines. Ch'o approached
him, but the boy ran into the cave and turned into a dragon. The three pearls were
inserted in his left ear. Ch'o took an axe daubed with drugs and chopped off the ear,
but the pearls had already disappeared."

On Things Seen

(One poem from a group of six)

The rebels' cavalry are everywhere:
our generals did battle over and over again.
Between heaven and earth, lost in broad daylight,
everything was hidden in yellow dust!

And so their blood flowed in rivers and lakes,
their bows and armor lay scattered, away from their bodies.
Who can write an ode, "Summoning Their Souls?"
I entrust my tears to the green reeds.

(p. 273)

——[Poet's note:] At the time, the two generals Wang and Hung had died in battle.

On Hearing That the Sea-Barbarians Are About To Attack Hu-chou—Expressing My Feelings to Tzu-yü

The troops brought enough suffering to the people;
now again comes the grief of red-feathered arrows!
Winds have raised waves on the distant seas,
and the tides flow in, swelling T'ai-hu Lake!
Heaven must burst from the drums and trumpets;
those killer-whales never seem to stop!
Here, the peach blossoms hide scenes of war:
do not ask for a fishing boat now!

(p.293)

——The "sea-barbarians" were undoubtedly the Japanese pirates who plagued the Chinese sea-coast during this period. Hu-chou was located slightly inland from the ocean, north of Hang-chou and south of T'ai-hu Lake. Tzu-yü was Hsü Chung-hsing (1517–78; see pp. 305–9), like Tsung Ch'en one of the Latter Seven Masters of Ming Literature, and a close friend of Tsung's. The poem ends with an indirect allusion to the story, *Peach Blossom Spring*, by T'ao Ch'ien (365–427). Ordinarily, one would want to follow the flowering peach trees to the paradise discovered by the fisherman in T'ao's story, but here, the peach blossoms "hide scenes of war" instead, so it would be best to remain safely at home.

Snowstorm: At a Gathering at Chang Chu-fu's House, with Tzu-yeh Attending, We All Wrote Poems on This Subject—I Got the Rhyme-Word, "Hu"

All night, the west wind blows over the capital;
we meet as northern snow fills the avenues.
Trudging through mud, our horses rear back;
entering the room, cold clouds float by in strips!
It's been a long road, ten thousand miles—
             we're startled by white hair.
Above a thousand mountains, the view to the south,
             completely cut off.
We grieve for our Han soldiers, with no winter clothes
             to wear,
still grasping their spears in the night,
             protecting us against the barbarians.

(pp. 390–91)

——Chang Chu-fu: Chang Chiu-i (1533–98), a poet and official. Tzu-yeh: Probably the painter and poet, Ch'en Ch'in (obtained degree in the *chia-ching* period, i.e., 1522–66).

——"Hu": One form of literary game involved a group of poets each arbitrarily being assigned a rhyme-word. Each poet would then write a poem on an assigned topic (in this case, the snowstorm), including that word in a rhyming position. Hence the use of the word *hu*, "barbarian(s)," to end the poem.

Snowy Mountains

A sudden snowfall comes in darkness,
black clouds hang, heavy and somber.
The mountains also can get grey hair:
don't be surprised that their sides are turning white!

(p. 433)

An Excursion to the Suburbs

(One poem from a group of six)

Side by side, we ride out of the city,
holding our whips and talking together.
There are willows everywhere, on every spring mountain:
which way should we go from here?

(p. 434)

Miscellaneous Words on the Lake

(Five poems from a group of twenty)

I.
The white-haired man, holding a fishing pole,
sits at Chiang-hua in the morning sun.
Don't let your hook go down too deep:
it might get stuck in the dragon king's cave!

2.

Glittering, glittering, fireflies in the grass:
they fly through the poplars, flit among the willows.
Who brought them here into my mountain hut?
Now constellations are moving on my walls!

3.

A scorching sun, enough to parch the Yangtze!
In home after home, they weep for the ruined grains.
Why can't the clouds over a thousand mountains
turn into a thousand mountains of rain!

4.

A night of rain on the autumn river:
everywhere, the schools of perch increase.
The fishermen run back and forth, and plan:
"At dawn, be ready with your bamboo cape!"

5.

White snow fills the lakeside village:
deep in the night, we walk out the door.
A thousand trees, along the lake-front:
every one of them, a crouching dragon of jade.

(pp. 437–38, 440–41)

Sent to Yü Te-fu Upon His Receipt of an Official Commission to the Two Che's

(One poem from a group of four)

When you enter Chin-hua Mountain
        with your tinkling pendant of jade
                among the autumn clouds,
when you see a green-eyed immortal
        sweeping away the fallen petals,
and innumerable sheep of stone
        grazing on ancient snow,
then you will know that you have arrived
        at the residence of Red Pine.

(pp. 460–61)

—— Yü Te-fu: Yü Yüeh-te (1514–83), a writer and official.

—— The two Che's: I.e., Chekiang, north and south of the Ch'ien-t'ang river.

—— Red Pine: A legendary Taoist immortal.

—— According to the *Biographies of Divinities and Immortals (Shen-hsien chuan,* a book the original text of which was supposedly written by Ko Hung [283–343]; possibly a later compilation), "Huang Ch'u-p'ing, at the age of fourteen, was herding sheep. A Taoist took him up Chin-hua Mountain. His brother searched for him and, finding him, asked, 'Where are our sheep?' Upon which Ch'u-p'ing answered, 'On the eastern slope of the mountain.' The brother went there, but saw only white stones. Ch'u-p'ing yelled at the stones, and they all arose to become several tens of thousands of sheep."

MO SHIH-LUNG (C. 1539–1587)

M O IS famous as a painter, and especially for his friendship with the major figure in later Chinese art theory, Tung Ch'i-ch'ang (1555–1636). The *Hua shuo (Discursus on Painting)*, a text sometimes attributed to him which broaches the important concept of Northern and Southern schools in painting, is now generally considered to be Tung's work, although Mo may still have contributed to the evolution of the ideas transmitted in it. It is a pleasant surprise to discover that as a poet, Mo demonstrates a delicate lyricism of considerable evocative power.

A Friend Comes To Visit on a Summer Night

Fanning away the heat
          I sit at night before the lamp;
chunks of ice are piled like mountains on my desk.
You are doing well, my friend,
          the times are right for you,
while I seem incapable,
          out of tune with the world.
We write poems under heavy clouds;
our friendship, deep—
          we look straight into each other's eyes.
My humble home has no entertainment or music—
When guests come, we spend our time
          discussing Buddhist sutras.

(p. 157)

Staying Overnight at Blue Cloud Temple

If you don't come to the mountains in autumn
you will never know the grandeur of the autumn scene.
Here are dried up riverbeds, filled with skinny rocks,
trees shedding leaves, revealing mountains underneath.
Wind-swept rain, like dancing dragons in pairs;
the traveler's heart, alone, between the sky and earth . . .
Early morning cold—impossible to sleep;
the temple bell echoes across the western peak.

(p. 190)

I Waited for Chuang Hsüan-yüan But He Never Came

Today you were supposed to come—
     evening draws on
and rain drops are drying in the silent woods.
The incense has burned out;
I've practiced calligraphy so long
     the brush-tip has gone limp.
A famous host once hid the linchpins
     of his guests' chariots;
now, alone, thinking of you,
     I stand leaning against the railing.
Who will dispel my loneliness for me?
Gulls and egrets crowd the shore.

             (pp. 251–52)

Gathering Lotus with Singing Girls

Boats of orchid-wood float on the river;
young girls compete in gathering lotus plants.
Sleeves flap in the wind—fragrance pervades the air;
reflections ripple beautifully on the waves.
Parasols of kingfisher feathers
     shield the girls from the autumn sun;
red makeup is lovely in evening light.
Here in Chiang-nan a new song will be sung,
transmitted through the generations of mist.

             (p. 249)

On a Cold Day I Climbed Tiger Hill With Professor Ho. At the Time, the Local Prefect Had Prohibited Pleasure Excursions and Feasts, But the Mountain Was Quiet and Tranquil, So We Stayed All Day.

The woods, the mountain, silent,
                facing the cold sunlight;
the ground half carpeted with wild moss—
                our horses, waiting.
Somewhere, a temple bell sounds dinnertime;
                our minds are transported.
The songs and flutes
                that were played here in the past
                                have completely disappeared.
Mists from the quiet pond chill our robes.
Faint fragrance of spray
                from a hidden waterfall
                                perfumes our wine . . .
Everyone tells us that feasting here
                is prohibited now—
that will not stop us—modern Shan Chien's!—
                from returning drunk tonight.

                                                (p. 326)

——Shan Chien (253–312) was famous for the feasts he held at Kao-yang Pond, at which
he inevitably became completely drunk.

Flower Shadows

Quiet, quiet
        spring clouds float
                across the garden wall,
at tips of branches
        under the leaves
                rising and falling.
In empty space
        suddenly
                "substance within void,"
mixed, confused patterns,
        forms hard to distinguish
                in the darkness.
Softly they dance
        beneath moon and clouds—
                all an illusion;
silently invade
        screen and curtain
                giving off no fragrance.
My boy servant
        takes them for lichens
                tries to sweep them away
but they are only
        shadows of flowers
                growing beside the winding balustrade.

(pp. 331–32)

Saying Good-bye to Feng the Hermit

Where will your strange pilgrimage take you next?
How far will you travel
            through southern trees, southern clouds?
Your boat winds its way
            past nine bends of the river
where Incense Burner Peak juts into the sky.
I know you will seek out all the famous mountains—
don't disappoint the immortals, they are waiting for you!
This may be the trip—you will experience wonders
and command flying dragons
            at the Cliff of Purple Sky.

(p. 335)

I Went to Gold Mountain to Visit a Ch'an Master But He Was Not at Home

A Buddhist monastery across a stone bridge—
here I would sweep away the dust of confusion
            and call upon the Hui-yüan of our day.
His home is between two śāla trees,
            among the cold clouds,
while he walks deep in the mountains,
            holding one sandal in his hands.
The roar of a waterfall
            sounds like pure Sanskrit chanting;
evening wind sings in pine trees
            beyond the courtyard.
Why cling to Causality and insist
            on seeing him face to face?

One reading of the poem he has left behind
            and my inner self
                  returns to the Void.

(pp. 352–53)

——Hui-yüan was a famous Buddhist monk of the early fifth century.

——Buddha entered the final Nirvana between two śāla trees.

——According to the *Record to the Transmission of the Lamp,* a major Ch'an Buddhist text
of the tenth century, after the death of Bodhidharma (the founder of Ch'an in China),
an envoy to the west met him on Onion Peak, holding a sandal in his hands. When
the envoy asked him where he was going, Bodhidharma replied, "To the Western
Paradise." The envoy informed the emperor of this, and the emperor had Bodhi-
dharma's coffin exhumed. In it was found only a single sandal.

Saying Good-bye to a Singing Girl Who Has Decided to Become a Nun

You have called at the gate of the True Vehicle,
            your worldly self is no more.
You have said farewell forever
                  to the golden chambers,
                        the wind and the dust.
Lightly you wield the yak-tail whisk;
                  your singing fan lies on the floor.
You learn to adjust your meditation cushion,
            and laugh at the dancer's mat.
No more resentment when rouge fades
            like red flowers;
no longer will the feathered hairdo appear in your mirror.
Mist, light, water—quiet Zen mind:
I know a new springtime
            will bloom
                  in the Realm of Emptiness.

(p. 448)

Drinking Wine

I don't believe in becoming a Buddha,
                    reborn in Paradise;
and talk of Immortals flying off in broad daylight
                    is nonsense.
All I'll do is swim my way through a lifetime of wine—
a much better plan than struggling to live for a thousand years!

(p. 483)

The Meditation Rock

Gnawed at by lichens,
                    covered by moss—
                                        a rock, old in centuries.
When was it
                    that the monk sat here
                                        to meditate in the silent woods?
Let the flowers
                    beside this rock
                                        scatter petals like rain—
they cannot distract
                    the mind of the monk
                                        who has entered deep trance.

(pp. 530–31)

To the Monk Wu-hsia on the Occasion of His Editing the Lotus Sutra

You have edited a thousand pages of palm-leaf manuscripts;
for years now, your mind has been devoted
              to the Buddhist canon.
I ask you the true meaning
              of Bodhidharma's trip to China:
no written word has ever explained this mystery.

                                         (p. 557)

T'ANG HSIEN-TSU (1550–1616)

POSSIBLY the greatest dramatist of the Ming dynasty, T'ang is especially well known for his masterpiece, *Mu-tan t'ing (The Peony Pavilion)*. He was a friend of Yüan Hung-tao (q.v.) and other figures in the late Ming individualist movement, and shared with them an appreciation for romantic love. Somewhat surprisingly, however, the arias in *Mu-tan t'ing* are if anything more erudite and even bookish than the writings of the orthodox masters themselves—virtually every line has embedded in it a literary allusion, and the play is therefore a kind of scholarly *tour de force*. T'ang's *shih* poetry, far less familiar, is beautifully crafted and shares with his arias an interesting fusion of lyrical tone and density of diction. For more on T'ang, consult Tang Xianzu (T'ang Hsien-tsu), *The Peony Pavilion,* translated by Cyril Birch (Bloomington: Indiana University Press, 1980); and Josephine Huang Hung, *Ming Drama* (Taipei: Heritage Press, 1966).

Descending the Ridge of Flying Clouds

At the top of this ridge I could whistle happily.
Down at the bottom—I'm feeling depressed!
Looking back now at the thousand peaks:
there—the one lost in the clouds is Mount Lo-fu.

(vol. 1, p. 423)

——Mount Lo-fu: A Taoist sacred mountain in Kuangtung, which T'ang visited when
he was banished to the south.

Evening View from the Bell Tower at P'ing-ch'ang

What a shame—the chaos of the city!
Straight up, I climb the tower, into the clouds.
Beneath a solitary tree, an old monk
    returns in the sunset;
the whole mountain is filled with roosting birds
    announcing the end of day.
I'm startled at first by Buddhist chanting
    piercing the void in serenity,
and —hidden in the sound—the peal of the temple bell
    heard in deep trance.
Then, suddenly, I'm amazed that the night
    is illumined by the Age of Stars:
now the gods must be driving off the armies of demons.

(vol. 1, p. 455)

——Age of Stars: In Buddhist mythology, a future age when many Buddhas will appear.

Twenty-two Quatrains on Receiving the Obituary Notice for My Son Shih-ch'ü

(One poem from the group of twenty-two)

My son, you loved telling the story of Prince Nata
who stripped off his own flesh, returned it to his mother,
        and gave his father his bones!
Now your flesh has gone to the Ninefold Springs
        —does your mother understand?
and your father must gather your bones
        and bring them home.

(vol. 1, pp. 555, 557)

——The poet's son died in 1600 in Nanking, where he had gone to take the official examinations. The "Ninefold Springs" is the underworld.

——According to a Buddhist text of the Sung dynasty, *Wu-teng hui-yüan* (ch. 2), "Prince Nata (the son of the guardian king of the north, Vaishravana) stripped off his own flesh and returned it to his mother, and took out his bones and returned them to his father. Only then did he manifest his True Body, wield his great spiritual power, and expound the dharma to his parents."

On the Day of Washing the Buddha in the Year *Ting-wei* (1607), I Dreamed That My Late Son Shih-ch'ü Was Holding a Book, and Appeared To Be Quite Happy. He Said That He Had Earned His *Chin-shih* Degree in the Underworld. After We Sighed and Laughed Together for a Long Time, I Woke Up and Wrote This Poem.

I have burned ten thousand volumes
        as paper money for you!

I have grieved at the death of such a talented son.
But do they really have an examination system
        down in the Yellow Springs?
How many of your fellow students
        have ascended to the Sixth Heaven of Desire?

(vol. 1, p. 628)

——On the eighth day of the fourth month in the lunar calendar, which was believed in China to be Buddha's birthday, images of Buddha would be washed in celebration.

——Shih-ch'ü had died seven years earlier in Nanking, where he had gone to take examinations leading eventually to the bestowal of the *chin-shih* degree, which would allow the candidate to enter the official bureaucracy. T'ang has been sending his son books to study from by burning them instead of the usual paper money, hoping that the books will reach him in the underworld (Yellow Springs).

——In Buddhist mythology, the Sixth Heaven is the highest heaven in the Realm of Desire. T'ang uses it as an image for obtaining the *chin-shih* degree.

——For an excellent discussion in English of paper money mythology, see Anna Seidel, review of Hou Ching-lang's book on the subject, *History of Religions* (February–May 1978), 17(3–4): 419–32.

The Cave of Gold Essence
—in Ning-tu

Year after year . . . how many millennia of worldly affairs,
while in this cave-paradise, phoenixes danced and sang?
Each midnight, purple mists fly into rain,
dripping a stream of precious drops on rocks of gold essence.

(vol. 2, p. 775)

——The cave is located in Ning-tu subprefecture in Chianghsi, and is one of the Taoist sacred caves.

The Paintings on My Wall Have Been Damaged by the Weather

When the southeastern wall was first put in,
                        it was fresh with bright designs,
but wind and rain have mildewed all the horns and scales!
For ten years now, wall and door have been peeling away:
well, let people laugh at these scabby unicorns!

(vol. 2, p. 784)

Inspector Hsü Claims He Has Found the Secret of Youth

Master Mo Tzu and Master Lao Tzu
                        had no method for turning back old age,
but for the beauties of the Imperial Gardens
                        it was quite commonplace.
And now you too speak of the Book of Cosmetics—
it can give someone with wrinkled chicken-skin
                        the complexion of a phoenix!

(vol. 2, p. 789)

Autumn River

Darkness marks the distance where river meets ocean;
I long for my friend—may he arrive with spring!
Vast, vast the moonlight scatters on the ripples;
in the sighing of the wind, fishermen's fires appear.

(vol. 2, p. 853)

Hsiu-chou

Rain dampens Sung-ling, spring fills with mist;
apricot blossoms and elm-seeds glitter
         in freshly sown fields.
If you wonder where to go to hear the most beautiful singing:
at Eastgate and Level Lake, there are boats moored night and day!

(vol. 2, p. 872)

Spending the Night on the River

Silent, the autumn river, fishermen's fires sparse.
I rise to watch the waning moon shine faintly on the trees.
Moonlight on the waves—the waterbirds are kept awake;
dew chilling the fireflies—they are too damp to fly.

(vol. 2, p. 876)

YÜAN HUNG-TAO (1568–1610)

YÜAN WAS the leader of the late Ming Kung-an School of literature, so named from the subprefecture in Hupei province where he was born. Tsung-tao (1560–1600) and Chung-tao (1570–1624)—his elder and younger brothers—were also important members of the circle. Yüan is known as an individualist, and he is, within the context of Ming literature, a highly eccentric figure. But his eccentricity falls well within the parameters of Chinese tradition and can even be seen as weighing the balance back toward moderation after decades of domination of the cultural scene by the extreme archaism of the orthodox masters. For more on Yüan, see my *Pilgrim of the Clouds: Poems and Essays from Ming China by Yüan Hung-tao and His Brothers* (New York and Tokyo: Weatherhill, 1978).

The "Slowly, Slowly" Poem

—Playfully inscribed on the wall

The bright moon slowly, slowly rises,
the green mountains slowly, slowly descend.
The flowering branches slowly, slowly redden,
the spring colors slowly, slowly fade.
My salary slowly, slowly increases,
my teeth slowly, slowly fall out,
my lover's waist slowly, slowly expands,
my complexion slowly, slowly ages.

We are low in society
        in the days of our greatest health,
our pleasure comes when we are no longer young.
The Goddess of Good Luck
        and the Dark Lady of Bad Luck
are with us every step we take.
Even heaven and earth are imperfect
and human society is full of ups and downs.
Where do we look for real happiness?
—Bow humbly, and ask
        the Masters of Taoist Arts.

(p. 12)

On Receiving My Letter of Termination

The time has come to devote myself to my hiker's stick:
I must have been a Buddhist monk in a former life!
Sick, I see returning home as a kind of pardon.

A stranger here—being fired is like being promoted.
In my cup, thick wine; I get crazy-drunk,
eat my fill, then stagger up the green mountain.
The southern sect, the northern sect, I've tried them all:
this hermit has his own school of Zen philosophy.

(p. 139)

Passing by the Hot Springs at Hua-ch'ing Palace

(One poem from a group of six)

Eastern mountains
    and western mountains;
land of Ch'in
    and land of Han.
Light, light clouds
    over the city;
flowing, flowing water
    through past and present.
Crumbling ruins,
    plowed under on terraced slopes;
woodcutters chatting
    as they come home at evening.
Even in decline
    there are "better" and "worse";
King Yu
    was worst of all.

(pp. 136–37)

——In 723, Hot Springs Palace was built on Mt. Li in Shensi; its name was changed to
Hua-ch'ing Palace in 747. King Yu, the twelfth king of the Chou dynasty (r. 781–771
B.C.), was killed and buried at Mt. Li.

A Record of My Trip to Mount She

1.

Yellow leaves spiral down through the air;
waterfall spray flies into raindrops.
Patches of moss darken Buddha's face;
the stones here have been brushed
                    by the robes of a god.
The monks are tranquil,
                    though their kitchen has few vegetables;
the mountain, cold—
                    not many sparrows in the flock.
Of themselves, my worries all disappear;
I do not have to try to forget the world.

2.

Height after height of strange mountain scenes;
new words, new ideas in our conversation.
Wild pines blow in the wind like hanging manes;
the ancient rocks are covered with mottled scales.
I enter the temple, seek the dream-realm of the monks,
thumb through sutras, feel the dustiness
                    of this traveler's life.
You, the Zen master, I, a lover of wine—
we are brothers, way beyond
                    the people of the world.

                                        (p. 130)

Climbing Mount Yang

Craggy rocks, crouching like elephants;
withered pine bark, mottled like fish-scales.
From which spot did the Crane Immortal take off?
Is the Dragon Mother possessed of real magic power?
The caves here have talking animals;
on the cliffs live people who never say a word.
The palace of Wu fell apart long ago—
where can the ruins be found?

(p. 78)

Pei-mang Cemetary

Old pine trees, their shaggy manes
               twirled in a dance by the wind;
row on row of tombs, one wisp of smoke
               rising from nowhere.
The lords and princes who once lived
               along Bronze Camel Avenue
have become the dust that settles on the traveler's face.
The white poplar on top of the mountain
               has turned into an old woman
who spends each night in the fields,
               chasing away tigers of stone.
Officials come to this place, face north
               toward the Mausoleum of Longevity,
and give thanks that the crows who perch here
               speak Chinese.

(p. 61)

On Board a Boat at Chi-ning

The mouth of the Wen River–240 feet wide,
a torrent like a cliff of water, all the way across.
In one night, the wind
        that blows the grain boats from the south
has swept us as far as the Nan-wang locks.
How many days since I left home?
In an instant, months and months have passed!
Traveling by canal, there's been no fixed schedule
but now we should be one stage from Peking.
For a hundred *li*—a storm of yellow sand
in a dry wind that sounds like ripped cloth.

I've long since been competing for a place at the table;
my body feels sullied by the muddy waves.
Thirty years old, and what have I accomplished?
Strive, strive—for a cluster of empty hopes.
Compare me to a boat, struggling upstream,
which gains one foot, and then loses two.

                                    (p. 22)

A Woman's Room in Autumn

Autumn colors trickle through the gauze curtains;
cold fragrance floats in, bit by bit.
The chirping of crickets rises from the dark walls;
fireflies flicker in the abandoned loom.
The bedroom fills with new moonlight;
frost on the bamboo screens—
        she changes to warmer clothes.
The migrating goose, the wanderer—
both are gone, only one
        will return.

                                    (p. 117)

Twenty-first Day of the Seventh Month

—A Memory Returned to Me and I Wrote This Down

Foggy moon, bird-calls in the flowers at dawn,
in cold willow branches, orioles trembled on the edge of dream.
The words, "Love Each Other" were written on the pillow,
and heavy incense curled from behind the curtains.

Her emotion had the lucidity of calm waters—
red color came to her cheeks as she smiled!
Back turned to the lamp, she changed her damp nightgown
and asked her lover to gather up her earrings.
Their tears of parting moistened the fragrant quilt,
tenderness of love, fragile as the wings of the cicada!
With silver tongs she stirred the ashes in the brazier
and traced these words: "As Long as the Sky . . . "
Lanterns hung from each story of the building;
the red railing of the balcony gave on the avenue below.

This was the scene of our love that year—
now I see only a tomb, overgrown with grass.
From the roots of the maples, I hear the whispering of a ghost
bearing the traces of her southern voice.
The stagnant clouds of this woman's soul
have been swept into rain
             over a mountain I do not know.

                                                      (pp. 28–29)

THE PLATES

Plate 1: Wu Chen (1280–1354). *Fisherman.* Handscroll: ink on paper. H. 9 3/4″, W. 17″. The Metropolitan Museum of Art, Promised Gift of John M. Crawford, Jr., 1981. (L. 1981.126.58)

The poem inscribed on the painting is translated on p. 52.

Plate 2: Yang Wei-chen (1296–1370). Calligraphic colophon to painting by Tsou Fu-lei, *A Breath of Spring* (dated 1360), detail. Handscroll: ink on paper. H. 13 7/16″, W. 88″ (complete work). Courtesy of the Freer Gallery of Art, Smithsonian Institution, Washington, D.C.

鶴東樓路
雨後海
神仙中
人殊不俗
小復解
巢

Plate 3: Ni Tsan (1301–74). *Wind Among the Trees on the Stream Bank* (dated 1363). Hanging scroll: ink on paper. H. 23 1/2″, W. 12 1/2″. The Metropolitan Museum of Art, Promised Gift of John M. Crawford, Jr., 1981 (L. 1981.126.27)

The poem inscribed on the painting is translated on p. 70.

江渚暮潮初落風林霜葉渾稀
秋柴門聞犬聲人山色依微至癸
卯九月望日戲為
騰伯徵君寫此并賦小詩倪瓚

Plate 4: Chang Yü (1333–85). *Spring Clouds at the Pine Studio* (dated 1366). Hanging scroll: ink on paper. The Metropolitan Museum of Art, Gift of Douglas Dillon, 1980. (1980.426.3)

Plate 5: Hsü Pen (1335–80). *Streams and Mountains* (dated 1372). Hanging scroll: ink on paper. H. 26 7/10″, W. 10 1/5″. Mr. and Mrs. A. Dean Perry Collection.

The poem inscribed by the painter in the far upper left-hand corner is translated on p. 121.

Plate 6: Shen Chou (1427–1509). *Poet on a Mountain Top.* Leaf from an album: ink on paper. H. 15 1/5″, W. 23 7/10″. The Nelson-Atkins Museum of Art, Kansas City, Missouri. (Nelson Fund)

The poem inscribed on the painting is translated on p. 172.

白雲如帶束山腰石
磴飛空細路遙獨倚
杖藜舒眺欲因鳴
澗答吹簫 沈周

Plate 7: T'ang Yin (1470–1523). *Ink Bamboo,* detail. Handscroll: ink on paper. H. 11 1/4″, W. 59″ (complete work). The Metropolitan Museum of Art, Promised Gift of John M. Crawford, Jr., 1981. (L.1981.126.33)

The poem inscribed on the painting is translated on p. 206.

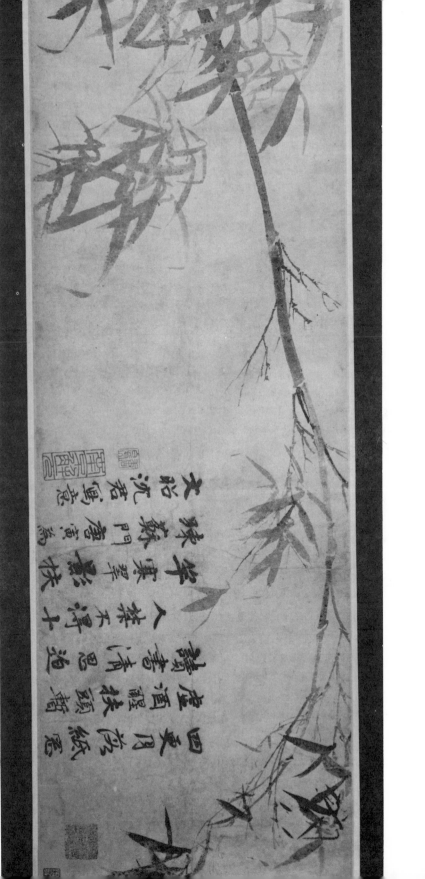

天將蘇軾蘇門翠蒔天時思四家三白沈君摩運翠海為詩巴題織遠意為林十送庸護接頼絕意

Plate 8: Wu Wei-yeh (1609–72). *Landscape with Man in Boat.* Fan: ink on gold-flecked paper. H. 6 2/5″, W. 19 4/5″. Asian Art Museum of San Francisco, The Avery Brundage Collection.

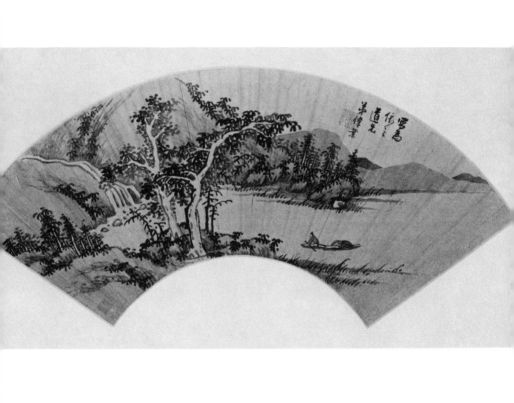

Plate 9: Yün Shou-p'ing (1633–90), after. *The Hundred Flowers,* detail of chrysanthemums. Handscroll: ink and colors on silk. H. 16 1/2″, W. 255 1/2″ (complete work). The Metropolitan Museum of Art, Promised Gift of John M. Crawford, Jr., 1981. (L.1981.126.42)

Plate 10: Tao-chi (1642–1707). *Drunk in the Autumn Woods.* Hanging scroll: ink and colors on paper. H. 63 1/8″, W. 27 5/8″. The Metropolitan Museum of Art, Promised Gift of John M. Crawford, Jr., 1981. (L.1981.126.53)

One of the poems inscribed by the artist—that in the upper left-hand corner of the painting—is translated on pp. 419–20.

III

CH'ING DYNASTY
(1644–1911)

CH'IEN CH'IEN-I (1582–1664)

C H'IEN IS a controversial figure, at once held in suspicion for serving the Manchu Ch'ing governement after having held office under the Ming, and admired for his disparaging comments about the Manchus, scattered throughout his voluminous writings and responsible for posthumously earning him the wrath of the Ch'ien-lung Emperor in the eighteenth century. He was a scholar of prodigious learning and an insightful critic; his *Lieh-ch'ao shih-chi hsiao-chuan*—a collection of critical biographies of Ming poets—is one of the most sophisticated books of literary criticism from the later period. Ch'ien's poetry is immensely erudite and difficult to penetrate; for the selections translated here, ample use has been made of commentaries by the Japanese scholar of Ch'ing poetry, Kondō Mitsuo, in his book, *Shinshi sen (An Anthology of Ch'ing Poetry)*, Tokyo: *Kanshi taikei* series, 1967. Like Wu Wei-yeh (q.v.), however, with whose name his own is often linked, Ch'ien is able to infuse his dense verses with a subtlety of lyrical feeling, and the effect can be quite moving.

Poem on Drinking Wine with the Degree-Holder Ku

No flowers!
    Let's blame the god in charge of flowers.
There's wine!
    Now that's convenient for us lovers of wine.
We'll simply sit on bamboo mats
    and pass our drinking cups;
if some guest, unhappy, slips out the back door,
    we won't pay any heed.
In the mulberries, cuckoos sing,
    urging on the farmers;
on the trees, "wine-jars" chirp,
    pressing us to drink.
I'm old, you're poor,
    what's for us to do?
Let's talk about becoming citizens
    of Intoxication-land!

(pp. 68–69)

No Flowers

As I travel, there are no flowers—
    alone, I stand in the tower;
I have no plans to go in search of spring;
    only vague resentment.
No flowers—yes, there is one thing
    convenient about that:
this year I will be able to escape
    the grief when flowers fall.

(p. 70)

Poem Written During a Dream on the Twenty-Third Day of the Intercalary [Month After The] Fourth [Month]

Tender mulberry leaves fill the basket-racks
        with their delicate green;
fine rain, delightful breeze—
        it's silkworm-raising time!
Outside, mud in beaks, the swallows are chattering:
"The news carried by summer cherries
        has now come to the south!"

                    (p. 71)

Miscellaneous Poems Written While in Jail

—No. 17 (of 30)

Frost-sad, clouds of white hair,
        locked behind iron doors:
tea-fragrance or dogwood wine—
        none of them for me!
In southern hat, old and weak,
        I yearn to wear black cap;
the jailor's footsteps, stumbling sound,
        I take for the white-robed messenger.
My wife, like the chrysanthemum,
        how gaunt has she become?
Myself, like a wild goose up north,
        when will I fly home?

Far away, I know throughout the world
   are mountain-climbing gatherings;
many men point to the Yen Mountains,
   pour libations in the setting sun.

(pp. 72–74)

——This poem, written in 1637, may be paraphrased as follows:

> My hair turned white, I'm locked in jail. It is the Double Ninth Festival (ninth day of the ninth lunar month), when people celebrate autumn by drinking tea perfumed with chrysanthemum petals and wine with dogwood blossoms, but I cannot share in these pleasures. I am a southerner, old and weak, wishing I were wearing the black cap of a hermit. Each time I hear the jailer approaching, I imagine it to be the white-robed messenger who brought wine to the great poet, T'ao Ch'ien (365–427). I think of my wife back home, undoubtedly grown gaunt like the chrysanthemums on T'ao Ch'ien's hedge. As for me, I am like a goose waiting to fly back south. I imagine people celebrating this festival by climbing mountains and pouring out libations in the hope of protecting the emperor in Peking, near the Yen mountains, from the invading Manchus.

In Lamplight, Watching My Wife Preparing a Flower Arrangement—Playfully Inscribing Four Poems

(Two poems from the group of four)

1.

Narcissus and chrysanthemum—
   lovely shapes together;
she places them in a porcelain vase,
   two or three of each.
Bending low beside the little window
   in flickering lamplight shadows,
my jade one has risen from her sick bed,
   braving the cold air.

2.

Clusters of cold-weather blossoms,
            standing quietly:
each branch weighted with mottled beauty now.
I think of consulting you for tips on flower arrangement—
but here they are before my eyes, in lamplight,
            against a white wall.

(pp. 75–77)

Miscellaneous Feelings at West Lake

My steps wander east of the mountains; I moor my boat by the
lake. Half the time, the sky is dripping rain—summer months that
seem like autumn. Dull thudding of embankments being built—
here land protects the foot of Wu. Full and rich, the mist and
dust—here heaven endows the horn of Yüeh. Yüeh Fei and Yü
Ch'ien—their paired mausolea still show green inscriptions;
southern, northern—these two peaks, covered with green haze as
if cut sheer. Think of the flourishing of lake and mountain, consider
the beauty of the city. The old dream is still here, the new self,
where should it go? Indeed, the scholars of this town have always
been moved by the flourishing crops here; while now, ordinary
citizens feel deeply the earth-shaking change. They boast of
practicing barbarian customs, speak a foreign dialect as if born to
it. What can be said of this? Alas, how far it has gone!

   In the past, when they moved south and established the capital
here—all that was left, this southern town—West Lake became a
place for reclusion rivaling West Mountain of old. Ah, the place
the same, but the men quite different: who can bear to lament the
past on the basis of today?

Clusters of long poems remain, and grievous short verses. The wine has taken, the lamp burned low. Across the river they are singing songs of Yüeh girls. The wind is brisk, the rain prodigious; I weep tears like those of travelers down the gorges of Szechwan. Respectfully I pronounce unto men of like mind: do not neglect the lesser plantings! I dare to leave these for the Poetry Collector to provide reading while trimming the lamp.

In the fifth month of the year *keng-yin* (1650), in the summer, I lived in a boat on West Lake for six days in all and wrote twenty poems. On the last day of the month, recorded on the road to T'ang-ch'i.

(Two poems from the group of twenty)

1.

Desolate poems of chaotic times—could I bear
        to hear them again?
Misty peaks like ochre wash,
        waters like burnt-out ash!
Beneath Po Chü-i's embankment of white sand,
        reeds from the era of T'ang;
beside the tomb of the Prince of O,
        clouds that date from Sung.
In the trees the orioles—
        today they are my friends;
perched on a branch, a cuckoo sings—
        in days of old, a king!
Like "K'un-ming Lake," after dissolution—
        a bell still sounds through the air:
coiling among the lakeside mountains
        it proclaims eventide.

2.

In hermit's robe, clean and simple,
　　　　with peaked cap on my head,
I climb to each red chamber,
　　　　then ride in painted boats.
Bamboo groves are fresh and lovely,
　　　　here where cranes were trained;
springtime breezes are mild and serene
　　　　in this paradise for flowers.
Butterflies flit through willow gardens,
　　　　greeting reddish pollen;
orioles sit on peachtree banks
　　　　awaiting winds and strings.
It must be that in times of peace,
　　　　tranquil days like these,
the lake and mountains easily
　　　　become the haunts of gods.

(pp. 79–85)

The long preface, in classical "four-six" prose, and the poems are filled with allusions to the history and lore of West Lake:

——Wu and Yüeh: Ancient names for Chiangsu and Fukien provinces, respectively.

——Yüeh Fei (1103–41), Yü Ch'ien (1398–1457): Two great military men, associated with loyalty to the Sung and Ming dynasties, respectively. Both were wronged by their enemies at court.

——West Mountain: The place of hermitage chosen by the legendary Shang-dynasty loyalists, Po Yi and Shu Ch'i after the accession to power of the Chou.

——Poetry Collector: An official supposedly charged in antiquity with the collection of folk poems to be used by the emperor to determine the mood of the people.

——Po Chü-i (772–846): The great T'ang poet was appointed governor of Hangchou in 822, and constructed the embankment across West Lake which still bears his name today.

——Prince of O: Yüeh Fei, whose tomb is located on the bank of West Lake.

——Cuckoo . . . king: According to legend, a king of Szechwan died of a broken heart because of his impossible love for the wife of his prime minister. His soul was transformed into the cuckoo.

——K'un-ming Lake: When Emperor Wu of the Han had the artificial K'un-ming Lake created, a patch of burnt earth was discovered. According to a sage from the far west, this was the remains of the cosmic fire which had ended an earlier era.

In Spring of the Year, *Ping-shen* (1656), I Came to
Ch'in-huai (Nanking) to Consult a Physician. I
Lodged in Mr. Ting's Water Pavilion for Two
Months. Before Leaving, I Wrote Thirty Quatrains,
Both in Parting and as Inscriptions, with No
Attention to Sequence.

(Two poems from the group of thirty)

1.

Pavilions of dance, terraces of song,
        clusters of lovely silks!
Yet now, no traces of visitors,
        only springtime wind.
"Treading the Green," unlimited
        feelings of lamentation
all absorbed into the setting orb
        of the Southern Dynasties.

——"Treading the Green:" A spring festival, when people would leave the cities, go out
    to the countryside, and celebrate the new year.

2.

Willow catkins beyond the garden wait for evening tides;
across the stream, leaves of peachtrees
        border the red bridge.
It is dusk: as I gaze in concentration
        at springtime like a river,
beyond the T-pattern blinds of the Ting Family house
        it is the Six Dynasties again.

(pp. 86–89)

WU WEI-YEH (1609–72)

W U IS one of the later Chinese poets most worthy of being
considered a major figure in the history of Chinese poetry,
and future work on him may indeed establish him as the preeminent
post-Sung poet. Like Ch'ien Ch'ien-i (q.v.), Wu held office under
the Ch'ing, but only briefly, and only after a failed attempt at suicide
upon the fall of the Ming dynasty, whereas Ch'ien had apparently
rushed to accept office and remained an official for a considerable
time. Wu never forgave himself for his lapse from perfect loyalty to
the Ming, and basically considered himself as one of the *Ming i-min*
(Ming loyalists). A poet of tremendous skill and power, Wu excels
especially at lengthy narrative poems unparalleled in the history of
Chinese literature for their unique use of oblique narrative technique
and lyrical evocativeness to convey historical events as experienced
by concubines and other peripheral participants in one of the most
tumultous periods in Chinese history—the transition from late
Ming to early Ch'ing. The *Ballad of Yüan-yüan,* translated here in
its entirety (pp. 362–67), is possibly his masterpiece in this mode,
which is ultimately traceable to Po Chü-i's *Song of Everlasting Sorrow,*
but which goes beyond Po in the direction of lyrical density inter-
woven with narrative ambiguity.

Although primarily known as a poet, Wu was a minor painter
as well. A fan-painting of his in the Asian Art Museum of San
Francisco is reproduced here in Plate 8.

Ballad of Yüan-yüan

This poem employs an oblique narrative style and many
allusions to tell the story of the geishalike singing girl, Yüan-yüan,
from the city of Suchou. The Ch'ung-chen Emperor, last of the
Ming emperors, was infatuated with his favorite concubine T'ien
(Wu Wei-yeh also wrote a long narrative poem about her), and
therefore ignored the Empress Chou. The latter's father, Chou
K'uei, a native of Suchou, purchased Yüan-yüan and presented her
to the emperor in the hope of thereby regaining the emperor's
favor. But the emperor remained infatuated with T'ien and paid
no attention to Yüan-yüan either, so Chou K'uei took her into his
own household. At this juncture, Wu San-kuei (1612–78), the great
general, saw her at Chou's house and fell in love with her; he
prepared to marry her, but was abruptly called away by the emperor
to lead the Ming troops into battle against the invading Manchus.
Eventually, Wu found himself pitted against the Manchu armies at
Shan-hai Kuan (called "Jade Pass" in the poem, as if Peking were
the T'ang capital of Ch'ang-an). While he confronted the enemy
there, the rebel leader Li Tzu-ch'eng took advantage of the stand-
off to invade Peking; the emperor committed suicide. Li sent a
messenger to urge Wu to surrender to him, but when Wu learned
that Yüan-yüan had fallen into Li's hands, he became infuriated,
immediately surrendered to the Manchu troops and, becoming
their vanguard, attacked and defeated Li Tzu-ch'eng, thus making
possible the rescue of Yüan-yüan from Li, but also the ultimate
triumph of the Manchu Ch'ing dynasty, for which Wu Wei-yeh is
criticizing him in this poem. (When Li heard of Wu's defection,
he ordered the death of Wu's entire family, including his father.)
    Subsequently reunited with Yüan-yüan, Wu proceded
westward in 1652 to engage the remnant troops of another rebel
leader, Chang Hsien-chung, taking Yüan-yüan with him.

At Tripod Lake on that day His Majesty quit this world,
to crush the enemy and recapture the capital
           Wu came down from Jade Pass.
Wracked with sobs, the six-fold army
           all wore mourning white;
but his hat rose—hairs bristling with anger—
           for a lovely face!
"A lovely face in dire straits
           is not what moves me now:
but rebellious bandits, against heaven's will,
           indulging in decadence!"
Like lightning he swept away Yellow Turbans
           and pacified Black Hills;
after lamenting for sovereign and father
           he got to see her again.
When first he saw her, it was at the home of T'ien or Tou:
noble mansion—singing, dancing, girls trooped out like flowers!
And they allowed the general to take the harpist then
to join the ranks of concubines in his lacquered cars.
Her home was in Suchou city,
           a neighborhood like Huan-hua;
Yüan-yüan was her childhood name,
           so charming in silk dress!
She dreamed of wandering in the gardens
           of King Fu-ch'ai of Wu:
palace women would usher her in,
           and the king would rise for her.
In former life she must have been
           a lotus-picking girl;
outside her door, an expanse of water—
           the embankment of Heng-t'ang.
From Heng-t'ang a pair of oars
           row out as if in flight:
a man of power from somewhere
           has taken her off by force.

At such a juncture how could she know
                    that her life was not to end?
At this moment, she could only
                    drop tears on her robe.
With excitement reaching heaven
                    they conveyed her to the palace
where lovely eyes and brilliant teeth
                    failed to move His Majesty to love!
Then they snatched her from those quarters
                    and shut her in the mansion
where they taught her to sing the latest songs
                    and astonish assembled guests.
The guests would fill their flying cups
                    as the sun set with red glow;
a song she'd sing with lamenting strings,
                    but who would hear her plaint?
A handsome, pale nobleman, youngest of the guests,
longing to pluck this blossom from the branch
                    often glanced at her.
As soon as possible he'd free
                    this charming bird from the cage:
when would they ever be able to meet
                    by crossing the Milky Way?
But, how frustrating! military orders
                    now urged him unto death!
Bitterly he left her with promises of meeting,
                    left her to cruel fate.
But promises of meeting may come from deep love—
                    still, how hard to meet!
One day the rebels like so many ants
                    overran Ch'ang-an!
How sad, the woman in her tower,
                    full with thoughts of him,
the willow she sees as catkins floating
                    off to the horizon.

Searching everywhere for this Green Pearl
                 they encircled the inner chambers,
shouting loudly for Red Tree to emerge
                 from carved balustrades.
If the brave warrior had not prevailed,
                 his troops preserved intact,
how could the moth-browed beauty ever
                 have ridden a horse back home?
"The moth-browed beauty is coming by horse!"
                 The news was shouted on;
her cloud-chignon in disarray,
                 her startled soul now calm.
With waxen tapers he greeted her
                 right on the battlefield:
tear-streaked makeup covered her face
                 with marks of smeary red.
Then on forced march with pipes and drums
                 they headed for Ch'in and Ch'uan;
along the Gold Ax Avenue
                 a thousand carriages moved.
In Slope Valley where clouds were thick
                 he built her a painted tower;
at Ta-san Pass as the moon sank down
                 she set out·makeup and mirror.
The news was transmitted until it filled
                 the entire waterlands;
the tallow trees had turned red leaves
                 through ten autumnal frosts.
The master geisha who taught her music
                 was happy to learn she lived;
her old companions at the silk-washing stream
                 remembered when they were friends.
Together in their nests of old they were swallows carrying mud,
but now she had flown to a higher branch,
                 transformed into a phoenix.

Forever among the cups of wine
          they would lament old age,
while one of them had found a husband
          lording it as prince!
In the past she only suffered
          from her burden of fame:
imperial relations and men of power
          vied to invite her then.
But each performance of *A Peck of Pearls*
          gained thousands of pecks of grief
as over mountains and passes she wandered,
          her limbs all wasting away.
Yet wrong it would be to blame the wild wind
          for blowing this blossom down:
now, unlimited colors of spring
          fill heaven and earth once more.
We hear of women so lovely
          they destroyed a country or town,
and yet they led to Master Chou's
          great legacy of fame.
Why should women be involved
          in these great events?
What can be done when heroes
          are smitten with such love?
The bones of his whole family
          have crumbled into dust,
while the rouge of the age's most lovely face
          glows on history's page!
Sir, do you not see:
    When Kuan-wa Hall was first erected
          the mandarin ducks there slept;
the beauty of Yüeh was like a flower—
          the king could not see her enough?
Now the fragrant paths are covered with dust,
          the birds sing there alone;
the corridors are deserted where her sandals stepped,
          the moss greens for no one.

There are changing notes and passing tones—
                ten thousand miles of grief;
there are pearl-like songs and feather-dances,
                and Liang-chou tunes of old.
But for you, Sir, especially I sing
                this ballad of the Palace of Wu,
like the River Han, flowing southeast,
                day and night forever.

(10/9a–12a; Fukumoto, pp. 120ff)

—— Yellow Turbans, Black Hills: Names of famous rebel armies in history.

—— T'ien and Tou: Surnames of imperial relatives.

—— King Fu-ch'ai,etc.: Yüan-yüan is compared to the famous beauty, Hsi-shih, the "lotus-picking girl."

—— Green Pearl, Red Tree: Famous concubines.

—— Master Chou: Chou Yü, the great general of the Three Kingdoms period who saved the beautiful Ch'iao sisters from the clutches of the evil Ts'ao Ts'ao, who would have made them his concubines had Chou not defeated him, according to the T'ang poet, Tu Mu (803–52).

—— Kuan-wa Hall: Built by King Fu-ch'ai for Hsi Shih.

—— Liang-chou tunes: The name of popular songs of the T'ang dynasty, Liang-chou being a frontier region. The beautiful concubine, Yang Kuei-fei, is said to have composed one.

Climbing P'iao-miao Peak

Precipitous point—river and lake
                bright beneath my eyes;
floatingly, as if about to take off on the wind.
Even here, the highest place, there is a smell of fish;
halfway up, already not the slightest sound of bird.
Fragrant grasses, blue and wild, mingle far and near;
evening sunlight, gold and emerald, transforms dark and clear.
King Fu-ch'ai's dictatorship has vanished utterly:
maple leaves, blossomed reeds, bobbing fishing boats.

(9/24b–25a)

Autumn Night—Sleepless

Autumn burgeons, sounds rise everywhere;
I lie sleepless, the night sinks deeper, deeper.
Time of chaos—plans to stay secure;
fragile life—fears about its end!
The neighbor's rooster, dream-fragment cut off;
window rainfall, one lamp in the depths.
In cutting chill, I pull on clothes and rise:
dawn crows already fill the trees.

(4/15a)

Country Scene

1.
The river Ching flows rapidly:
where can the wanderer's thoughts find rest?
White bones by the newly built fort;
green mountains, how many rings around?
Tall tower—sails pass in rain;
single pagoda—troops of clouds return.
At sunset, a sad flute starts to play;
cold crows flock on flock fly off.

2.
Fading, sick, again I hear of war;
sad, afraid, past things empty now.
This remnant village, beyond the autumn waters:
new ghosts in the brilliance of moonlight.
Trees rise from a fog of thousand sails;
the river bends through wind where one flute plays.
Who uses tears for years accumulated
in this high spot to mourn a road run out?

(4/31a)

Seeing Off Wang Yüan-chao—Reprise

Comings, goings, hard to settle down:
your baggage is light; suddenly you're ready
                     for the road.
Watching you, I stand beyond the trees;
boat advancing, you shout as you enter clouds.
Colors of the country: wild geese on flat sands.
Dawn light: reeds on cut-off shores.
The desolate feeling in all of this:
no one but you could paint it.

                                             (7/13b)

——Wang Yüan-chao: Wang Chien (1598–1677), a major early Ch'ing painter.

Seeing Off Sun Ling-hsiu on His Journey to Chen-ting

Success and failure are not our affairs:
in frosty woods, ten thousand things fade.
A northern wind blows down the avenue;
the wine of parting is served on the river bridge.
A driving snow turns back the journeying goose;
low clouds oppress the angry hawk.
Once you were an official in Yen and Chao;
your time of desolation is this morning.

                                       (7/21b–22a)

At the River Tower Parting from My Younger Brother, Fu-ling

Colors of the country, powerful river,
      thoughts without an end;
we climb this mighty tower and gaze,
      leaning into space.
Cloudy mountains on both shores
      in our wounded hearts;
falling snow, solitary city
      in our tear-filled eyes.
After illness, my whole life
      is like a shedding tree;
troubled times—and all my plans
      float off with tumbleweed.
At heaven's edge, two brothers feel
      the bitter grief of parting;
tomorrow, my little boat
      will follow the dawn wind.

                                          (6/1a)

Lamenting for My Late Daughter

In utter chaos no sooner were you born
than the family had to flee along the roads.
Afraid of your crying, I thought of abandoning you;
each time we escaped, my love for you would grow!
Children are crushed in times of disaster;
shields and halberds threaten young lives.
Rise and fall—these affect the world:
remembering, my feelings of sorrow grow.

                                        (10/15a)

Feelings Come As I Pass Through Wu-chiang

Sung-ling road in setting sunlight;
the embankment so long it nearly circles town.
A pagoda twists up, the lake is shimmering;
a bridge beckons where moon reflections come.
The city is silent: people have fled taxation;
the river, wide: travelers escape the troops.
My friends of twenty years ago—all scattered;
wine in hand, I sigh at fleeting fame.

(Fukumoto, pp. 141–42)

Poem of the Western Fields

Digging and building tire men out,
still, out in the country you have found nature's way.
Leisurely you came outside the northern wall
to study living beside the western stream.
The Tao is great, the hermit's life is hard;
the place remote, yet many speak of it.
And so I come for an unexpected visit,
rowing into this paradise of reeds.
The setting sun floats on distant trees;
the mulberries issue a delicate mist.
Now the way turns, the stream-path is lost,
a flock of wild ducks guides my boat.
Fragrance near—I smell chestnut and lotus;
lying down, enter where flowers are fresh.
Human voices come from weeping willows:
along the winding shore, fish-gaffs everywhere.
You take my hand, look at me and smile,
"This place is my western field!
I often have scholars like you, Sir, call

and together we linger, taking joy in nature.
Sit on the grass—we'll pour a jug of wine
and bring happiness to our remaining years."

(2/20a–b)

——Western Fields: The estate of the great painter, Wang Shih-min (1592–1680).

At the Mountain of the Mysterious Tomb Visiting Master P'ou

One monk, you have dissolved phenomena;
the lone peak is occupied by your mystic incense.
Sutra-chanting purifies the bones of stone;
Buddha's face chills the luster of the lake.
Petals fall—you carry on the cross-legged posture;
clouds return—I recognize the lecture hall.
Deserted pond reflecting tonight's moon,
with gong and drum you bless the ancient king.

(2/31a–b)

Setting Out at Dawn

Setting out at dawn from T'ung-lu county,
green mountains thrusting through the fog.
River village—empty inn with moon;
country fort—frozen flag in wind.
My clothes, all stuffed with cotton, warm;
my face, all flushed with wine, is red.
The sun goes higher, my horse slips as I ride;
killing sadness comes to this old man.

(4/19a)

Ancient Feeling

Beloved, you are like thread in the loom
woven into a flowering tree of love!
I am like the flowers on your robe:
the spring wind blows but they won't drop off.

(4/15a)

The Broken Lampstand

I remember when you shared my insomnia:
how can I bear to cast you off today?
In joy, you were with me, beside the chilly window;
in sorrow, you added to the depth of my old room.
Now I must read in neighbors' reflected light;
I will sink into dream beneath Buddha's altar lamps.
I've no regrets that the orchid-oil is gone—
those clever rats no longer will invade.

(Fukumoto, pp. 143–44)

Song to the Tune, *Perching Crows*

Sandalwood the hawser-ties, silk the puller ropes;
in a pool of pure white jade, a skiff of kingfisher blue.
Lotus blossoms shake off water, mandarin ducks bathe:
Master Lu tonight is sleeping here inside his boat.

(1/23b–24a)

——Master Lu: Either one of the youths sent to recover herbs of immortality by the First
Emperor of the Ch'in dynasty, or the hero of the famous T'ang-dynasty tale of a man
who dreamed an entire lifetime while his gruel was being prepared.

Garden Living

Outside the town I've built this little place
beside water, stuck in sparse hedging.
The bank is curved—flowers hide the angler;
the windows, high—cranes hear chessmen move.
My bed is carried, a long way up stone steps;
I call for tea, a long time cross the stream.
Myself I savor the joy of quiet living;
no one comes here to find out how I live.

(3/14a)

Impromptu

Chang Liang's face was like a young woman's;
Li Kuang was quite sincere—and ugly.
Yet with one blow Chang nearly killed the Dragon;
with ape-arms Li shot arrows like a god.

(5/12a)

——Chang Liang: An important figure in early Han history. He came close to success in
his attempted assassination of the "Ancestral dragon," Ch'in Shih Huang-ti.

——Li Kuang: The great general, an expert archer.

Reading the Annals of Emperor Wu of the Han Dynasty

The temples of Mount T'ai greeted the sun in the east;
the source of the Yellow River spoke with heaven in the west.
Late in his reign, his noble plans ran out
and quack wizards took the place of immortals.

(5/14a)

Passing By Huai-yin I Have Feelings

Climbing high, sadly I gaze at the Mountain of
                              Eight Immortals:
those trees of jade and cinnabar cliffs
            I've never been able to ascend.
I do not expect to meet Yellow Stone
            and get the mystic charm;
I would settle for using the mighty treasure
            to hold the face of youth!
There is but one flaw in this floating life of ours
            and that is death!
The dusty world affords no means
            of knowing ninefold elixir.
Basically I am like the chickens and dogs
            of the Prince of Huai,
except I did not follow him to heaven—
            I fell back to the world of men.

(6/4b–5a)

——The allusions in this poem all imply failed attempts to obtain the elixir of immortality.
Wu is apparently lamenting his failure to join the true Ming loyalists in death. We
are told that "when the Prince of Huai-nan took the elixir and ascended to heaven,
he left some excess elixir behind in the courtyard; the chickens and dogs licked it up
and also ascended (*Shen-hsien chuan*)."

Distant Roads

Distant roads in the aftermath of war;
cold journey, worse as illness lingers.
Stuffed with cotton—threads sewn by my wife;
"medicine enclosed"—letters from my friends.
Evening crossing, horse at river ford;
morning ice, cart at roadside inn.
Withered, desolate, trees of my home garden:
I've so betrayed the mountain-facing hut.

(5/5b)

WU CHIA-CHI (1618–84)

WHEREAS Wu Wei-yeh (q.v.) guiltily accepted office under the new Ch'ing administration, Wu Chia-chi withdrew into retirement in the remote and impoverished saltlands of southern Chiangsu province, remaining in his little native village of An-feng in T'ai-chou prefecture. Disillusioned with the moral failure of Ming leadership, he turned instead to the common people around him for exemplars of *chung* ("loyalty") and *hsiao* ("filial piety"), key Confucian virtues, and recorded acts of these people which he believed bore testimony to the ongoing vitality of these virtues. The long narrative poems in which he transmits their acts may be seen as evolving out of Po Chü-i's New *Yüeh-fu* poems—just as Wu Wei-yeh's more lyrically toned historical narratives are traceable back to Po's *Song of Everlasting Sorrow*. Wu Chia-chi's poems in this mode have a stark, uncompromising power as impressive in its way as Wu Wei-yeh's beautiful tapestry of metaphors and allusions.

Many of Wu's narrative poems, such as *The Grainbarge Wife* (pp. 384–85) and *The Woman Née Wú* (pp. 385–87) relate exemplary deeds of moral courage by ordinary people, deeds proving the ongoing vitality of the basic virtues of *chung* and *hsiao* at a time of great national suffering. It appears to have been Wu's goal to show that the survival of these virtues held out hope for a spiritual and moral regeneration in China.

Quatrain

The old saltman, hair turned white,
                    in his hovel of thatch:
the sixth month come, he boils down the salt
                    beside the blistering fire.
He steps outside and stands a while
                    in the raging sun:
for him, this moment out of doors
                    counts as cooling off.

                                              (p.10)

[Alternate version]

East of the salt village, low and narrow—
                    the huts of the seaside folk.
The sixth month come, they boil down the salt,
                    as if boiling in water themselves!
They step outside and stand for a while
                    in the raging sun:
for them, this moment out of doors
                    counts as cooling off.

                                              (p. 467)

——This poem is said to have moved the Ch'ien-lung Emperor (r. 1736–96) to "open the
national treasury to give succor to the saltmen."

Returning to the Alluvial Fields

(One poem from a group of four)

In the morning they build embankments against floods;
in the evening, dig the roots of wild reeds.
This is to feed their hungry stomachs
and for the generations to come.
I have heard that before the year *chia-shen*
this place was Peach Blossom Paradise!
Chickens and dogs along mountains and streams,
thick groves among the neighborhoods.
When frost fell, grain crops reached their peak;
oranges perfumed every village.
At sunset, fishing boats returned;
laughter and conversation sounded from each home.
I picture that time of serenity:
house after house, wine brimming in the jars.

(pp. 156–57)

——*Chia-shen:* I.e., 1644, The year of the founding of the new Ch'ing dynasty.

My Hut

My hut, beside the crystal stream,
is growing old: half has fallen down.
So much for the part that's fallen down—
but the part that's standing soon will topple too.
The old plum tree slants sideways with the house,
propping up the wall above the water.

A friend, concerned my house will soon collapse,
has sent some grain to pay for the repairs.
Sacks are carried in, startling the neighbors,
just a few pecks to pay the workmen's wage.
Still we lack the stone and wood we need:
tomorrow, we will have to sell one pig.
"Why is everyone working so hard?"
My dumb son pesters the old housemaid.
Before too long, the windows let through light,
and the path again is clear from end to end.
My wife begins to get a little greedy—
pointing at the old foundation stones,
she says she wants to pawn some of our clothes
to pay for an extension to the house.
With a smile, I remind my wife:
"Outside, the cold is just beginning.
Let's keep this little bit of open land
and wait until the springtime breezes blow.
I myself will carry out a hoe
and plant a vegetable garden in the yard."

(p. 1)

To Ch'eng Fei-t'ao

In degenerate times, people love extravagance;
the masses blindly follow suit.
In the city and all four directions
they ape each other with no end in sight.

(There is an old proverb: "When high chignons are fashionable in town/They rise a foot in villages all around.")

In Kuang-ling, fatuous excess thrives:
people build homes like those of dukes and princes!
They stuff on meat, and wear fine silks,
exhausting ingenuity to please their petty selves.
The pursuit of pleasure has rendered them obtuse,
and as ill luck would have it, they possess excessive wealth.
As for me, it's Ch'eng Chung-tzu I love,
residing in dignity among fishermen and saltmen.
The springtime wilds are overgrown with weeds
but amongst them grows this elegant orchid.
How can one set a different tone in life?
Try the style of this pure-blowing breeze.

(pp. 159–60)

Woman Tung

I was passing through the village of mottled bamboo;
there was a woman weeping in the fields.
The land stretched wide, few signs of man;
the woman was leading a calf by a rope.
It nibbled the grass below,
a vast expanse of greenery.
How sad was the sound of her weeping;
oxen and sheep heard it and stood still.
And I too stopped traveling,
approached and questioned her.

Moved by the kindness of her old master,
she wanted to speak, but tears continued to flow.
"My master was Degree-Holder Han,

(named Mo)

who made his home in Yangchou City.
When the city fell, the troops slew and slaughtered;
my master and his wife committed suicide.
His wife (née Hsiao) hanged herself from the rafters,
and he drowned himself in the well.
They had two young sons, the elder of them
followed his noble father in death.

(His name was Yen-ch'ao)

The younger (named Wei) was still at mother's breast,
and she entrusted him to my old self!
I remember how the mother, about to hang herself,
held the child close and suckled him.
How many times had the boy been fed before?
And now in turmoil the two of them must part!
Outside, corpses were piled high;
it was late in the day—should we go east or west?
I bundled up the baby, so he wouldn't cry,
and together we entered among the dead!
The dead bodies covered our living bodies,
blood smeared red all over us.
For five days they killed and killed;
their camels neighed along Shu Ridge.
Crawling, at night I left the city,
to field-paths under clear skies and ripened wheat.
I plucked wheat-ears and fed them to the boy,
then hid in a village where hearth-fires still burned.
The boy and I both managed to survive;
the farmers sighed in amazement.

That year the wheat ripened,
the next year wheat ripened . . .
and soon the boy was called, Young Sir!
His body grew just like his father's;
his eyebrows were especially full.
His writing brush spun essays and poems
and he associated with friends of quality,
wishing to bring glory to his house.
And where is the Young Sir now?
With book and sword, beneath the Yen-shan Mountains.
The Yen-shan Mountains, 3,000 *li* away:
longing for him, my heart is broken!"
Done speaking, she said good-bye to me;
leaning on the calf, she gazed toward the north.
Along the northern road, a donkey approached;
she rushed toward it, and shouted from far away:
"Young Sir, you've not abandoned me!
Today, have you returned?"
Her mistake she was ignorant of herself;
she thought it strange when no one answered her.
The sparrows return to their village;
mist turns cold, trees sink into darkness.
I too return, covering my ears:
the woman's cries are too painful to hear.

(pp. 357–59)

——The historical event underlying this poem was the Yangchou massacre of May 20–
30, 1645, perpetrated upon the population by the troops of the newly established
Ch'ing dynasty and intended as a warning against any further resistance. The Woman
Tung was a family servant of a certain Han Mo, famous for his protest suicide together
with his wife, elder son, and daughter. The Young Sir, Han Wei, was an acqaintance
of the poet. An alternate account by the poet's friend, Wang Mou-lin *(chin-shih* degree,
1667), implies that Han Wei was not quite so cold-hearted; he did ignore Tung while
studying, but later returned and gave a feast for her—then left again. She always
grieved in his absence.

The Grain-Barge Wife

Autumn winds blow along the river,
blow upon a man in hunger;
he has a wife lovely as a flower,
but no means to put food on her plate!
Toward sunset with great clamor
a grain barge moors in the harbor.
The officer in charge sits at the prow;
gazing about, he sees the lovely face.
He sends a man with an urgent message:
"I have plenty of clothes and food.
You are going to starve to death—
why not join me, and we'll work together.
Work with me for one year,
and I'll send you home for a fee.
Work with me for three years,
and I'll send you home for free!"
The husband pleads with his wife:
"I urge you to do what he asks.
If you don't, we will starve to death,
and then we'll be parted forever."
He lifts his wife—lifelong companion—to her feet;
her tears fall like drops of rain.
One day a wife in her bedchamber,
the next, a boatman's mistress!
When the man's cronies hear he may have a son
they prepare a feast, the fatted calf and wine.
They come in boats from south of the river;
they come in boats from north of the river.
The boatman is delighted in his heart;
with his own hand he pours out goblets of wine.
He tells himself that lovely piece of goods
is like a bird, caught within his nets.

But the netted sparrow has a mate,
the woman has a husband.
How could they know this woman's will
could never be bent or broken?
Her husband, weeping, clings to her:
"Follow what he says, lower your eyes!
Work for him for three years' time,
and he'll let you return for free."
The woman remains silent, not a word;
as people sleep, the moon sinks at the window.
Quckly she leaves the boatman's place,
determined to seek ghostly companions.
Clutching a rock, she jumps into the Grand Canal:
the waves stop flowing for her.
Passers-by wipe their tears and stare
at her body floating in the water.

(pp. 119–20)

The Woman Née Wú

The woman née Wú had the personal name Wǔ. She was a native
of An-feng village and was married to Lu Kao. Kao's father became
seriously ill; he had heard that in the village there was a man who
had sliced his own flesh as a cure for his parent's illness, and he
told his family about this, expressing the desire that Kao would
imitate the other man's action. But at the time, Kao himself was
ill. So the woman resolutely took his place. Cutting with a knife,
she sliced off flesh from her left forearm. The blade was sharp and
cut to the bone. The blood flowed for twelve days and nights, and
then she died. Those who witnessed this all grieved at it.

The dodder twines around the *huang-po* tree,
sharing with it the mist and rain.
But the tree's branches and leaves are rooted:
the dodder alone encounters a bitter fate.
                              —First Stanza

The marriage occurred at an auspicious time;
a magpie carried a plum branch in its beak.
Everybody said, "The bride is beautiful!"
The go-betweens enjoyed their glory.
                              —Second Stanza

As broths and roasts were cooking in the kitchen,
in the hall calamity approached!
Just as the go-betweens were sent off to the west,
from the east, the doctor was ushered in.
                              —Third Stanza

"For drinking, hot soups are inappropriate;
for eating, he'd better not eat gruel."
The ghost chief was pressing this man's fate;
the ghost boss was anxious for his flesh.
                              —Fourth Stanza

The great man had no weak daughter,
nor had he any other son.
Sick with consumption, his flesh wasted away,
how could his one son bear to cut and slice?
                              —Fifth Stanza

At night the woman rises, beneath the constellations,
a knife at the ready in her hands.
Before the god she kneels and worships, and then
the sharp blade moves along her arm.
                              —Sixth Stanza

"Gee-oo, gee-oo," ghosts wail and weep;
the lamp goes out, extinguished by the wind.
In the valley sway grasses and trees, all wild;
outside, pigs and sheep squeal and bleat.

—Seventh Stanza

Cutting her body, could she be following custom?
Bearing the pain, because she's taken her husband's place.
And does she grudge the blood, drop after drop,
for twelve days and nights, flowing?

—Eighth Stanza

Having obtained this flesh, father-in-law is pleased;
having taken husband's place, the woman has died.
Alas, alas, all family members weep:
can anyone now bring her back to life?

—Ninth Stanza

Her in-laws compete to be the first to visit;
her fragrant fame spreads through the neighborhood.
In the past she was the twining dodder;
now she is a grove of orchid bloom.

—Tenth Stanza

(*Lou-hsüan shih,* 5/39b–40a)

YÜN SHOU-P'ING (1633–90)

YÜN IS known as one of the great "orthodox" painters of the early Ch'ing dynasty, although only in relation to the "fantastic and eccentric" masters who were also an important force in Ch'ing painting. His flower paintings are actually quite individualistic, combining the lyrical expressiveness of literati art with the meticulous detail of the academic tradition. As a poet, Yün is a virtuoso of the *chüeh-chü* quatrain (especially as inscribed on paintings), ringing seemingly endless, delightful variations on the themes of the relationship between art and life, and of the aesthetic richness of nature.

Seeing Off Mr. Yang on His Journey to Wu-wei Prefecture

(One poem from a set of two)

War ships, cold tides,
        ancient troops of clouds,
crows like crazy dots of ink
        splashed against the dying sun:
here, on the west bank of the Yangtze,
        at Ju-hsü entrenchment,
as the spring waters start to rise
        I say farewell to you.

(p. 17)

Inscribed on a Snowscape

Blown in the wind—the silver river
        of the Milky Way;
halfway to heaven, hibiscus flowers of jade.
The Jasper Lady, dazzling
        among trees of pearl,
a white phoenix, dancing among pine trees
        on a cliff.

(p. 18)

Sadness in the Autumn Chambers

Autumn winds blow in from Chieh-shih Mountain;
thousands of trees turn sparse and bare.
Wild geese fly beyond the cold sands;
hibiscus is moist with drops of rain.
Like silken threads, the moonlight
                 glimmering on the loom;
written on silk, the letters
                 that come in dreams.
Her man has been gone for one year now—
in the high chamber she spends the whole night alone.

(p. 29)

Inscribed on a Painting by Shih-ku

(One poem from a group of four)

Through the windy valley,
                 clear sound of a hidden spring.
In the mountain courtyard,
                 the dawn especially bright.
Since last night, the pines
                 have been heavy with snow;
the cranes and gibbons, frozen,
                 utter not a sound.

(p. 30)

——Shih-ku: Wang Hui (1632–1717), one of the major "orthodox" masters of early Ch'ing
painting, and Yün Shou-p'ing's closest friend.

Green Banana Leaves

I sit here long, the lamp burns dim;
sound of rain, swept by the wind past my house.
The tears of the banana leaves, outside the window:
for whom are they falling tonight?

(p. 35)

Inscribed on a Painting of Sailboats on the River— Seeing Off Yen-chi on His Journey to Ch'ang-an

Floating clouds, before my eyes,
        the old country lost in haze,
and, from beyond the skies,
        the sound of orioles.
Since this morning, I have not been grateful
        for the brisk river wind:
willow catkins and sailboats
        all rushing toward the west.

(p. 38)

Early Summer in the Year Jen-tzu (1672)—Playfully Painted in the Manner of Ts'ai Yün-hsi

Stone cliffs, no clouds,
          deserted gully path;
wild, wild bamboo leaves
          after a night of wind.
My mind wanders among old trees
          and withered vines,
poetry lies hidden in the cold mist
          and the wild grass.

(p. 41)

——Ts'ai Yün-hsi: Ts'ai Chih-po (1272–1355), an important painter of the Yüan dynasty, known for his old trees and rocks.

Hearing a Flute at Broken Bridge

On misty waters, vast and vague,
          floating in a painted boat.
From a stone railing along the bank,
          gazing at the cold sky.
One note from the jade flute—
          moon of a thousand autumns;
scattering, scattering, plum blossoms
          over the twelve bridges.

(p. 48)

In the Tenth Month of the Year Jen-tzu (1672) the Imperial Censor Tan Chiang-shang, Mountain Man Wang Shih-ku and I Traveled by Boat to Pi-ling and Moored There. We Lingered Among the Frosty Trees and Red Leaves. Wang Was Entrusted with the Task of Painting a Picture, and We Each Wrote Twelve Poems to Record Our Delightful Experience.

(One poem from a group of twelve)

Scorpions' tails, silver hooks:
               masterful calligraphy!
The villa at Wang-ch'uan, the bamboo of Ch'i Garden:
               a picture worthy of a god!
Please do not talk about this cold, stark beauty
with people who live in the dusty world, and eat meat.

(p. 43)

——Tan Chiang-shang: Tan Chung-kuang (1623–92), a painter, calligrapher and poet who was a good friend of Yün's.

——Wang-ch'uan: Site of the private estate of the great T'ang dynasty poet and painter, Wang Wei.

——Ch'i Garden: The beautiful bamboo here are mentioned as early as the *Book of Songs* (compiled c. 600 B.C.).

On a Painting: *Ancient Trees and Flowing Stream*

True feelings come from my innermost heart,
when—suddenly—face to face with the Master!
It's not that I set out to follow Ni Tsan,
but my painting has Ni Tsan's spirit!

(p. 51)

——Ni Tsan (1301–74): One of the Four Great Masters of Yüan dynasty painting, famous
for his sparse compositions which are suffused with an austere nobility. Ni was one
of the painters who exerted the greatest influence on Yün's generation of artists. See
pp. 66–75.

Mourning for Lü Hui-chiu

(One poem from a group of four)

—Though he was extremely ill, Lü still commissioned Wang Hui,
at an unusually generous rate, to paint a large hanging scroll of
mountains and streams, and then had it hung on the wall.

Facing you, on the wall, across from your bed:
mountains like skinny bones,
                    rising loftily above table and desk.
Half the wall covered with craggy peaks and valleys;
seriously ill, you still loved the mountains
                    of Fan K'uan.

(pp. 51–52)

——Fan K'uan (active c. 990–1030): One of the great masters of Chinese painting.

A Painting of Chrysanthemums in the Boneless Style of Hsü Ch'ung-ssu

I face the yellow flowers,
      silent, saying nothing.
The yellow flowers face me
      as if they had feeling.
Slender stems, leaf after leaf
      touched with frosty breath;
heavy flowers, petal after petal
      alive with the clarity of autumn.

(p. 108)

——Hsü Ch'ung-ssu: Hsü Hsi (d. before 975) was a great master of flower painting. The "boneless method" associated with his name consists of defining the forms entirely through the use of colored washes, without enclosing outlines. Yün Shou-p'ing's greatest fame as a painter was achieved though his mastery of this style.

——This poem is inscribed on a painting in the Shanghai Museum. See René-Yvon Lefebvre d'Argencé, ed., *Treasures from the Shanghai Museum* (catalogue of an exhibition organized by the Shanghai Museum and shown at a number of American museums in 1983 and 1984), color pl. XLI.

Written on the Night of the Twenty-ninth of the First Month

Wooden bridge, gaunt willows—
      here the thatched hut stands open.
By the stream, the mountain boy announces
      that a guest has come.
Together we sit in the cold mist,
      among the pines and bamboo,
warm up wine in the snow and gaze
      at the plum blossoms in the courtyard.

(p. 110)

On the Painting, *Mist Over Ten Thousand Mountains* by Shih-ku

(Two poems from a group of five)

1.

I listen to a waterfall
       without getting up from my desk,
travel through mountains
       without going out the door.
This painting will never be rolled up
       and put back in its case:
I will leave it on the wall,
       watch it give birth to mist and fog.

2.

Nature's workings made this gentle place,
a magic realm that came from no mind.
Stop plucking the strings and listen to the pure sounds:
such music was never played by the finest lute.

(p. 112)

On a Landscape by Myself

In the blue-green shadows
       the morning clouds lie smooth.
Wild grasses look like mist,
       the gully path is bright.

When can I come here
    to build a home in the mountains
and listen forever to the wind in the pines,
    the sounds of monkeys and birds?

(p. 118)

A Painting of Yams

I still remember the time at the mountain hut,
    going to bed late at night . . .
I called a friend over
    and we chanted poems
        in the cold lamplight,
then, over a pinewood fire in the brazier
    we roasted yams,
and when we stood up to open the window,
    saw the snow outside.

(p. 121)

Inscribed on a Painting

Who needs a raft that can invade the stars?
Crystal bright, I see the jasper towers!
I'll ride a cloud to travel through the air
and pluck the moon from the autumn sky!

(p. 124)

A Lament for Myself

—Shown to my friends

(One poem from a set of two)

As old age approaches
        my faculties grow numb;
I do things alone,
        people think I'm strange!
The frightened fish
        is saddened by the net,
the tired bird
        cannot find a roost.
My wife and children
        are tired of my poems,
my clothing lets through
        the chill of ice and snow.
Selling my writings,
        still a traveler through life,
have I betrayed my pledge
        to become a hermit
                at Deer Gate Mountain?

(p. 128)

On a Painting of Mushrooms

A single rock from Cinnabar Hill
and glittering on it: mushrooms of five colors!
Eat them and you will grow wings.
Swallow them—they are good for your complexion.

(p. 131)

On the Day of the Mid-Autumn Festival of the Year *Ping-yin* (1686), Together with Chang Han-chan, Ching-fan, and Ching-t'ien, I Saw the Kuei Blossoms at the Northern Garden of Jade Peak

(One poem from a group of ten)

In a hidden spot on the northern mountain,
      reached by a wooden bridge,
the mountain spirit quietly keeps watch
      over a grove of flowering *kuei*.
Fearing that the autumn winds may blow the blossoms down,
I will sleep among these flowers tonight,
      along with the cranes and gibbons.

(p. 137)

Chrysanthemums

(One poem from a set of two)

As we say farewell to autumn
      we think of the flowers
and gather a group of friends
      to drink wine
          among the chrysanthemums.
On all sides—flaming lamps,
      in the center—great torches:
the flowers burn with points of light
      on every branch.

(p. 143)

Waterside Village

West of the bridge
      they dry the nets
            on the road to the fishing village.
Noble in the frost, bare of leaves,
      the trees along the cold bank.
Mountains reflected in the lake,
      mist among the reeds:
I want to bring my whole family with me
      and come here to live!

(p. 145)

Inscribed on a Painting

(One poem from a group of three)

Magic mists twirl through the sky;
the sounds of nature are heard in the silence.
Why go searching for herbs of immortality?
You can eat these white clouds for breakfast!

(p. 163)

A Painting in the Style of Secretary Kao

The mountain is the father of the clouds,
the clouds are the children of the mountain.
They lean against the mountain all day long
and the mountain does not even seem to know.

(p. 164)

——*Secretary Kao:* Kao K'o-kung (1248–1310), an important Yüan dynasty painter of
landscapes.

On the Painting, *Joys of Village Life*

For a hundred miles, the west wind carries the fragrance
           of millet;
the water is low in the cold stream,
           the grain is on the threshing-floor.
The old buffalo, done with his task of plowing for today,
chews some grass as he lies in the sunset
           on the hill.

(p. 165)

——This is actually a variation on a poem by the Sung poet, K'ung P'ing-chung.

Landscape

(One poem from a group of three)

Brush in rocks, draw a stream:
　　no end to the inspiration!
The blossoming ink can change form
　　like the clouds in the sky.
Why bother to put on your sandals
　　and go off in search of mountains?
Ten thousands gullies and a thousand cliffs
　　are here before your eyes!

　　　　　　　　　　　　　　　　　　　　(pp. 233–34)

Autumn Plants, Flowers, Bamboo, Rocks

Autumn colors
　　on the leaves;
autumn sounds
　　in the bamboo.
Evening wind,
　　morning frost:
these things
　　make solitude beautiful.

　　　　　　　　　　　　　　　　　　　　(p. 235)

——This poem is written in the unusual form of four lines with four characters in each
line *(ssu-yen chüeh-chü)*. As each character is a single syllable, this makes for a total of
sixteen syllables, one less than in the well-known Japanese *haiku*.

A Lament for the Willows Outside the City Walls

—At the time, an embankment was being constructed along the
Yellow River in the north, and the authorities requested that
nearly all the local willows be transplanted there.

When the universe goes up in flame
         it is hard for trees and plants to survive:
the long branches, the short leaves,
         all turned to dust.
In a thousand villages, no catkins can be seen
         floating in the air:
what damage they have done to the third month of springtime
         here in the south!

(p. 236)

In My Boat, Painting a Picture of
Going Home by Boat

(One poem from a set of two)

The essence of ink
         is brushed into fog,
                  cold as autumn:
half the surface of this fine silk
         is swept by mist and rain.
And in the fan painting is a man
         painting another fan:
look closely among the flecks of mica dust
         and you'll see him in a little boat.

(p. 238)

——*Mica dust* was sometimes used to decorate the surface of a fan.

WANG SHIH-CHEN (1634–1711)

WANG'S PRIMARY IMPORTANCE in his day was as an arbiter of literary taste; his declared interest in the poetry of Wu Chia-chi (q.v.), for example, set the stage for what little fame Wu was to enjoy in his lifetime. In the realm of literary theory, too, Wang was a primary representative of what James J. Y. Liu has termed the "metaphysical" school of poetic criticism; he called for attention to *"shen-yün"*—"spirit-resonance"—in poetry. As a poet, Wang was prolific and varied, ranging from exquisite landscape vignettes in the Wang Wei manner to grandiose historical meditations inspired by archaeological objects, as in the *Song of the Ch'in-Dynasty Mirror* translated here (pp. 410–12). Such a poem can probably be traced back to poems on the archaic stone drum texts by Han Yü (768–824) and others in the T'ang and Sung dynasties, as well as to Mei Yao-ch'en's (1002–60) several poems on ancient artifacts.

Thinking of the Past on an Autumn Night at Tz'u-jen Temple

Traveler's homesickness, sad and lonely,
        below embroidered Buddhas;
cloudy mountains, dark or pale,
        sky now turning cold.
Back from dreams, still I remember
        that temple south of West Lake:
evening chanting, morning bell ringing,
        now ten years have passed.

(Takahashi, p. 25)

Things Seen

Dark, dark, far mists rise;
swish, swish, sparse woods echo.
Setting sun, west mountains disappear;
a man is plowing the ancient plain.

(Takahashi, p. 28)

Mooring at Night at Kao-yu

In cold rain at Kao-yu
        at night I moor my boat;
the southern lake is newly swollen,
        water touching sky!

A man of romance like Ch'in Kuan
        is nowhere to be found:
how desolate this world of ours
        the last five hundred years!

(Takahashi, p. 31)

——Ch'in Kuan (1049–1100), the great poet and a native of Kao-yu.

Echoing Old Man Mu's Poem, "Inscribed on Shen Lang-ch'ien's Little Landscape, *Autumn Willows at Stone Cliff*"

The mist in the palace willows
        holds all the grief of Six Dynasties,
each catkin fearful of autumn at Yeh-ch'eng.
So heartless! In this painting
        they meet the time of falling leaves:
overnight, the west wind has swept through
        Stonetop Hill.

(Takahashi, p. 52)

——Old Man Mu: Ch'ien Ch'ien-i (1582–1664), one of the most important early Ch'ing poets (see pp. 353–60).

——Shen Lang-ch'ien: Shen Hao (1586 to after 1661), a late Ming painter.

Crossing the Yangtze in a Strong Wind

Red-head swallows swoop and clip the waves in pairs,
                                so light!
Petals fly from riverbanks, rippling wavelets rise.

Heading south or north, boats pass,
　　　　　no time to yell, "Hello!"
Windswept sails swiftly slice their way
　　　　　across the Yangtze River.

(Takahashi, p. 59)

Quatrain at Chen-chou

Along the river most homes here
　　　　　belong to fishermen;
willow embankments and chestnut ponds
　　　　　are scattered everywhere.
But it's most beautiful after sunset
　　　　　when the wind calms down:
a riverside of trees all red
　　　　　and people selling perch.

(Takahashi, p. 71)

Bamboo Branch Song of Han-chia

The mountains beyond the city fade to nothingness;
the clear waves below the city reveal Lake Yü-ku.
White pagodas, red boats returning for the night:
Chia-chou, it seems, has a West Lake of its own.

(Takahashi, p. 119)

——Han-chia: Chia-chou in Szechwan.

Mooring at Night at the River Mouth, I Heard a Flute—Sent to My Elder Brother Hsi-ch'iao

Cloud and water, lonely, desolate:
where now is the flute's voice coming from?
Sighing, sighing—full of autumn thoughts;
unawares come feelings of separation.
Chilly moonlight on water by the tower;
west wind in the city on the river.
What need now to hear the Wu-ch'i Song
with its bitter resentment at southern journeys?

(Takahashi, pp. 88–89)

Lamenting for My Wife

I.
Sick, you said goodbye to me
                as I left for Szechwan;
moved by parting, our tears of sorrow fell.
I'll always remember the place
                where crying gibbons broke my heart:
a river station at Chia-ling
                where rain fell like particles of dust.

2.

The door lock, sealed by green moss,
   stayed locked through the autumn;
the ceiling was covered with cobwebs—
   I let them gather dust.
All that was left of your possessions
   was the gold embroidered skirt:
how could I ever be so heartless
   as to give it away?

         (Takahashi, pp. 135–37)

——The poet's wife died in 1676.

Seeing Off Editor Wang Chou-tz'u and Secretary Lin Shih-lai on Their Mission as Envoys to the Ryūkyū Islands

Congealed vapors surge in vast space;
you ride the flow, and set out for the Great Wild.
You hear the Ocean God, whistling and singing;
striking the waves, approach the cosmic tree!
Sun and moon are swallowed and spit out;
dragons, leviathans plunge down and hide away.
You come to know the vastness of the world:
when Tsou Yen spoke of nine continents,
   he was not telling lies.

         (Takahashi, pp. 147–48)

——Wang Chou-tz'u: Wang Chi (1636–99), a poet and scholar sent as envoy to the Ryūkyū Islands in 1682. Wang has left two texts in which he records his impressions of the islands.

——The cosmic tree: The "Fu-sang" tree in the distant east, from which the sun was said to rise.

——Tsou Yen: A thinker of the fourth century B.C. noted for his writings on geography and other matters.

After Rain, Visiting the Temple of Heavenly Peace

At break of day we leave the western gate;
the temple has been through a storm.
The sun comes out, we meet no one:
filling the courtyard, windbells' whispering.

(Takahashi, p. 149)

Song of the Ch'in-Dynasty Mirror
—Written for Yüan Sung-li

Flashing light, this ancient mirror,
            twin dragons writhe thereon.
Tradition says it once belonged
            to the palace at Hsien-yang.
This bright moon of Ch'in times
            still survives today:
scrape away the muddy sand—
            its luster shines again.
In those years, when Ch'in engulfed
            all six of China's states,
to inner palace were consigned a thousand lovely eyes!
Gecko-juice smeared on their limbs,
            inner organs mirrored:
yet through his reign of thirty-six years
            the emperor knew them not.

—[Poet's note:] When the Han Ancestor (the first emperor of the Han dynasty) entered Hsien-yang Palace (the palace of the defeated Ch'in emperors), he found a square mirror, four feet and nine inches across, which could reflect the five viscera. This is recorded in [the book,] *Hsi-ching tsa-chi* ("Miscellaneous Accounts of the Western Capital").

Then the envoy on Hua-yin road met the Mountain God;
the imperial carriage traveled east
    when the ancestral dragon died.
The beautiful women, bells and drums
    all scattered like the mist,
and this mirror, desolate,
    passed through the market place.
Remember when the emperor
    requisitioned all weapons in the land,
and twelve images of giant men
    were then cast from the bronze!
He must have used the excess metal
    to make this mirror and case;
the God of Oneness peered down from heaven,
    dragons were amazed!
Then Lius came forth as Yings died out—
    how rapidly they fell:
the golden lessons of a thousand autumns
    weighed feather-light to them.
Mirror of Ch'in, in vain they boast
    you coldly image gall:
you do not show the many bones
    of dead men at Great Wall!

                        (Kondō, pp. 181–85)

——Yüan Sung-li: Yüan Fan, a friend of the poet's and the owner of the mirror.

——Hsien-yang Palace: The palace of the emperors of the short-lived Ch'in dynasty (221–206 B.C.).

——Gecko-juice, etc.: It was said that if one fed quantities of cinnabar to a gecko, then pounded it and smeared the juice on a woman's limbs, a red mark would appear which would fade only if she engaged in sexual activity. Also, the Hsien-yang Palace was said to contain a mirror which could reveal the inner organs. If a woman harbored licentious thoughts, her heart would be seen to palpitate rapidly and her gall bladder to swell. The First Emperor of the Ch'in Dynasty would have any woman so discovered executed immediately.

——Ancestral dragon, etc.: According to the *Basic Annals* of the First Emperor of the Ch'in Dynasty as recorded by the great Han historian, Ssu-ma Ch'ien (145–c. 90 B.C.), in the thirty-sixth year of the dynasty (211 B.C.), an envoy from Cheng traveling through Hua-yin met a mountain god who predicted that the "ancestral dragon," i.e., the First Emperor, would die that year. After he died, Li Ssu, the Prime Minister, concealed the fact of his death by secretly placing his corpse in an imperial carriage and carrying on with government business as if nothing had happened.

——Lius, Yings: The imperial surnames of the Han and Ch'in rulers respectively.

TAO-CHI (1642–1707)

IF YÜN SHOU-P'ING (q.v.) is one of the great orthodox painters of the early Ch'ing, Tao-chi is the preeminent "eccentric" master of the period, an innovator expanding the limits of the Chinese visual imagination. As a descendant of the Ming imperial house, he was quite naturally loyal to the memory of the Ming dynasty, although merely two years old at the time of its fall. Tao-chi has attracted a good deal of attention from art historians, and was one of the first Chinese painters to be given a one-man show in modern times *(The Painting of Tao-chi,* at the Museum of Art, University of Michigan, 1967). As a poet, Tao-chi has a quirky obliqueness of expression which can be reminiscent of Wu Wei-yeh or Ch'ien Ch'ien-i (qq.v.) in its indirectness, although not as richly orchestrated. One sometimes suspects the presence of political undertones and allusions which would no longer yield to explication.

Tao-chi is also known by his sobriquet, Shih-t'ao. For more on this poet-painter, consult Richard Edwards, *The Painting of Tao-chi* (catalogue of the exhibition) (Ann Arbor: Museum of Art, University of Michigan, 1967).

A Trip to the Village of the River of White Sand

Blue-green bamboo, white sand, village on the river;
evening breeze among the flowers, water lapping the gate.
As I walk home, the moon is a delicate lady;
no words can describe the fragrance, the serenity
                              in my tea cup.

                                        (Fu Pao-shih, p. 22)

Inscribed On a Painting of a Wu-t'ung Tree by Myself

A wu-t'ung tree a hundred feet tall,
                    half an acre of shade;
each branch, each leaf filled with the heart of autumn.
When will I be able to leave my bones behind
and fly back here on a phoenix
                    to hear the white zither in the moonlight?

                                        (Fu Pao-shih, p. 23)

——Wu-t'ung tree: The Chinese paulownia, associated with the season of autumn and
   considered the only tree on which the phoenix will deign to perch.

Inscribed on My Ink Landscape Painting

From the top of Dragon Gate
              I gaze down at West Lake:
Wu Tzu-hsü's hill, townsman's retreat,
              props me from behind.

A sound of flute wafts on fragrant breeze
              from amongst the lotus:
my soul melts, bit by bit,
              at this scene within a painting.

(Fu Pao-shih, p. 23)

Inscribed on a Painting

The little boat floats by the dock,
              no one rows the oar:
truly this is a quiet spot
              far from the noisy world!
Filling the path, verdant shade,
              I rise now from my nap
and joy to watch the flowing river
              swell with tides of spring.

(Fu Pao-shih, p. 23)

Inscribed on My Large Landscape Hanging Scroll, *Listening to a Waterfall*

Sheer cliff, far mountains,
              blue-green shadows flow;
the wild goose flies off in space,
              the southern sky so vast.
What year will I construct a home
              here, beneath the pines,
and sit to listen to the waterfall,
              cold in summer months?

(Fu Pao-shih, p. 23)

Inscribed on My Little Painting of Plum Blossom and Bamboo

One ring of clear chimes through the evening mist;
the waters ebb, the sands lie flat
        east of the deserted courtyard.
Here, beneath the trees, a lady:
        where did she come from?
Outside the window, a good friend,
        suddenly met again.
Desolate, the country inn,
        no fine brew to drink;
quiet, lonely, the isolated village,
        just this old man is left.
White-haired, let us agree to meet, you and I together;
we'll pour our hearts out, and avoid
        the ordinary flowers.

                        (Fu Pao-shih, p. 24)

Riding a Boat on Wu-ling Stream

At the mouth of Wu-ling Stream,
        petals bright like clouds;
in a boat I follow them,
        more and more inspired.
Then return to my little home—
        the feeling still with me:
brushtip filled with springtime rain
        I paint this flowering peach.

                       (Fu Pao-shih, p. 7)

——Wu-ling Stream: Supposedly the stream lined with flowering peach trees which led the fisherman to his discovery of the lost land, Peach Blossom Spring, in the famous story.

A Trip to Hua-yang Mountain

One peak, stripped sheer,
        another peak circles round;
the shortcut twists and turns
        along the emerald stream.
Inches away, the heavens open
        just above the trees;
writhing, meandering, 10,000 gullies
        rise from your eyebrows!
A flying bridge of natural stone
        leads to misty light;
a man beneath a shoulder-pole
        looks down from bird-paths.
We would explore the source of the stream,
        the deepest spot of all,
but flowing cloud, so vast and vague,
        hides the immortals' altar.

(Treasures, color pl. XLII)

——This and all subsequent poems by Tao-chi are inscribed on surviving paintings by him. See the references in *Treasures* and Edwards for reproductions and further details.

Inscribed on the Wall at the Temple of the Auspicious Talisman

The traveler who wants to stay
        at the Temple of the Talisman
first goes to the hot spring to take a bath.
He washes off completely a hundred ages of dust
and then climbs to the highest peak
        softly chanting poems.

(Edwards, p. 97)

Searching for Herb Brazier and Cinnabar Well, I Also Saw the Waterfall of Singing Strings. Alongside Was the Cliff of the Lord of the Mountain.

Cinnabar Well—I don't know where it is;
Herb Brazier still spits smoke.
In what year did this Stone Tiger arrive
and lie down to listen to the Fall of Singing Strings?

(Edwards, p. 98)

——Herb Brazier, etc.: These are names of famous sights within the Yellow Mountains of Anhui Province.

[Untitled]

The mood comes on—I want to cross Hsi-ling
and so my tiny boat floats in this painting.
Clear ripples, rippling in the breeze
have the power to open up my heart.
What a shame! That traveler on a raft
uselessly traveled to the stars and back.
How much better, the paddle in my hands,
moving, stopping—this is real calm.

(Edwards, p. 106)

——Hsi-ling: An alternate name for West Lake at Hangchou.

The Flower-Rain Terrace

—When I resided in the Ch'in-Huai area, at sunset after people
   had gone home, I would climb to this terrace. Having chanted
   poems, at times I would also paint the spot.

Outside the city, desolate, an ancient terrace;
the story still is told—it once rained flowers here.
Winds whistle through the great gorge,
                   a thread of smoke floats up;
birds accompany reed sails
                   on tall masts as they return.
The ruined temple has a bell,
                   lonely in the dawn;
clear-voiced gibbons, dreamless,
                   cry out in sorrow at night.
Floating clouds I watch disperse
                   here, above my cup;
for some reason, in this land of the immortals
                   I think of the end of the world.

                                            (Edwards, p. 135)

—— Ch'in-huai area: i.e., the city of Nanking and environs.

[Inscribed on *Drunk in the Autumn Woods*]

In just an instant mist and cloud
                   can bring back times gone by:
everywhere, trees all red set fire to the sky!

I ask you, Sir, to get quite drunk
                    beneath my black brushstrokes
and, lying there, watch frosted forests
                    twirl leaves down through the air.

(Edwards, p. 154)

——The painting is reproduced here as Plate 10.

[Untitled]

Bend after bend, the long embankment,
                    lined with fallen flowers;
trees upon the eastern mountain
                    linked with lovely homes.
In one of them, a man opens a window
                    to get a better view;
smiling, he points where breezes ripple
                    the petals on the water.

(Edwards, p. 177)

CHIN NUNG (1687–1764)

TOGETHER WITH Cheng Hsieh (q.v.), Chin Nung was one of the so-called Eight Eccentrics of Yangchou who dominated Chinese painting in the eighteenth century. They were the equal of Tao-chi in eccentricity, but gentler and without the wildness sometimes suggested by Tao-chi's art. Chin Nung perfected a slow-moving, self-consciously archaic "clerk script" *(li-shu)* calligraphy, and a related style of painting for landscapes, plum blossoms, and human figures. In his poetry, he openly refers to supporting himself by selling or exchanging his art works.

Evening Scene at Twin Forests

Like a bolt of silk, the rippled course of this southern river
                bends and turns back.
The distant mountains sink in silence, pressed by the setting sun.
No trace of people—just the sound of passing oars
and a pathway opening among the duck weed plants.

(p. 14)

On Twisting River Is the Old Home of My Father. Now That My Illness Has Eased Up, I Have Written These Six Poems About the Place.

(One poem from the group of six)

I remember when he took me on a trip to this place;
the prefect was a member of our company.
With ten sailboats in the springtime
we covered every part of Lake T'ai-hu.
For thirty miles, the trees on the shore
were as sparse as the hairs of an ox!
We inscribed poems at Great Thunder Mountain,
and searched for mysterious remains from the past.
And even today, in my cold dreams,
I am startled by the roar of the waves.

(pp. 14, 16)

Mooring in the Rain at Sung-ling

Once again, my luggage packed, I'm returning to Wu;
my path lies in the wilds now—I'm like a wild duck!
All night, the sound of rain on my sail, among the reeds—
drop after drop leading my dreams through the rivers and lakes.

(p. 24)

Thirty Poems of Longing for People

(One poem from the group of thirty)

I get so drunk, I could be called the Earl of Dissipation!
Every morning I get dead drunk, forgetting my advanced age.
Sometimes you try to trick me into stopping completely:
you're afraid I'll go to heaven, and become a prisoner
of the Wine Star!

(p. 29)

Written at the End of Master Ho-ching's Collected Works

You never married, never took a job—you went completely astray!
And yet your fame has inspired admiration for centuries.
There are even people here at your burial site,
offering paper money to your soul, caring for the grave,
wearing the hempen cloth of mourning.

(p. 37)

——Master Ho-ching: Lin Pu (967–1028), a major poet of the early Sung dynasty.

Inscribed on the Wall of a Rice Cake Shop

Scallion stands, gruel shops—half are run by ex-scholars!
Here on this thoroughfare, selling rice cakes,
                    is another Philosopher in Hiding!
Tell me—in the cold, flickering light of the oil lamp,
have you managed to finish one chapter
                    of the Kung-yang Commentary?

                                                    (pp. 102–3)

I Have Recently Edited My Unworthy Poems in Four Chapters, Copied Them Out in My Own Hand, and Entrusted Them to My Daughter to Keep. Five Miscellaneous Poems.

(One poem from the group of five)

In the silences between peals of the bell
                    I knit my brow, and think.
As the sun slips away, I chant lines out loud.
Even a single word must come through painstaking effort,
like searching for a golden hook in all the sands
                    of the Ganges.

                                                    (p. 144)

Wearing a Worn-Out Coat

—To the Retired Gentleman Ting at the Riverside

This sheepskin coat may be worn out,
    but it is loved by me!
Over the years, the hairs have fallen out—now
    it is no longer thick.
But in my poverty, I love the old leather,
    and can't throw it away—
old things can be the same as old friends!
Here in this province, there is snow in the ninth month;
the plants all wither and the insects stop their chirping.
When I put on this coat, it doesn't warm me up
    as much as one cup of wine;
my body may not be comfortable, but my heart is full of warmth.
Would it be worth a single cent at the doors of the rich?
Compared to it, regular hemp would be better
    for turning back the wintry breath.
My hands are chapped, and I wish to find
    an "anti-chapping ointment."
How are you doing, bleaching silk there by the river?

(p. 106)

——Last two lines: According to *Chuang Tzu,* ch. 1, a family in Sung had a recipe for making an anti-chapping ointment, but used it only to help them in bleaching silk. A more enterprising man bought this recipe, and sold it to the King of Wu, whose troops used it to defeat the armies of Yüeh in a sea battle (it helped in the handling of their weapons). This man was rewarded with a fief. Here, Chin Nung may be asking Ting for a new coat in an extremely oblique manner. Ting may be Ting Ching (1695–1765), a master of the art of seal-carving and a friend of Chin Nung.

An Inkstone Inscription for the Blind scholar Ho Yung-kuang

This Tzu-hsia of Hsi-ho,
brilliant in classical scholarship:
he may be blind in his eyes
but he is not blind in his heart.

(p. 171)

——Tzu-hsia of Hsi-ho was one of Confucius's best disciples.

I Discuss the Past and Not the Present. What Men of Today Are Worth Discussing? May the Men of the Past Not Blame Me for My Discussion of Them.

(One poem from a group of three)

Who bought a mountain and became a hermit there?
      —Kuo Wen-chü!
Who quit his job because he was afraid of becoming too rich?
      —Wang Hsiu-chih!
These days, where can we find men like these?
The fine moon, the fine breeze—who are they waiting for?

(pp. 208–9)

——Kuo Wen-chü: Kuo Wen of the Chin dynasty, who loved mountains ever since he was a child.

——Wang Hsiu-chih: Son of Wang Tsan; an official under the Liu-Sung and Southern Ch'i dynasties.

Inscribed On a Lichen-Covered Wall in My Hut

(One poem from a group of three)

Three lines of "clerk script" calligraphy—
        reclining waves!
One branch of ink bamboo—
        swept by the wind!
My boy servant takes them to town to barter for rice:
in whose home will I become famous now?

(pp. 209–10)

On New Year's Eve of the Year *Hsin-wei* (1751), Drinking Alone and Sadly Chanting Poems, I Remembered My Aged Wife Who Is Living at Twisting River

(One poem from a group of three)

A traveler, I've been through a thousand changes.
Thinking of home, my insides turn over nine times!
Here in Yangchou they have good local wine:
What a pity that I'm drinking alone!

(p. 211)

CHENG HSIEH (1693–1765)

L IKE CHIN NUNG (q.v.), one of the Eight Eccentrics of
Yangchou, Cheng Hsieh was deeply influenced by Hsü Wei
(q.v.) in his calligraphy and in his highly individual paintings of
bamboo and orchids. Both his paintings and his calligraphy display
a delicate, fluttering, dancelike motion which is instantly identifiable.
Cheng's's poetry is full of humor and a bold searching for unusual
subject matter; there is also a moralizing tendency.

Yangchou

(One poem from a group of four)

The west wind has come again to the "tower of makeup."
Withered grasses reach the horizon, the sunset brings sadness.
Heaps of tiles and rubble—woodcutters sing in the evening.
Layers of chilly clouds—swallows dart through the autumn sky.
The glory lasted a moment; people remember it with nostalgia.
The lamentation has gone on for a thousand years;
                    the waters have stopped flowing!
I wonder—here, beside the overgrown mounds of the graves—
how many farmers' plows have struck hairpins of jade?

(pp. 11–12)

Seven Songs

(Two poems from the group of seven)

1.
Master Cheng is thirty—and doesn't have a job!
He's studied books, practiced swordsmanship—and gotten
                  nowhere!
He would drag his young companions into bars to drink,
and they'd spend their days banging on drums,
                  or blowing into mouth-organs.
This year, his father died, leaving him an inheritance
                  of old books,
but the tattered volumes with torn pages
                  can't be appraised that fast.
Meanwhile, the stove is cold, the firewood has nearly run out,
and the debt collector is beating on the front gate!

Oh, alas! this first song is one of hardship;
I'm rushing through all those books—
            but how can I read them on time?

——Master Cheng: Cheng Hsieh himself.

2.

When I was three years old, my mother passed away,
but it's hard to sever the tender love
            of a child in baby clothes:
I climbed into her bed, and tried to nurse,
            clutching her prone body—
not realizing she was already dead, I kept calling out to her!
Before, when I would cry at night—cry on and on—
my mother, ill as she was, would be wakened by my voice,
and, ill as she was, she'd caress me and whisper to me
            until I'd fallen asleep.
Then the lamp went out, and my mother would cough
            by the chilly window . . .
Alas, This second song is sung at midnight
when perching crows are restless, and branches
            snap from the locust trees in the courtyard.

(pp. 15–16)

Mourning For My Son Jun-erh

(Two poems from a group of five)

1.

At the dawn of your life, you ate gruel,
            and so you grew;
now, full of shame, I face you—my son—
            tears streaming down my face.
Today, I pour you a spoonful of gruel as an offering:
can I call you back, to taste it again?

2.

When a wax candle burns down, ashes are left behind;
when paper money floats away, it merges with the dust.
I seem to recall that the Buddhists speak about Three Births:
my son's karma was hardly used up—perhaps he will return!

(pp. 18–19)

Song of Surfing on the Bore

The boys of Ch'ien-t'ang practice riding the bore:
with firm poles and long oars they stroke and plunge!
One boy, alone, stands on each deck as if cast in iron,
face the color of ashes, his eyes unblinking, fixed.
The bore rolls in like a mountain—they shoot their boats ahead;
masts and sculls flip over sideways
        as the boats stand up on end!
Then—suddenly, they all disappear, without a trace . . .
then reappear on the slow after-waves, a fleet of boats again.
Now the bore has gone down, the waves flow softly,
        the boats follow the gulls.
The boys sing and laugh, the mountains are green,
        the blue water laps the shore.
This is the way we all should go through the troubles of life:
put up with them while they last—calm waters lie ahead.

(pp. 42–43)

——The bore: "An abrupt rise of the tide which breaks in an estuary, rushing violently
up the channel." *(The American College Dictionary)*. In China, the mouth of the Che
River at Hangchou (also known as the Ch'ien-t'ang River at this location) is famous
for this phenomenon.

On A Painting of a Knight-Errant

Snow fills heaven and earth—
where are you going, traveling with your sword?
I want to speak to you of what is in my heart:
let us go together to a wine shop.

(p. 47)

To Chin Nung

With wild hair, you block out your characters.
Deep in the mountains, you engrave your poems.
Don't even mention this man's "bone and marrow"—
who could even imitate his "skin?"

(p. 66)

——Chin Nung (1687–1764; see pp. 421–27): Like Cheng Hsieh, one of the "Eight
Eccentrics of Yang-chou," and a major painter and calligrapher. His calligraphy is
indeed characterized by the blocklike style of the *li-shu* ("clerk script") characters he
writes.

Collecting Antiques

In this age of decadence people love antiques
and willingly submit to deception.
For thousands in cash they buy calligraphies and paintings,
for hundreds they have them remounted.
Old jade tokens missing a corner,
bronze seals decorated with tortoises and dragons;
inkstones made from the tiles of Bronze Sparrow Tower
                    on lacquered tables,

gold lion incense burners on ivory supports;
a cup, a beaker, or any ancient vessel—
they consult old texts to verify inscriptions.
Far and wide they seek and search,
into old age, as if they were obsessed.
Blood relatives sue each other in the courts,
close friends grow suspicious of each other.
These things cost thousands to those who are rich,
but when you're poor—you wouldn't give a rice cake for them.
Now I have here some ancient antiques
which—alas!—the men of our times do not know.
The Eight Trigrams, drawn by Fu Hsi;
the *Appendix* to the *Changes* by King Wen and Confucius;
the *Great Plan*, based on the *Document of Lo River*,
transmitted by Yü of Hsia to Chi of Shang;
East Mountain and the *Seventh Month:*
how variegated in their beauty!
All of these are things of high antiquity,
which appeared in sequence during the Three Dynasties.
They don't cost you a single cent—
your bookshelves are already piled high with them.
And even the least of these treasures
consists of such things as Han Yü's prose
                    or the poems of Li and Tu.
Use them to nourish your virtue and conduct
and you can expect to live for a hundred years.
Use them to regulate the empire,
and the hundred peoples will return to the age of peace.
But people are unwilling to love this true antiquity;
they follow each other in repeating vulgar ways.
The neighbor to the east owns a Hsüan-te incense burner,
the neighbor to the west, a Ch'eng-hua porcelain!

These blind men treasure vulgar things,
they are the "stupid of the lowest class,
who cannot be changed."

(pp. 69–70)

——The Eight Trigrams, etc.: I.e., the Confucian classics, the *Book of Changes, Book of Documents,* and *Book of Songs.*

——Hsüan-te, Ch'eng-hua: Two reign-periods in the Ming dynasty (1426–35, and 1467–87, respectively) famous for their fine ceramics.

——"Stupid of the lowest class:" A quotation from the *Analects* of Confucious (XVII, 3, as translated by James Legge).

A Poem For My Wet Nurse

My wet nurse, surnamed Fei, was a serving woman in the service of my grandmother, Lady Ts'ai. When I was three, I lost my mother, and was subsequently brought up by Fei. At the time, there was a famine, and Fei was working at outside jobs as well as performing her duties at home. Every morning when she got up, she would take me into town with her, and for one cent she would buy a rice cake which she then put into my hand. Only after this did she turn to her jobs. If she happened to get some fish or fruit she would always give me some first, and only then would she herself or her family eat any.

After some years, Fei found it even harder to make ends meet, so her husband decided they should go elsewhere. Fei did not dare say anything, but the signs of tears could always be made out on her face. Every day, she continued to take my grandmother's old clothes and wash and mend them, and to draw water with which she filled our storage jars and buckets. She also purchased the firewood—several tens of bundles—which she piled beneath the stove. But after a few days, she did in fact leave. That morning

I went into her room. It was desolate and empty, except for a broken bed and table lying in disorder. The stove was still warm, and there was a bowl of rice and one of vegetables stored within a cauldron. It was these that she usually served me from. I wept bitterly and couldn't bear to eat them.

Three years later, she came back, and again served my grandmother and helped to raise me even more warmly than before. Thirty-four years later, she died at the age of seventy-five.

The year after Fei returned, her own son Chün received the official posts of Inspector of River Works *(Ts'ao-chiang)* and Provincial Secretary Stationed in the Capital *(T'i-t'ang)*, and he repeatedly offered to have his mother come and live with him at his expense. But she never went, because of her feelings for my grandmother and for me. When I finally obtained my official *chin-shih* degree, she was very happy, and said, "The young master I cared for as wet nurse has become famous, and my own son is an official of the eighth rank—what more need I concern myself about?" And indeed, she had no further worries for the rest of her life.

I felt such love for you,
you were more than a wet nurse to me!
But I regret that my success came so late,
and my shame before you lasted so long.
The road to the Yellow Springs is long and difficult,
and I am old now, unseemly with my white hair.
I have an official's salary now,
but it cannot compare with that single rice cake
in my hand!

(pp. 79–81)

The Girl from Ch'ang-kan

The girl from Ch'ang-kan is just fourteen years old:
on a spring ramble, she comes upon a temple
                            from the Southern Dynasties.
With her elegant, soft hairdo she bows slowly to Buddha,
lowers her head—and drops a gold hairpin to the ground!
A young man who visits the temple that day
picks up the hairpin with its inlay of kingfisher.
He takes it home with him, not knowing whose it is,
and stands unhappily, smelling its fragrant odor
                            again and again.

                                                        (pp. 81–82)

The "Contest Snake"

In the Yüeh region (Kuangtung and Kuanghsi), there is a snake
which likes to have contests with people to see who is longer or
taller. If the snake is longer than the person is tall, he eats the
person. If not, he kills himself. But the snake will always let the
person see him face to face—he does not compete in secret. Some
people who travel through the mountains thrust their umbrellas
straight up above their heads when they encounter the snake, so
the snake loses and dies.

You like to have contests of size with people,
emerging from forests to cut them off
                            on mountain roads.
But although you may die, you leave behind a name for honesty:
you never compete behind people's backs.

                                                        (p. 83)

Twenty-eight Characters Sent to Tung-ts'un on the Subject of the Poems He Burned

I hear that you have burned ten thousand of your poems—
all of them, not a single one left!
Now I know that I—the Plank Bridge Recluse—
　　　　　　　do much too much talking:
when this poem reaches you, if it bothers you
　　　　　　　—please, just burn it right up.

(p. 95)

—— Tung-ts'un: Possibly the poet Wang Ming-lei, from Fan-yü in Kuangtung.

"Mother-in-law is Cruel!"

An old poem says, " 'Mother-in-law is cruel?' 'Mother-in-law is cruel?' No, it's not that she's cruel, just that my fate is bad!" This can be said to be the height of loyalty, and it captures the traditional purport of the Three Hundred Poems. But the mother-in-laws do not appear to repent of their ways, so I have written this poem to describe in detail what the daughter-in-law's life is like, in the hope that it will act as an exhortation.

A young girl, only eleven,
leaves home to serve her in-laws.
How could she know how it feels to be a wife?
It's like calling her elder brother, "Husband."
The two young people feel bashful with each other;
they try to speak, but can only mumble.
Father-in-law sends her to the women's quarters
to embroider some new ornaments.

Mother-in-law gives her all kinds of awful jobs,
and sends her to the kitchen, knife in hand.
She tries dicing meat, but can't cut perfect cubes:
instead, she serves up ugly chunks on the tray.
She tries making soup, but gets the spicing wrong,
failing to distinguish "sour" and "hot."
Cutting firewood, she tears her soft hands;
tending the fires, the skin on her fingers
                                        wrinkles and dries.
Father-in-law says, "She's still young—
we must be patient in teaching her."
Mother-in-law says, "If she can't be taught when young,
who'll be able to handle her when she's grown up?
Haughty and proud, she'll take advantage of us
                                        when we're old and decrepit.
Arrogant and lewd, she'll drive our son to his knees!"
So today, she curses and scolds her,
and the next day has her whipped and beaten.
After five days of this, the girl has no untorn clothes
                                        to wear;
after ten days, even her skin is completely torn.
Facing the wall, she moans and weeps,
with sounds of sobbing and bitter sighs.
Mother-in-law says, "You're casting spells!
Bring the stick! Bring the knife and saw!
Your flesh can still be cut—
you're pretty chubby, not too skinny at all!
You still have hair on your head—
we'll pull it all out so your head looks like a gourd!
I can't live in the same life as you,
if you live, then my life is done!"
The old witch glares in anger
as if she's about to slaughter her.

And the husband?—He watches a while,
then joins in and shouts, "Have you no shame?"
Father-in-law tries to calm down his wife,
and gets yelled at himself: "You stupid old slave!"
The neighbors try to find out what's going on,
and they're yelled at too: "None of your business!"
Oh, this poor, poor girl from an impoverished family:
why doesn't she just jump into the river?
She can become a meal for the fish and turtles,
and escape this terrible suffering.
Oh, how cruel of heaven to allow this evil!
and to hear nothing of her cries.
A girl who becomes a young wife in this world
will suffer pain and unjust accusation.
Better to be a cow, a sheep or a pig:
you eat your fill—then one cut of the knife ends it all.
When her parents visit,
she wipes her tears and pretends that she is happy.
When her brothers visit,
she bears the pain, and says, "Mother-in-law is exhausted."
Her scars she covers with tattered clothes,
her bald head she explains as illness.
If she said a single word against mother-in-law
her life would end in a minute.

(pp. 141–44)

———The title of the poem, *ku-e* in Chinese, is said to have been the sound of the cry of a
certain water bird. This also happens to be the sound of the words, "Mother-in-law
is cruel" in Chinese. The Sung poet Su Shih (1037–1101) has a poem on this bird in
which he says that it was believed to be the spirit of a daughter-in-law tormented to
death by her mother-in-law. Cheng Hsieh in his introduction refers to this work as
an "old poem" and quotes from it.

YÜAN MEI (1716–98)

A RTHUR WALEY'S fine book, *Yüan Mei: Eighteenth Century Chinese Poet* (New York: Macmillan, 1956; later reprints by Grove Press and Stanford University Press), was for years virtually the only western-language book on a single poet of the later period, and remains one of a tiny handful of volumes in this field. Waley's choice of Yüan Mei was inspired—he is beyond doubt one of the most attractive of the later poets, a latter-day Po Chü-i who combines humor with affection for the details of everyday life. His *Sui-yüan shih-hua (Comments on Poetry from the Sui Garden)* is one of the best compilations of poetic criticism from the later period, a veritable treasure-trove of insightful discussions of poems and poets.

On the Way to Pa-ling

From Lake Tung-t'ing we travel west
        to the Shrine of the Goddess;
here to comfort weary travelers
        are women with painted brows.
The mountain town is desolate,
        shops close at early hours;
the fortress tower's light still far,
        we're late to moor our boat.
The dialect here I do not speak—
        I'll hire interpreters;
such strange birds—I don't know their names,
        ashamed as a scholar of the *Odes*.
How rare to find a boatman
        who understands my heart:
each time I open the cabin window
        there's a branch of blossom on shore.

                              (p. 1)

——Ashamed, etc.: One of the benefits to be derived from studying the classic *Shih ching* ("Odes"), according to instructions by Confucius to his disciples, is that the reader learns the names of animals and birds.

Returning Home

The view from far: beside the gate
        they've set up a colored pole;
the whole family comes out to greet me
        and ask me how I am.
Everyone's glad I've come home early
        from the Immortal Park;
they tell me it was difficult
        to get letters from Ch'ang-an.

On the wall, my degree announcement,
                gold pale from the rain;
outside the window, plums and willows,
                chilled by the spring air.
So cute and brash, my little sister
                admires her brother's glory:
she asks if I will let her have
                my court robe to try on.

(p. 6)

Fog at Liang-hsiang

No rain, and yet my saddle is damp,
and so I know we're traveling in fog.
Morning blossoms—hard to tell their colors;
river water—only hear the sound.
The man beside me seems miles away;
all day the sky is as before the dawn.
The road ahead has always been a dream:
why insist on seeing it all clear?

(p. 9)

The Next Day the Fog Was Even Worse

All night, the camel-back saddle-cloth was invisible;
sketched here is a picture of utter nothingness.
At this time, should the immortals
                look down from above,
would they be able to tell
                if we were down here in this world?

(p. 9)

Miscellaneous Feelings in the Sui Garden

1.

Joy and anger are not caused by outside things:
they simply happen to arise in the heart.
Rising and falling are not matters of fate:
one simply happens to encounter them.
Reading a book and finding nothing there,
I drop the volume, get up, and take a walk.
I think I'll go to the bamboo grove
where I can listen to the springtime water flow.

2.

Let them knock at the bramble gate—
the host is in a dream!
Startled awake, I search for my socks;
I must have lost them east of the thatched hut.
At night, with nothing on my mind,
in dream I watched the bamboo growing tall.
Should guests arrive now at my garden,
barefoot I will see them off.

3.

Classics, Histories, Philosophers, Belles-Lettres:
these the four branches of literature.
Pavilions I have built, libraries—
one for each kind in four different spots.
In each one I have placed an inkstone
as well as several brushes to write.
Mornings I rise, wash my face,
then let my feet lead me where they will.
Circulating among all four,
happily I pass the day's twelve hours.

4.

When they hear me stop reading out loud,
the farmers come from all around.
The healthy ones shoulder hoe and plow,
the fragile ones wear their hempen shoes.
The happy ones bring piles of bamboo mats,
the tired ones have bundled fire wood.
They invite me to sit with them under the trees:
we all open our hearts to each other!
"This year we've suffered from wind and rain,
and still can't plant good sprouts.
We hear you chanting out loud from books:
could it be you prepare for exams?"
I love these people, their true, sincere nature,
and the way they speak, like little children!
Each one drinks a cup of wine
and we lie in a heap on the moss.

5.

Do not mock me for building this tower tall:
of course a tower should be tall!
If you approach from three miles away,
already I'll see you from here.
When you visit, come not in a carriage:
the carriage's racket will terrify my birds.
And when you visit, don't come on a horse:
the horse's teeth will decimate my grass.
Also, when you visit, please, don't come at dawn:
we mountain folk hate to rise too early.
And when you visit, don't wait until dusk:
by then the flowers will all have withered away.

6.

The Master of Sui Garden in the past
first built buildings here beside these hills.
Terraces, pavilions summoned clouds and mist;
wine cups glittered in the candlelight.
The old men here all say to me
that this Master was no vulgar man.
He took this garden and passed it on—to whom?
How could he know it would be me!
Long, long the thirty years;
and now I come, to help the flowers and bamboo.
"Follow Garden": the meaning timely now;
no need to change the garden's name at all.
Consider my present-day happiness
continuation of the Master's joy.
Does it really just all "pass away"?
Past and present, still the same chess game!
And who will follow after I have left?
I ask the mountain, but it does not say.

(pp. 18–19)

——"Follow Garden": The meaning of the name of the garden, *Sui yüan,* in Chinese.

Ma-wei

Don't sing *The Song of Everlasting Sorrow*
       written in days gone by:
here too, in the world of mortals,
       Milky Ways keep lovers apart.
In Shih-hao Village the man and wife
       when they said goodbye

wept more tears than ever were wept
      in the Palace of Long Life.

                                                (p. 26)

———In this poem, Yüan Mei interweaves references to two famous narrative poems of the
    T'ang dynasty: *The Song of Everlasting Sorrow* by Po Chüi (772–846), which tells the
    story of Emperor Hsüan-tsung's ill-fated infatuation with his concubine, Yang Kuei-
    fei (he was compelled to execute her at Ma-wei to placate his angry troops), and *The
    Sheriff of Shih-hao Village* by Tu Fu (712–770), which relates how an old woman
    volunteered for military service to protect her husband from being drafted. Perhaps
    the idea is that the sufferings of lovers in romantic stories cannot compare with the
    actual sufferings of ordinary people under the pressure of cruel governmental policy.

Words from the Goblet of Wisdom

I often read the writings of the sages
and now I understand enlightened rule.
"Enrich them and teach them," we are told,
yet not a word on how it's to be done!
"Sufficient arms and sufficient food";
but no details listed here at all.
Yet if we wish to be like Eastern Chou,
in just one year we could do it now.
The "well-field system" spoken of in schools:
not one word of it need bother us at all.
When T'ang and Yü instructed Kao and K'uei,
"Be dignified," they said, two words alone!
So great, the hearts of these sage men:
Yao and Shun and Confucius as well.
We are simply tasked with emulation;
measures taken will follow naturally.
As to whether it is possible,
that depends on how we act ourselves.
When Mencius discusses the government of kings
already we feel a buzzing in our ears.

Later scholars were even wordier,
so pedantic with their piles of books.
The "Ever-Stable Granary" plan sounds great,
but Eastern Han saw troubles burgeon forth.
"Chariot Warfare" surely was the best,
yet General T'ao was wiped out on the field.
People at peace—but government grew;
if people are to live, statutes must first die!
No surprise that the spirit of the Three Golden Ages
long ago came to a grinding halt.

(pp. 26–27)

——The poet's message is that the ancients achieved a harmonious society by stressing self-cultivation, rather than mechanisms for implementing agricultural or military policy: moral tone rather than governmental action. This is essentially classical Confucianism.

Things Seen on Spring Days

Spring's second month,
  the lovely peach trees
    bloom and block the path;
with a cane of bamboo wood
    I come through, treading moss.
Walking mountains, most I love
    the sudden gusts of wind:
flower petals strike my face
    like drops of falling rain.

(pp. 34–35)

Things Seen

Apricot about to fade, raindrops quiet now;
filling the paths, patches of moss,
                the green has stained my clothes.
The wind is strong—I cannot get the little window shut:
flower petals and my poems
                go flying through the air.

(p. 35)

Writing My Feelings

1.

I had no desire for life—
suddenly, I was born in the world!
Just as I learned to love life—
suddenly, I found death drawing near.
Not yet born or already dead:
they both feel just about the same.
So if you're dissatisfied here in this world
you just need to wait around a while.

2.

Birds and animals end up cooked as food
simply because they know nothing.
Parrots, however, because they can speak words
are prized and pampered by men.
Thus a man who does not want to learn
is like a zombie walking in a daze.
So why not exercise a tiny bit of effort
and let your mind sink into books and poems?

(p. 35)

Five Poems on Returning to Hangchou

1.

I gaze at this, my hometown,
as if reentering a former life.
So vague and formless, everything has changed,
yet clear, detailed the dream remains.
I've been away for forty years
and so there's no roof to shelter me.
For now I rent a cell
                in an old monk's cloister;
a place to stay, dare I complain it's small?
Children cluster round to stare—
they think I'm a visitor from another world.
And I do feel sad and alone,
and see myself as a visitor here.
In the morning I go out, spirits bright,
but come back in the evening unbearably lonely.
A guttering lamp glimmers from the wall,
a northerly wind howls outside the window.

2.

Of my flesh and blood, only one remains,
my sister, ten years older than me.
I go to see her, knocking at her door;
white hair hangs about her face.
When she hears the sound and knows her brother's here
she comes out to greet me, in fine spirits.
She speaks many words with much self-awareness,
sitting upright, instructs me forcefully.

And we agree that the next day
together we will visit mother's tomb.
In years past, to wait upon
           her compassionate visage
there were only my sister and myself.
In the morning, we pour the wine libation,
not knowing if her soul can drink or not.
Sister is a woman in her seventies,
and I—the brother—have come a thousand miles.
Who will be able to visit here again?
Unbearable, the sadness that we feel.

3.

One morning I call for a sedan-chair man;
his face shows amazement as he looks at me.
"Can it not be possible
that you and I have met once in this life?"
The bearer rubs his eyes,
looks again, and sighs again.
He says that when I was first married
it was he who pushed the marriage car!
Now that scholar, so young and handsome,
has changed appearance like the morning mist.
How is it that the second time we meet
I should have become so very ancient?
Before the bearer has finished talking
a secret pain is born in my heart:
It's like meeting the old man
         of the T'ien-pao era
to hear tell again of the Yellow Millet Dream!

——The last two lines allude to the famous story of a man who dreamed an entire lifetime
of events while his millet-gruel was being warmed up.

4.

Of all the famous Hangchou sights
everyone says that West Lake is the best.
I happen to have come in a dry winter
when West Lake is smaller than before.
Even brisk winds do not raise waves;
mudbanks emerge, covered with reeds.
But still I go floating in a little boat,
to view the scene and clarify my mind.
Hills and gullies—I recognize the new and old;
pavilions and terraces—classify the skillful and clumsy.
Clouds congeal, it darkens in broad daylight;
the trees all shed, the mountain is desolate.
I laugh at myself for being such a fool;
to be so late in coming for the view!
What I've gotten is lots of cold wind:
there's very little inspiration now.

5.

The bird in flight parts from the old wood,
chirps and cries as if full of pain.
The nomad horse longs for his old trough,
neighs sadly, his feet not surging forth.
And here I am, in my parents' land;
it's not that I didn't want to come before!
But I was kept at White Gate for so long
that it was hard to find a time to come.
Now I take advantage of this moment:
I could not bear to miss the slightest chance.
People that I only half knew once
knock at the door to say hello.
The earth I trod on when I was a boy:
each spot bears the imprint of my shoes!
Daylight ends, I light the evening candle;
I glance back each step of the way.
People ask, "So how are you doing?"
I just smile, and point at my white hair.

(pp. 61–62)

Moments of Fulfillment—Writing Down Miscellaneous Quatrains

1.

Three magnolias, identical,
            planted at one time:
two of them wither and fade away,
            one of them blossoms and grows.
If plants and trees so clearly differ
            amongst themselves like this,
how much truer must it be
            of people in this world?

2.

As I grow old, and weaker grow my eyes,
returning yellows and changing greens
            I barely recognize.
Falling petals float and dance
            in dangling spider webs:
And I see them mistakenly as flying butterflies.

3.

My whole family floats out on the lake
            in a little boat,
my younger sister raises sail,
            my elder sister steers.
Ecstatic, my little son, both hands trembling now:
as he tugs his fishing line
            a single shrimp jumps out.

4.

Do not say that time once gone can never be returned!
The feelings, scenes of youthful years
            are captured in our poems.
Fragments of lamplight, memories of wine,
            dreams of nights in spring:
every time you chant a poem
            again they're conjured up.

(p. 69)

Miscellaneous Poems on Growing Old

1.

I write characters in lamplight,
           dots and strokes all coarse;
I climb the stairs very slowly—
           someone must prop me up.
My remaining teeth remind me
           of the general at Liao City:
alone he guarded the empty town—
           the troops had all withdrawn.

2.

Long robes or short,
           wide or narrow hats:
the changes of these thirty years
           have been ridiculous!
Luckily I went on wearing
           the same clothes as before
and now again my ancient fashions
           are considerd à la mode!

3.

Old habits it seems cannot be swept away:
beneath my lamp I go on studying whenever there's leisure time.
I copy things, takes notes on them,
           forget them right away
yet still remember all the books
           I studied as a child.

4.

After half a minute of conversation
            I feel short of breath;
before I've walked three steps outside
            I want to call a carriage.
All that's left are my two eyes,
            muddled as they are:
they long to see the flowers
            in this foggy world of ours.

                                                        (p. 77)

Ballad of Peach Blossom Spring

—with preface

Starting with [T'ao] Yüan-ming, no fewer than ten or so old poets
wrote poems about the Peach Blossom Spring at Wu-ling. But
poems about the Peach Blossom Spring at T'ien-t'ai Mountain have
been lacking. I have visited the place, and now supply the poem.

T'ien-t'ai Mountain is tall,
            thousands and thousands of feet!
And in the mountain are secret caves
            concealing the immortals.
They say that in the Han dynasty,
            two men—Liu and Juan—
came to the highest peak of this mountain
            to gather medicinal herbs.
They passed peach trees and more peach trees,
            crossed stream after stream,
the blossoms reflected in the water,
            clouds of misty red.

They glanced around—no other men,
        but suddenly, a sound:
a pair of women, lustrous jade,
        came towards them through the mist.
Blowing breath like orchid fragrance,
        they spoke to those two men:
"Before you got here, gentlemen,
        we knew you would arrive!"
On golden trays they offered them
        ambrosia of sesame
and jeweled leaves on which were written
        poems of nuptial bliss.
Who would be groom? Who be the bride?
        Who be married to whom?
They opened the mandarin-duck tablets
        and all was written there.
They only sensed that days grew long
        high up in the mountains;
they did not realize that down below
        people were growing old.
After years in that immortal realm
        they remembered the human sphere,
and thought of exchanging the world of white clouds
        for the world of red dust below.
Alas, the moment this vulgar thought
        was born within their minds
the line was clearly drawn between
        the human world and heaven.
The women tried to keep them there
        but the young men would not stay,
so the women escorted them as far
        as the mountain's peak.

A whinnying snort upon the wind,
        their piebald horses neighed;
looking back, they still could glimpse
        the women's lovely forms.
Home again, they knocked once more
        upon the bramble gates;
how could they have known—as oceans turn to land—
        that everything had changed?
Their spouses from the previous year
        they remembered very well,
but grandsons here in the seventh generation
        they did not know at all.
The two men looked at each other,
        and felt confused and scared;
they were regretful now that they
        so lightly left that place.
Their links of fate with the immortals
        no one here understood,
though they did invite their neighbors over
        and told them of it all.
To find the immortals beyond this world
        they set out once again
and for thousands of generations
        disappeared
            into the setting sun.
Nor do we know if in the end
        they rejoined immortal mates;
the peach blossom trees tell nothing—
        they only put forth blossoms.

                                      (pp. 80–81)

——T'ao Yüan-ming: T'ao Ch'ien (365–427), the great poet and author of the original
    poem and account on the hidden land of Peach Blossom Spring.

Rough Ridge

My servant wakes at break of dawn,
ties on sandals and comes to say,
"Today the road ahead is hard—
that ridge up there is known as 'Rough.'"
And sure enough that stretch of half a mile
takes half a day of trudging along.
We twist left, and turn back to the right;
above, sharp peaks, below the fall is sheer.
If not a conch, crawling round a spiral,
we are a snail inching through a hall.
Twisting, turning, as if in prostration;
bending, writhing, dazed we'll lose our way!
At first unhappy, but later rather glad;
at first quite frightened, later with a smile.
Crossing mountains is like reading books:
you must go on a while before it gets good.
And it is also like making friendships:
how can you suddenly have total trust?
Although I make apologies to Master Ching,
this place reminds me of his personality!
For now, I'll follow Ch'ang-li's example:
be thankful for short rests, don't rush ahead!

(p 81)

——Master Ching and Ch'ang-li: The major poets and political figures, Wang An-shih (1021–86) and Han Yü (768–824). The last four lines may refer either to the personalities or the poetic styles of the two men.

Rains Pass

Rains pass, the mountains' face is washed;
clouds gather, the mountains enter dreams.
Clouds and rain come and go like this,
and yet the mountains never once have moved.

(p. 103)

Flying Bells

What place have the bells come flying from?
They hang in mid-air like green roof-tiles.
As if on purpose, avoiding being rung
they willingly stay silent through the years.

(p. 103)

——Flying Bells: Undoubtedly the name of a natural rock formation of some sort.

I Know Inside . . .

The age of seventy is gone,
        and now four springtimes more;
I know inside that I no longer
        have my former spirit.
Guests—I invite men of my age
        since I can talk to them;
poems—afraid of senility,
        I work even harder on them.

My books and paintings—
      I never tire
         of putting them in order;
my pavilions and terraces—
      I renovate them, have them all rebuilt.
It's like chess pieces on a board,
      the game drawn to a close:
you gather them and get things ready
      for the next man's game.

                 (p. 109)

In Late Spring of the Year *Keng-hsü* (1790), I Stayed at the Sun Family's Gemstone Mountain Villa at West Lake. Before Leaving, I Wrote These Poems as Mementos.

I.
Once again to see West Lake!
      I open my mouth and laugh,
which makes the birds and fishes here
      startled and amazed:
"Look! That geezer with white hair
      covering his head
said he'd never come again,
      and yet he is right here!"

2.
The peonies below the stairs
                    are still there, fading red;
the willow trees beside the pavilion
                    sway in the blue air.
Monocolor, lake like glass,
                    spread out for ten miles:
as soon as I am out the door,
                    I am a fisherman.

3.
The old house from my childhood,
                    west of the woodplank bridge:
again I visit this scene of the past,
                    even the dream confused.
The one thing left, beside the window,
                    the red-bark cassia tree:
it sees me and it smiles with joy,
                    it sees me and it weeps.

                                        (p. III)

Night of the Fifteenth, Second Month

"Dark fragrance, sparse shadows,"
                    east of the zigzag balustrade:
a thousand trees of flowering plum,
                    a single old man.
White hair like white blossoms,
                    white blossoms like snow;
late at night, in the moonlight,
                    it's hard to tell the difference.

                                        (p. 148)

——"Dark fragrance," etc.: A well-known passage from a famous poem on plum blossoms
    by Lin Pu (967–1028).

Busy

The flowers need irrigation,
            the cranes need food to eat:
digging pools and piling rocks,
            "control and regulate."
Hermit Ch'ao and Hermit Yu
            caring for the garden
end up being just as busy
            as Ministers Kao and K'uei.

(p. 148)

——"Control and regulate": a passage from the classic, *Shang shu (The Book of Documents)*.

Finding Serenity

1.

This spring, the sky is leaking,
            clouds hang thick and heavy;
we'll have one day of deceptive clearing,
            then ten days of cloud.
Tree after tree of crab-apple flowers,
            weeping tears of red:
they seem to be lamenting to us,
            "This rain is hard to take!"

2.

In old age, life's affairs
            are supposed to leave one at peace;
how could I foresee that every morning
            as soon as I wake, there's grief?
Requests for inscriptions, calls for forewords,
            poems to be written on paintings:
busy as ever in the world of men,
            I coldly meet their requests.

3.

Setting brush to paper has always been hard
                because I want perfection:
each poem I'll change a thousand times
                before I am content.
The matron it seems continues to act
                like an adolescent girl—
until her hair is perfectly combed
                no one's allowed to look.

4.

In snow and mud the goose leaves prints
                then flies off hurriedly:
catching sight, it's hard to keep
                my old eyes from reddening.
A letter from my family, written sixty years past,
suddenly falls floating from the pages of my book.

5.

Become an immortal? Become a Buddha?
                —It's all so hard to tell!
I'll just go and transform again
                in the Creator's furnace.
But if I do appear before the Emperor of Jade,
I'll ask, "Now, really, beyond the sky,
                is there another sky?"

(pp. 117–18)

Arriving at Hangchou

Two years now since I last came
          to visit at West Lake;
I have returned, the scenery
          is lovelier than ever.
Mulberry leaves, stripped from branches,
          green and soaked in rain;
wild vegetables with yellow flowers
          reach to the horizon.
In deserted temples, monks no longer
          sound the bells and chimes;
above the tombs of families,
          smoke from paper cash.
The lake's surface is like a mirror,
          my hair is white as snow;
reflected in the water,
          my life is clearly seen.

(p. 122)

On the Twenty-First Day of the Fifth Month, I Reached Home

I return from my second T'ien-t'ai trip:
again, no seven hundred years have gone by!
Meeting me at the door, my wife laughs:
"I guess you didn't become an immortal!"

(p. 123)

——The poem wittily refers to the young men, Liu and Juan, who did encounter the immortals on Mount T'ien-t'ai and remained there for seven hundred years. See the poet's *Ballad of Peach Blossom Spring* (pp. 454–56).

Happy About Being Old

1.

My elder sister stays by my side;
soon she will celebrate her hundredth birthday.
My old wife too is eighty years old,
and still lifts the tray when she serves.
My servants all have heads of white hair—
frost and snow mottle their temples.
People say, "This place is the Land of the Geezers!"
For me, it's the lost paradise of Emperor Fu-hsi.
And then there are others who want to have long life;
they bring in their children, and beg for a favor:
they want me to rub the childrens' heads with my hand—
they think it will bring them good luck!
Whenever I go out, in any direction,
people come running around for a look.
They seem to think that seeing me face to face
is better than meeting an immortal.
As for me, I just laugh out loud:
"There could be money in this business of being old!"

2.

When I was born, I cried myself;
when I die, others will cry.
When I cried, others were happy;
when others cry, I too should feel joy.
"Alas, it passes away so fast!"
The windblown wheel, rolling like a carriage.
They change the torch, but not the fire:
the later flame is still the older flame.

How laughable, the people of this world,
frantically making offerings to Buddha and immortals!
Spiritual alchemy just exhausts the body,
and bowing in worship hurts your head.
In the end, all return to the vastness,
like wind whose form never can be grasped.
Indeed, when called
          that is when I'll go;
with a smile, I follow with the crowd.

(pp. 140–41)

——"Alas," etc.: A lamentation uttered by Confucius upon viewing a swift-flowing
stream.

LIU E (1857–1909)

L IU E is famous as the author of *The Travels of Lao Ts'an,* at once the last great traditional novel in the history of Chinese fiction, and the first in which modern elements appear. The publication in 1980 by the Ch'i-Lu Publishing House in Chi-nan (Jinan), Shantung province, of a small MS of Liu's poetry which had been kept by his descendants establishes him as possibly the last truly great practitioner of traditional *shih* poetry. (Political events rendered earlier publication impracticable or impossible.) *The Travels of Lao Ts'an* had contained some skillful poetry by Liu, although the needs of the narrrative—especially the visit to the Yellow Dragon in the central chapters—made it necessary for much of that poetry to be obscure and riddlelike. In the poems of the MS, many of which were written during two trips Liu made to Japan and Korea in the spring and again in the fall of 1906, a simpler and yet more profound poetic voice emerges. For more on Liu, consult Liu T'ieh-yün (Liu E), *The Travels of Lao Ts'an,* translated by Harold Shadick (Ithaca: Cornell University Press, 1952).

I Remember

I remember when we made our first promises of love—
behind a door-curtain shadowed with blossoms
                    you played the zither for me.
We only wanted the candle to drip and drip with silver wax,
and paid the water clock no heed as it sounded hour after hour!
You would throw open the lattice shades
                    to let in the chattering swallows,
or put aside your music
                    to hear the orioles sing.
Hand in hand we didn't hope for titles or high station,
only to pass through this life together perched on the same branch.

(pp. 5–6)

Poem on Falling Leaves

Falling leaves leave the trees
float and flutter with the wind.
A traveler with no place of my own,
my sorrow is the same as these.
But think of how the falling leaves
are used for kindling in the valleys
to light the cooking fires there
and feed the hungry people.
They are nothing but the leavings of trees,
and yet they have at least this virtue.
Oh, oh, it seems that I
must be more useless than a falling leaf.

(pp. 44–45)

——In the original text, this poem is primarily written in the archaic meter of four
    characters per line, characteristic of the ancient classic, the *Book of Songs*.

On the Twenty-fourth: Improvisations

I.

Beautiful women—we've vowed to be lovers!
famous mountains—I've climbed up most of them.
How many really joyful things are there in my life?
Number one is romance, after that comes travel.

2.

Academics? Politics? I've nothing to do with them!
Still less have I come for commerce or business!
"Well then, may we inquire what *is* your purpose here?"
Half to travel to beautiful places,
            half to see women like flowers!

(p. 32)

A Teahouse at Hoshioka

A girl in poor clothes, her skin lustrous as jade:
the scenery here in Hoshioka is really wonderful!
Tonight there are no intoxicating songs or sensuous dances,
only this woman of noble nature, discussing poetry.

(p. 35)

Boiling Falls

Maple leaves fill the emerald mountain,
leaf after leaf of brilliant flame!
The Milky Way—when did it spill from the sky
and fall to earth in this place?
She seems to be a woman warrior,
full of power, but sensuous as well!
She spits out vapors into rainbows;
heavy with blossoms, her cloudy hairdo falls.
Spray and foam sprinkled on our whiskers,
we sit on rocks by the steam.
And who is the most deeply moved of all?
—This "China-guy" right here!

(p. 38)

New Year's Eve

The north wind blows, cracking the earth,
in sadness, seeing off the old year.
The servant announces we're out of rice,
and a creditor has come, asking for money.
A hungry crow caws in evening snow;
a wild goose cuts through cold mist.
This is the way my life is now:
others are even worse off.

(p. 11)

On the Night of the Sixteenth of the Eight Month: Watching the Moon from the Deck of the Ship, Aimo-maru, in the Black Water Sea

I.

In the sky, not a sliver of cloud.
On earth, not a speck of dust.
The water is blacker than ink,
the moon more brilliant than silver.

2.

The waves thrust up and sink,
the boat races like a thoroughbred.
Will Master Ch'eng-lien ever come?
I too am a man whose heart has been transformed.

(p. 35)

——Master Ch'eng-lien: According to the text, *Explanations of the Titles of Old Yüeh-fu Songs,* attributed to Wu Ching (670–749), "Po-ya studied the *ch'in*-zither with Master Ch'eng-lien. After three years, he had mastered the instrument. But when it came to quieting the spirit and concentrating the heart, he still had not reached the goal. Ch'eng-lien said, 'My own master, Fang Tzu-ch'un, lives in the eastern sea. He can transform a man's heart.' He then led Po-ya to the P'eng-lai Isles of the Blest, and parted from him, saying, 'I'm going to find the Master.' With this, he punted his boat away, and after ten days had still not returned. Left behind on the island, all Po-ya could hear was the slapping and crashing sound of the waves, the deep silence of the woods, the sad cries of the birds. With a long sigh, he said, 'So, Master, you have transformed my heart after all!' Whereupon he played the zither and sang. When the song was done, Ch'eng-lien, punting his boat as before, suddenly returned. Po Ya later became the supreme zither player of the world."

Liu E, with his deceptively simple allusion to this parable of artistic initiation, intimates that his trip to the "eastern sea," like that of Po-ya, was a step on the path to artistic maturity. But unlike Po-ya, whose newly perfected art was implicitly acknowledged in the return of Master Ch'eng-lien, Liu E still awaits some acknowledgement of his own achievement.

Poems for Yukiko of Tamba

I.

Last year, with jade hands you offered cups of tea
boiled with snow brushed from the petals of plum blossoms!
"I'll recite fine poems for you, and serve you fine tea:
you'll remember forever the fifth house on West Bank!"

2.

"Next year you must come again
              and taste our tea once more
when the whole mountain is covered, front and back,
              with blossoming cherry trees.
Please write a letter and let me know
              when you'll be getting here—
I'll take you myself to pay a visit
              to Miss Imamura, the geisha of them all!"

(p. 39)

Pleasures of Shinbashi

Entertained by song and dance here in this wine pavilion,
truly a palace of paradise where the soul melts completely away!
Having mastered all the "postures of joy" the Buddhists talk about,
in one spring evening, twenty-five cases
              of perfect enlightenment!

(p. 33)

——Shinbashi: Refers here to one of the pleasure quarters where Liu E seems to have
spent much of his time in Japan.

The House of Red Leaves

In the House of Red Leaves are the most beautiful dances:
swirling snowflakes, twirling winds, in time
                                       to the beat of the drum!
Filling the air, frosty maple leaves flutter down
                                       before our wine cups,
as if a goddess were scattering blossoms,
                                       a rainfall of red from the sky.

(p. 34)

On the Road to Pyongyang—An Improvisation

A thousand miles of pure river water,
far, far, the pavilion for seeing off guests.
Is this the place where soldiers died for their country?
The local gods have long since lost their power.
In rain can be heard the sound of weeping;
the mountains and streams still smell of blood.
This lonely minister has no more tears to weep:
full of grief, he faces a dimming lamp.

(p. 41)

On the Fifteenth Day of the Eighth Month: Watching a Rainstorm from a Tower in Seoul

1.
My thoughts flow in streams around this tower;
the rain slants in, splattering the room.
Sadly I stare at clouds like mountains,
        remembering home far away.
There tonight is celebrated the Festival of Mid-Autumn.

2.
Cotton blankets let in the cold,
        dreams will not take shape;
in this hotel room the guttering lamp glimmers,
        nearly goes out.
Midnight, two o'clock, four in the morning—
        no human sounds at all.
I listen to the wind, listen to the rain,
        listen to the sound of the pines.

(pp. 34–35)

Waiting for the Ferry at Inchŏn

1.
Gazing west—the isles of paradise,
        beyond an expanse of mist;
alone, I stand in my mountain room,
        lost in reverie.
Ocean vapors rise like steam,
        turn into multicolored clouds:
wild mountains, innumerable,
        floating in the sky.

2.

Fresh flowers, brimming with dew,
            fill the women's chambers:
beautiful women, their window-leaves
            thrown open to the view!
At the horizon, a single thread,
            dark and thin, like a hair:
one woman points to it, and says,
            "The tide is coming in!"

3.

The fishermen haul in their nets
            as the evening tide returns;
I lean on the railing, into the wind,
            and watch this scene from a painting.
This is the moment when the setting sun
            touches the mountain's edge:
the whole catch is glistening
            with scales of brilliant red!

4.

The wail of a bugle shatters my dream,
            awakens me at midnight:
the ocean's exhalation brings chill
            in mid-summer.
At just the moment when loneliness
            seems impossible to dispel,
through a clear night sky the glowing moon
            comes toward the balcony.

5.
Past midnight, all is quiet,
        total calm.
The wind has stopped—beneath a vast sky
        the night air is fresh.
Lighthouse beams are turning, disappearing
        and reappearing:
firefly lights, glittering
        in the midst of the ocean.

                                                        (pp. 40–41)

——Inchŏn: One of (South) Korea's major seaports, located on the west coast of the
Korean peninsula on the Yellow Sea, to the southwest of Seoul.

——Isles of paradise: According to the poet's grandson, this conventional phrase refers
here to Japan, as it often does. Looking westward from Inchŏn, however, the poet
would actually be gazing in the direction of China, where he is returning after a stay
in Japan.

List of Poets with Editions Used

THE POETS are listed in the order in which they appear in this book (i.e., in chronological order of their birth dates). For each poet, the name of the edition used is given. The page numbers inserted after each individual poem or set of poems refer to these editions. In some cases where more than one edition is listed, the first is considered to be the primary edition and page numbers with no further qualification refer to this edition.

The following abbreviations are used in the list:

MSPT: Shen Te-ch'ien 沈德潛 and Chou Chun 周準, eds. *Ming shih pieh-ts'ai* 明詩別裁. Hong Kong: Shang-wu yin-shu kuan, 1961 reprint of 1738 publication.

MST: Chu I-tsun 朱彝尊, ed. *Ming shih tsung* 明詩綜. Taipei: Shih-chieh shu-chü, 1962 reprint of 1705 publication.

SKCSCP: *Ssu-k'u ch'üan-shu chen-pen* 四庫全書珍本.

SPTK: *Ssu-pu ts'ung-k'an* 四部叢刊.

SPTK, syp: *Ssu-pu ts'ung-k'an so-yin-pen* 縮印本.

Yoshikawa: Yoshikawa Kōjirō. *Genmin shi gaisetsu* 元明詩概說. Tokyo: Iwanami, 1963.

1) Tai Piao-yüan 戴表元 (1244–1310)
Shan-yüan Tai hsien-sheng wen chi 剡源戴先生文集, in SPTK, syp.

2) Chao Meng-fu 趙孟頫 (1254–1322)
Sung-hsüeh-chai wen chi 松雪齋文集, in SPTK, syp.

3) Ma Chih-yüan 馬致遠 (?1260–?1334)
a) Lo K'ang-lieh 羅忼烈. *Yüan ch'ü san-pai shou chien* 元曲三百首箋. Hong Kong: Lung-men shu-tien, 1967.
b) Wu-chi Liu and Irving Yucheng Lo, eds. *K'uei yeh chi*. Bloomington: Indiana University Press, 1976.

4) Yü Chi 虞集 (1272–1348)
Tao-yüan hsüeh-ku lu 道園學古錄, in SPTK, syp.

5) Wu Chen 吳鎮 (1280–1354)
Mei Tao-jen i-mo 梅道人遺墨, in *Mei-shu ts'ung-k'an* 美術叢刊, vol. 2. Taipei:
Chung-hua ts'ung-shu pien-shen wei-yüan hui, 1964.

6) Yang Wei-chen 楊維楨 (1296–1370)
T'ieh-yai hsien-sheng ku yüeh-fu 鐵崖先生古樂府, in SPTK, syp.

7) Ni Tsan 倪瓚 (1301–74)
Ch'ing-pi-ko ch'üan chi 清閟閣全集. Taipei: National Central Library, 1970.

8) Chang Yü 張羽 (1333–85)
Ching-chü chi 靜居集, in SPTK, series III.

9) Yang Chi 楊基 (c.1334–c.1383)
Yang Meng-tsai Mei-an chi 楊孟載眉菴集. Taipei: National Central Library,
1971.

10) Hsü Pen 徐賁 (1335–80)
Pei-kuo chi 北郭集. Taipei: Taiwan hsüeh-sheng shu-chü, 1970.

11) Kao Ch'i 高啓 (1336–74)
a) Iritani Sensuke 入谷仙介. *Kō Kei* [Kao Ch'i]. Tokyo: Iwanami (in the
   series, Chūgoku shijin senshū), 1962.
b) MST

12) Yang Shih-ch'i 楊士奇 (1365–1444)
Tung-li ch'üan chi 東里全集, in SKCSCP, Series VII.

13) Hsieh Chin 解縉 (1369–1415)
Wen-i chi 文毅集, in SKCSCP, Series IV.

14) Shen Chou 沈周 (1427–1509)
a) *Shih-t'ien hsien-sheng chi* 石田先生集. Taipei: National Central Library,
   1968.
b) Richard Edwards. *The Field of Stones: A Study of the Art of Shen Chou.*
   Washington, D.C.: The Freer Gallery, 1962. (Reproductions of paintings
   with inscriptions.)

15) Li Tung-yang 李東陽 (1447–1516)
a) MST
b) MSPT
c) Yoshikawa

16) Chu Yün-ming 祝允明 (1461–1527)
Chu Chih-shan ch'üan chi 祝枝山全集. Taipei: National Central Library, 1971.

17) Wang Chiu-ssu 王九思 (1468–1551)
Mei-p'o chi 渼陂集. Taipei: Wei-Wen Book & Publishing Co., 1976.

18) T'ang Yin 唐寅 (1470–1523)
a) *T'ang Po-hu hsien-sheng ch'üan chi* 唐伯虎先生全集. Taipei: Hsüeh-sheng shu-chü, 1970.
b) Marc F. Wilson and Kwan S. Wong. *Friends of Wen Cheng-ming: A View from the Crawford Collection*. New York: China House Gallery, 1975. (Reproductions of paintings with inscriptions.)

19) Wen Cheng-ming 文徵明 (1470–1559)
Fu-t'ien chi 甫田集. Taipei: National Central Library, 1968.

20) Li Meng-yang 李夢陽 (1473–1529)
a) MST
b) MSPT

21) Wang T'ing-hsiang 王廷相 (1474–1544)
Wang-shih chia-ts'ang chi 王氏家藏集. Taipei: Wei-Wen Book & Publishing Co., 1976.

22) K'ang Hai 康海 (1475–1541)
Tui-shan wen chi 對山文集. Taipei: Wei-Wen Book & Publishing Co., 1976.

23) Pien Kung 邊貢 (1476–1532)
Pien Hua-ch'üan chi 邊華泉集. Taipei: Wei-Wen Book & Publishing Co., 1976.

24) Ho Ching-ming 何景明 (1483–1521)
a) MST
b) MSPT

25) Yang Shen 楊慎 (1488–1559) and his wife, Huang E 黃娥 (1498–1569)
Wang Wen-ts'ai 王文才, ed. *Yang Shen tz'u ch'ü chi* 楊慎詞曲集. Chengtu: Szechwan People's Publishing House, 1984.

26) Li K'ai-hsien 李開先 (1502–68)
Li K'ai-hsien chi 李開先集. Shanghai: Chung-hua shu-chü, 1959. All references to vol. 1.

27) Hsü Chung-hsing 徐中行 (1517–78)
Hsü T'ien-mu hsien-sheng chi 徐天目先生集. Taipei: Wei-Wen Book & Publishing Co., 1976.

28) Hsü Wei 徐渭 (1521–93)
Hsü Wen-ch'ang san chi 徐文長三集. Taipei: National Central Library, 1968.

29) Tsung Ch'en 宗臣 (1525–60)
Tsung Tzu-hsiang chi 宗子相集. Taipei: Wei-Wen Book & Publishing Co., 1976.

30) Mo Shih-lung 莫是龍 (c.1539–87)
Shih-hsiu-chai chi 石秀齋集. Taipei: National Central Library, 1968.

31) T'ang Hsien-tsu 湯顯祖 (1550–1616)
T'ang Hsien-tsu chi 湯顯祖集. Shanghai: Chung-hua shu-chü, 1962.

32) Yüan Hung-tao 袁宏道 (1568–1610)
Yüan Chung-lang ch'üan chi 袁中郎全集. Taipei: Shih-chieh shu-chü, 1964. All references to *shih chi* 詩集 section.

33) Ch'ien Ch'ien-i 錢謙益 (1582–1664)
Kondō Mitsuo 近藤光男. *Shinshi sen* 清詩選. Tokyo: Kanshi taikei series, 1967.

34) Wu Wei-yeh 吳偉業 (1609–72)
a) *Wu Mei-ts'un shih chi chien-chu* 吳梅村詩集箋注. Shanghai: Ku-chi ch'u-pan-she, 1983.
b) Fukumoto Masakazu 福本雅一. *Go I'gyō* [Wu Wei-yeh]. Tokyo: Iwanami (in the series, Chūgoku shijin senshū), 1962.

35) Wu Chia-chi 吳嘉紀 (1618–84)
a) Yang Chi-ch'ing 楊積慶, ed. *Wu Chia-chi shih chien-chiao* 吳嘉紀詩箋校. Shanghai: Ku-chi ch'u-pan-she, 1980.
b) *Lou-hsüan shih* 陋軒詩. Preface dated 1679 (Library of Congress copy).

36) Yün Shou-p'ing 惲壽平 (1633–90)
Ou-hsiang-kuan chi 甌香館集, in *T'u-shu chi-ch'eng*.

37) Wang Shih-chen 王士禎 (1634–1711)
a) Takahashi Kazumi 高橋和巳. *Ō Shi-shin* [Wang Shih-chen]. Tokyo: Iwanami (in the series, Chūgoku shijin senshū), 1962.
b) Kondō Mitsuo. *Shinshi sen* (see Ch'ien Ch'ien-i above).

38) Tao-chi 道濟 (1642–1707)
a) Fu Pao-shih 傅抱石. *Shih-t'ao shang-jen nien-p'u* 石濤上人年譜. Taipei: Wen-ching ch'u-pan-she, 1970 reprint of 1948 edition.
b) Richard Edwards. *The Painting of Tao-chi*. Ann Arbor: Museum of Art, University of Michigan, 1967. (Reproductions of paintings with inscriptions.)
c) René-Yvon Lefebvre d'Argencé, ed. *Treasures from the Shanghai Museum*. Catalogue of an exhibition organized by the Shanghai Museum and shown

at a number of American museums in 1983 and 1984. (Reproduction of a painting by Tao-chi with inscription.)

39) Chin Nung 金農 (1687–1764)

Tung-hsin hsien-sheng chi 冬心先生集. Taipei: Hsüeh-sheng shu-chü, 1970.

40) Cheng Hsieh 鄭燮 (1693–1765)

Cheng Pan-ch'iao ch'üan chi 鄭板橋全集. Taipei: Han sheng ch'u-pan-she, 1971.

41) Yüan Mei 袁枚 (1716–98)

Sui-yüan ch'üan chi 隨園全集. Hong Kong: Kwong Chi Book co., undated reprint of edition published in 1934 by Ta-ta t'u-shu kung-ying-she, Shanghai. All references to *shih hsüan* 詩選 section.

42) Liu E 劉鶚 (1857–1909)

Liu Hui-sun 劉蕙孫, ed. *T'ieh-yün shih ts'un* 鐵雲詩存. Chi-nan: Ch'i-Lu Publishing House, 1980.

Index of Poets in Alphabetical Order

Translations from the Oriental Classics

Major Plays of Chikamatsu, tr. Donald Keene   1961

Four Major Plays of Chikamatsu, tr. Donald Keene. Paperback text edition   1961

Records of the Grand Historian of China, translated from the Shih chi of Ssu-ma Ch'ien, tr. Burton Watson, 2 vols.   1961

Instructions for Practical Living and Other Neo-Confucian Writings by Wang Yang-ming, tr. Wing-tsit Chan   1963

Chuang Tzu: Basic Writings, tr. Burton Watson, paperback ed. only   1964

The Mahābhārata, tr. Chakravarthi V. Narasimhan. Also in paperback ed.   1965

The Manyōshū, Nippon Gakujutsu Shinkokai edition   1965

Su Tung-p'o: Selections from a Sung Dynasty Poet, tr. Burton Watson. Also in paperback ed.   1965

Bhartrihari: Poems, tr. Barbara Stoler Miller. Also in paperback ed.   1967

Basic Writings of Mo Tzu, Hsün Tzu, and Han Fei Tzu, tr. Burton Watson. Also in separate paperback ed.   1967

The Awakening of Faith, Attributed to Aśvaghosha, tr. Yoshito S. Hakeda. Also in paperback ed.   1967

Reflections on Things at Hand: The Neo-Confucian Anthology, comp. Chu Hsi and Lü Tsu-ch'ien, tr. Wing-tsit Chan   1967

The Platform Sutra of the Sixth Patriarch, tr. Phillip B. Yampolsky. Also in paperback ed.   1967

Essays in Idleness: The Tsurezuregusa of Kenkō, tr. Donald Keene. Also in paperback ed.   1967

The Pillow Book of Sei Shōnagon, tr. Ivan Morris, 2 vols.   1967

Two Plays of Ancient India: The Little Clay Cart and the Minister's Seal, tr. J. A. B. van Buitenen   1968

The Complete Works of Chuang Tzu, tr. Burton Watson   1968

The Romance of the Western Chamber (Hsi Hsiang Chi), tr. S. I. Hsiung. Also in paperback ed.   1968

The Manyōshū, Nippon Gakujutsu Shinkokai edition. Paperback text edition. 1969

Records of the Historian: Chapters from the Shih chi of Ssu-ma Chien. Paperback text edition, tr. Burton Watson. 1969

Cold Mountain: 100 Poems by the T'ang Poet Han-shan, tr. Burton Watson. Also in paperback ed. 1970

Twenty Plays of the Nō Theatre, ed. Donald Keene. Also in paperback ed. 1970

Chūshingura: The Treasury of Loyal Retainers, tr. Donald Keene. Also in paperback ed. 1971

The Zen Master Hakuin: Selected Writings, tr. Philip B. Yampolsky 1971

Chinese Rhyme-Prose: Poems in the Fu Form from the Han and Six Dynasties Periods, tr. Burton Watson. Also in paperback ed. 1971

Kūkai: Major Works, tr. Yoshito S. Hakeda. Also in paperback ed. 1972

The Old Man Who Does as He Pleases: Selections from the Poetry and Prose of Lu Yu, tr. Burton Watson 1973

The Lion's Roar of Queen Śrīmālā, tr. Alex & Hideko Wayman 1974

Courtier and Commoner in Ancient China: Selections from the History of the Former Han by Pan Ku, tr. Burton Watson. Also in paperback ed. 1974

Japanese Literature in Chinese, vol. 1: *Poetry and Prose in Chinese by Japanese Writers of the Early Period,* tr. Burton Watson 1975

Japanese Literature in Chinese, vol. 2: *Poetry and Prose in Chinese by Japanese Writers of the Later Period,* tr. Burton Watson 1976

Scripture of the Lotus Blossom of the Fine Dharma, tr. Leon Hurvitz. Also in paperback ed. 1976

Love Song of the Dark Lord: Jayadeva's Gītagovinda, tr. Barbara Stoler Miller. Also in paperback ed. Cloth ed. includes critical text of the Sanskrit. 1977

Ryōkan: Zen Monk-Poet of Japan, tr. Burton Watson 1977

Calming the Mind and Discerning the Real: From the Lam rim chen mo of Tsoṅ-kha-pa, tr. Alex Wayman 1978

The Hermit and the Love-Thief: Sanskrit Poems of Bhartrihari and Bilhana, tr. Barbara Stoler Miller 1978

The Lute: Kao Ming's P'i-p'a chi, tr. Jean Mulligan. Also in paperback ed. 1980

Modern Asian Literature Series

Neo-Confucian Studies

Studies in Oriental Culture

Companions to Asian Studies

Approaches to the Oriental Classics, ed. Wm. Theodore de Bary   1959

Early Chinese Literature, by Burton Watson. Also in paperback ed.   1962
Approaches to Asian Civilizations, ed. Wm. Theodore de Bary and
Ainslie T. Embree   1964

The Classic Chinese Novel: A Critical Introduction, by C. T. Hsia.
Also in paperback ed.   1968

Chinese Lyricism: Shih Poetry from the Second to the Twelfth Century,
tr. Burton Watson. Also in paperback ed.   1971

A Syllabus of Indian Civilization, by Leonard A. Gordon and Bar-
bara Stoler Miller   1971

Twentieth-Century Chinese Stories, ed. C. T. Hsia and Joseph S. M.
Lau. Also in paperback ed.   1971

A Syllabus of Chinese Civilization, by J. Mason Gentzler, 2d ed.   1972

A Syllabus of Japanese Civilization, by H. Paul Varley, 2d ed.   1972

An Introduction to Chinese Civilization, ed. John Meskill, with the
assistance of J. Mason Gentzler   1973

An Introduction to Japanese Civilization, ed. Arthur E. Tiedemann   1974

A Guide to Oriental Classics, ed. Wm. Theodore de Bary and Ainslie
T. Embree, 2d ed. Also in paperback ed.   1975

Ukifune: Love in The Tale of Genji, ed. Andrew Pekarik   1982

Introduction to Oriental Civilizations
Wm. Theodore de Bary, Editor

Sources of Japanese Tradition	1958	Paperback ed., 2 vols., 1964
Sources of Indian Tradition	1958	Paperback ed., 2 vols., 1964
Sources of Chinese Tradition	1960	Paperback ed., 2 vols., 1964